NEW
BLACK &
AFRICAN
WRITING

NEW
BLACK &
AFRICAN
WRITING

A CRITICAL ANTHOLOGY
VOL. 1

C. SMITH
IRCALC-GHANA

GMT EMEZUE
EBONYI STATE UNIVERSITY

Handel & IRCALC

NEW BLACK & AFRICAN WRITING Vol. 1
Editing and Introduction: C. Smith, GMT Emezue
    includes bibliography of works cited
    includes index listing

World-Wide Sponsors:

Africa Research International
The International Research Confederacy on
African Literature and Culture, IRCALC
Website: <http://www.africaresearch.org>

Front and Back Cover: African Books Network
Published by African Books Network for
Handel Nigeria
6/9 Handel Avenue
AI
Email: handelbook@yahoo.co.uk

Marketing and Distribution in the U.S. UK,
Europe, N. America (US and Canada),
and Commonwealth countries outside Africa by

African Books Collective Ltd.
PO Box 721
Oxford OX1 9EN
UK
Email: orders@africanbookscollective.com

ISBN: 978-9-7835-0356-4

A Handel Book Publication

Visit our Website:
<http://www.africaresearch.org/handel.htm>

An IRCALC Educational Project
<http://www.africaresearch.org/ircalc.htm>

*To the entire board
of IRCALC Editors
for their diligence
and resourcefulness*

Contents

Introduction 9-13

Section A1.

1. POSTCOLONIAL VOID: ACHEBE, VASSANJI, WA THIONGÓ
15-28

2. COUNTER DISCOURSE: COETZEE
29-49

3. FEMALE SILENCING: ANDREAS, HEAD, VERA
51-66

4. WRITING BACK: ACHEBE, DANGAREMBGA
67-83

5. CHILD HEROES: OYONO, WA THIONGÓ
85-102

6. FREE WOMEN: LOPES
103-117

7. TRADITION VS MODERNITY: CE, LAYE
119-136

8. CULTURAL TRANSLATION: AIDOO, ONWUEME
137-156

9. REWORKING THE CANON: OSOFISAN
157-174

10. CONFLICT AND TURMOIL: UWAYS
175-198

11. SURREALISM IN DIASPORA: BESSORA
199-214

12. CHORIC/ANIMISTIC SELF: COUTO
215-235

13. COMPLEMENTARY REALISM: ACHEBE, CE
237-260

Section B1.

14. GRIOT TRADITIONS: CHINWEIZU 263-278

15. POWER AND POLITICS: MAPANJE 279-287

16. FOETAL SEARCHING: BRATHWAITE 289-303

17. NEO ROMANTICS: CE 305-318

18. NAMIBIA IN POETRY: KAHENGUA 319-327

19. POETIC HUMANISM: ENEKWE 329-343

20. GUINÉ-BISSAU AND CARRIBEAN POETRY: CABRAL, TCHEKA, PROENCA, YTCHYANA, BORGES AND MILLER 345-356

BIBLIOGRAPHY OF WORKS CITED 357-383

INDEX OF FEATURED WRITERS 383-389

Introduction

The Critical Anthology Vol.1

PUTTING together a critical anthology of Black and African Writing is rather ambitious but not novel since previous anthologizing and creative presentations of black expressions had been part of several movements for cultural renewal in Africa and the Diaspora attendant with rising Pan African awareness of common history. Agreeably Africa altered significantly by the historical contact with Europe: the scattering of generations of her peoples across the Western hemisphere via slavery, the conquest and pacification of indigenous nationalities, a century of colonialism and entrenched Western Capitalism all of which had left their scars on the continent. Yet succeeding generations of the black world continue to adapt and forge new realities from this and other global impacts on their economic, political and social conditions as evidenced by the literary historicization of the collective experience.

It had been noted that the celebration of Black writing in the fifties and sixties had seen her writers turning from old problems of colonialism and racial discrimination to new issues of political independence.[1] This trend survived twenty-first century African writing with its concern with historical and political experiences of modern African republics. A new tenor is being led by an avant garde of younger energies envisioning and rewriting postcolonial power relations in various individual, national and cultural environments. Conflicts of citizenship, gender relations and of minority ethnicities within an exploitative majority structure have loudly trailed the new

---

[1]King, Bruce and Ogungbesan, Kolawale. A Celebration of Black and African Writing. Kaduna: Ahmadu Bello University Press, 1975 viii

critical discourse on African literatures.

This first volume of criticism of black and African writing emerges mostly from journal research projects of the International Research Confederacy on African Literature and Culture aimed at furthering the imaginative approach to Africa's leadership and development concerns through providing an online network for independent discourse on Africa's literatures and cultures, inclusive of writings from the Black Diaspora that lend meaning and support to this African vision. At IRCALC we have maintained, and rightly so, that until African countries evolve more imaginative, more progressive states beyond their present ephemeral stages of social and political turmoil, not to talk of the intellectual mimicry of western thought in their educational and cultural programs, the growth of national literatures should move along with the canon and imperative of a continental cooperation.

Arranged with writer-comparative foci and cutting across various nationalities of the continent, these selected chapters offer contemporary perspectives on black literatures as a tributary of the Renaissance that had stirred older black and African traditions. Africa's emerging body of writing is still grounded on the historical and cultural need for black emancipation but new visions are introrsely directed at the reconnaissance of past and present temporalities in a fluid and progressive unity. Now here lie some evidence of modern critical traditions through which challenges of globalization and international cooperation give new meanings and new relations to aging concepts. Theoretical questions of realism or fantasy, ethnicity or universalism, terrorism or pacifism, feminism, womanhood and the interrogation of power as they affect the whole planet of black literary traditions are consequently redefined for wholesome aesthetic and didactic purposes of African art. All these are corroborated by prevalent historical forces which lie at the heart of the emerging literary dialogues from Africa and the black world.

It is most apparent that this critical evaluation of new writings is not just intended to encapsulate the proud zest of Pan African idealism and black racial legacy. Indeed what has been called the conscious understanding, or continuous reassessment of heritage, is borne from the vision which some of Africa's great founding fathers had so selflessly, and courageously, espoused. For this volume, the anchor on individual concerns within an all-inclusivist continental heritage is the core of its contemporary relevance.

A noticeable effort has been made to expound the significance of a work in each chapter through an intensive argument on the discourse, the objective being to cast some illumination on contemporary art in the varied genres of African poetry, drama and prose from innovative perspectives. Also, most of the featured writers have had not less than three published works within, or otherwise across, the genres of poetry, drama and fiction by which a critical tradition might emerge from continuing reading of their works in subsequent volumes of the project. Many theoretical considerations as they apply to textual analysis and elucidation of new writings have been employed. The critical approach is aetiological, descriptive and explanatory rather than prescriptive and argumentative. Its scholarly emphasis is practical as against pre- or non-reading theoretic or mere articulation of ideological preferences. A common thread further connects the chapters in the crystallization of new perceptions that originate or hybridize the links and influences or possible confluences and divergences in present and future worldviews of recent Black and African writing.

There is no doubt that modern African writing and its criticism should reflect the distinctive imaginative landscape of the continent defined by its collective colonial and unique national experience. Neither is there a doubt that these trends and developments shall continue to offer a healthy comparative opposition to the literary movements of other parts of the Western world.

C. SMITH
GMT EMEZUE   April 2009

 **Section A1**

1

L Nesbitt

Achebe, Vassanji, wa Thiongó

IN THE last half of the twentieth century many postcolonial cultures have found themselves out of balance. During colonization the people lived a kind of non-existence, a living void; their identities had been stolen. To establish dominion, the colonial power eradicated previous religions, educational structures, and languages. Although the indigenous person adopted a Western identity through the colonizer, it was an illusion, empty of meaning, because the native culture, in all its complexity, was not recognized by the colonizer. Essentially the people became impostors of themselves. Their personal and cultural history had been destroyed as one of the implications of colonial rule. Since the complex identity of the native was not acknowledged, the native essentially never existed as a unique individual in the colonizer's eyes.

The identity inflicted on the indigenous person was a meaningless stereotype masking the true identity that had become void. This vacancy will be explored from the context of abuse of power. This void is the denial of identity and a life with no meaning; the mask of colonial identity covering the void is an illusion. Taking off the mask in the postcolonial world does not necessarily reveal a full individual; the colonial erasure of cultural and personal identity appears to be permanent.

The enduring exploitation of formerly colonised nations has been defined using the term Neo-colonialism. The term implies a nation with a continued reliance upon the former imperial power and the West in general, but more specifically neo-colonialism also implies a persistent state of confusion of selfhood for the individual and for the whole nation. We spend our lives constructing unique personal traits and individually recognizable selves created from different sources. In the globalisation of today's society, the notion of identity is becoming increasingly complex, especially with an added complication of post-colonization. Many individuals do not communicate in their indigenous language, were not schooled using textbooks reflecting their particular social and cultural situations, or had Western instructors; even their religions did not reflect their own indigenous religious history. The definition of one's self has become multi-layered and essentially fractured. The departure of the colonizing power forced the postcolonial world out of balance placing the formerly colonized nations into a new and continued version of dependence upon the West.

M.G. Vassanji's novel, *The In-Between World of Vikram Lall*, covering fifty years of Kenyan history, focuses on neocolonial imbalance and the elaborate postcolonial reappraisal of cultures. In the beginning of the text, the Kenyan people are on the lowest rung of the social ladder with Whites and Indians in power. In 1965 after

Kenya assumed political independence and Jomo Kenyatta became president of the new nation, an elaborate repositioning of the classes occurred. This tumultuous period contributed to a chaos that fed lawless activities, realigning individuals in Western nations with Kenyan politicians and private citizens in the extortion that harmed the Kenyan people yet again. Vassanji's elaborate novel depicts an international racketeering allowing some individuals like the protagonist, Vik, to get very rich. The novel begins with a confession:

> My name is Vikram Lall. I have the distinction of having been numbered one of Africa's most corrupt men, a cheat of monstrous and reptilian cunning. To me has been attributed the emptying of a large part of my troubled country's treasury in recent years. I head my country's List of Shame. (3)

Through his employer Vik is involved with an illegal scheme in which private individuals essentially operate their own bank with no government restrictions, providing the government no financial benefit. Kenya is a "country of ten millionaires and ten million paupers" (259). Vik is in the middle of a handful of Kenyans who profit enormously from European and American fraud.

Vik's illegal activities essentially contribute to the death of his childhood friend, Njoroge. Njoroge, is a symbol of the Kenyan people and their resistance movement. In the beginning of the novel, Njoroge sympathizes with the Mau Mau, refers to Jomo Kenyatta as the Black Moses, and takes Vik to a meeting of "former freedom fighters Mau Mau, as they used to be called" (153). Later in the novel, Njoroge realizes that Jomo Kenyatta, the man he believed would lead the Kenyans to a better future, had become corrupt and the Mau Mau have been betrayed. Njoroge is killed by a political rival of Kariuki, the honest man he hopes will become president, who is also the rival of Jomo Kenyatta, the man Vik is enabling to profit from the illegal scam. This complicated entanglement leading to Vik's enormous profits essentially links Vik's actions to Njoroge's murder. At the end of the novel Vik's realization of the ramifications of his scam leads to his suicide.

Kenya is out of balance; its people suffer because of a corrupt government with corrupt politicians and self-serving, greedy men and women. Kenya is also still economically dependent upon the West. Vik is the middle-man in a lucrative hustle that brings American dollars into the country so that Jomo Kenyatta's government will stay in power. Paul Nderi, Kenya's Minister of Transport and Vik's boss, tells Vik:

> These are donations to our party from well-wishers abroad. ...Honest-to-God donations from private individuals. I would like you to find your Indian contacts and have them change this money and stash it; like in a bank. . . . And when our different constituencies need money for their operations, they will be paid by those Indians. (257)

Although there is no direct implication by Nderi of any Western nation, it is clear that corruption has spread throughout all cultures in Kenya and throughout the West. Even though Nderi is not a trustworthy character, the reader can believe that the two men with whom Vik exchanges money-stacked suitcases are American citizens. While it is possible that millions of dollars are given by private American citizens who are concerned about the possibility of a "great danger from the communists" (256); it is also highly unlikely that one individual would have access to so much cash and would be altruistically concerned solely with the Kenyan government. Therefore, this draining of Kenya's wealth is an example of neo-colonialism, an enduring exploitation of a formerly colonised nation creating a continued reliance upon the West, implicating the

American government. The people who suffer the most grievously are the majority of the Kenyan people. As a symbol of those people, Njoroge is the only true innocent.

Throughout the essay "On National Culture," Frantz Fanon argues that a native writer assists in the process of cultural and personal re-identification by acting as a communicator of the national struggle to the people. It is the writer's task and unique ability to use literature to describe the illusion, the void, and thereafter, the imbalance created. He can evoke the identification process from the culture of which he writes. Fanon clarifies this potential in his interpretation of a poem by Keita Fodeba: "The understanding of the poem is not merely an intellectual advance, but a political advance. There is not a single colonized person who will not perceive the message that this poem holds" (231). By using his own heart for exploration, the native author communicates the struggle to the people, and thereby helps the people to begin to define a new voice. In removing his own colonial mask of illusion, the writer assists each individual in their own private struggle to remove the illusory mask.

On the one hand Fanon implies that there is an old identity in which the indigenous person can be re-attired. However, he also acknowledges that the old identity is extinct. Relying on the security of a past identity is problematic:

> The artist who has decided to illustrate the truths of the nation turns paradoxically toward the past and away from actual events. What he ultimately intends to embrace are in fact the castoffs of thought, its shells and corpses, a knowledge which has been stabilized once and for all. But the native intellectual who wishes to create an authentic work of art must realize that the truths of a nation are in the first place its realities. He must go on until he has found the seething pot out of which the learning of the future will emerge. (225)

If the artist puts on a destroyed mask, it reinforces the abstraction of stereotype and the idea that the ghost of the past is an empty white sheet. Even though Fanon believes it is possible to re-wear that stereotype, he also believes it is worthless and that no future exists by wearing the empty mask. It is the chaotic present that holds the essence of the future. Moreover, it is only the first of three stages that the native intellectual will progress through before he becomes "an awakener of the people" (223). While the present may contain elements of the past, for example language, even the native language itself is in the process of transformation; and it is that transformation that is the key to progress. Fanon's argument for a people's revolution focuses on Algeria and the still present French colonialist power of 1963; but the reasoning behind his argument can be generally applied to many, if not all states. His notions are relevant to a postcolonial world and the issue of neo-colonialism. The native intellectual must analyze and communicate the struggle to the people in a language they will understand; this is empowering to the most vulnerable class, those without money and power, the majority of the population.

Ngugi wa Thiong'o, whose first novels were written in English, the colonizer's language, has long chosen to write in his native Gikuyu rather than English. Historically the Gikuyu people are an oral culture. According to Ngugi, although the Gikuyu may not have the money to buy his books, they discuss his ideas in community gatherings. By his choice of language, Ngugi accepts and acknowledges the importance of his role as communicator and facilitator these discussions:

> It was easy for people to write in the language of their colonization because it was the language of their conceptualization, the language of education, the language in which they attempted to intellectually grasp the world around them.

I believe that the language issue is a very important key to the decolonization process. What is really happening now is that African thought is imprisoned in foreign languages. (*Interviews* 30)

In other words, African identity has been stolen. When the colonisers replaced the Gikuyu language and when the education system was translated into a Western one, it weakened Gikuyu identity. When the writer communicates to the people in Gikuyu, he is making a conscious decision to communicate to the majority of the people in a language they can trust and understand. Potentially there are unique thoughts within the Gikuyu language that can only be expressed with that language.

Paradoxically, language is a portion of the old identity, but it is also a tool which can transform and be manipulated to shape the present, becoming an essential part of the new identity. Moreover, the development of a new language creates new identity; it does not resurrect an old one. Accordingly, since the texts chosen for this paper are written in English, perhaps there might be something missing or lacking. However, what can be gained from the cultural variety of the three texts is the notion that the postcolonial void ignores international boundaries. The colonising agents of education, religion, and language erase individuality and contribute to instability in the world. Each text depicts a different stage of colonial power: the imposition of rule, the initial occurrences of strikes against colonial authority, and the effects of colonization.

In Chinua Achebe's first novel several things fall apart with the imposition of colonial rule: a man's life; his tribe; and his country. Achebe begins *Things Fall Apart* by quoting the first four lines of 'The Second Coming' by W.B. Yeats:

Turning and turning in the widening gyre

21

> The falcon cannot hear the falconer;
> Things fall apart; the centre cannot hold;
> Mere anarchy is loosed upon the world.

Yeats' notion that humans have created a dark and foreboding future with no connection between their own humanity and spirituality is implicit and explicit in Achebe's novel. There is a loss of common purpose, instability, and great unrest in a world spinning out of control.

Things Fall Apart is replete with symbolism emphasizing these notions. For example, several of Achebe's characters function as symbols. While Okonkwo, the protagonist, is a complex character, he also symbolizes traditional Igbo society; he is defined by his culture, clan, and his rigid role in that clan. He is also a flawed character with some of his destruction being self-inflicted. For example even though he is warned not to participate in the killing of his surrogate son, he fears "being thought weak" and so strikes the fatal blow (43). This blow destroys his family since it drives his son to the colonizer's religion where he is given a new self-identity, "Isaac" (129). On the one hand Okonkwo's resolute behaviour kills him and contributes to the fracturing of his tribe; however, his daughter, Ezinma, symbolizes the future of the clan when she crawls into the cave and womb-like safety of Africa, transported on the back of the oracle, Chielo.

Religion is clearly represented as a colonising agent; the missionaries reject the authenticity of indigenous beliefs and thereby contribute to the colonising process by stripping away the already present and functioning religion and converting its members through Western education. For instance, missionaries are responsible for sending Okonkwo's son to a British school where he is renamed. Therefore, Okonkwo's determined nature is only a part of the destructive force: "From the very beginning religion and education went hand in hand" in the colonization of Nigeria (128). The benevolence of both education and religion reduce Okonkwo and his whole clan to "not a whole chapter but a reasonable paragraph" in the colonial text: "The Pacification of the Primitive Tribes of the Lower Niger" (147-8). Therefore, missionaries contribute to the death of the clan since they are responsible for the loss of their next generation: "Nwoye, who was now called Isaac, [is sent] to the new training college for teachers" (129).

The dichotomy is that the Igbo will let the white people stay and worship their own gods: "It is good that a man should worship the gods and the spirits of his fathers. Go back to your house so that you may not be hurt. Our anger is great but we have held it down so that we can talk to you" (134). The Igbo are a very peaceful culture and will accept a Western god; but, their welcoming nature contributes to the destruction of their clan, since Western religion does not recognize any other gods. The distinctiveness of the Igbo culture is eradicated through religion and education:

> Our own brothers who have taken up his religion also say that our customs are bad. How do you think we can fight when our own brothers have turned against us? The white man is very clever. He came quietly and peaceably with his religion. We were amused at his foolishness and allowed him to stay. Now he has won our brothers, and our clan can no longer act like one. He has put a knife on the things that held us together and we have fallen apart. (124-5)

Okonkwo is aware of how some white men have colonized and destroyed another village. He cannot allow other white men to destroy his own village since his own sense of self is represented by traditional Igbo culture; the destruction of his village would imply the destruction of himself. Clearly, for Okonkwo he must kill the white messenger. He then hears members of his tribe questioning his actions. He now understands that his tribe has fallen apart; therefore,

23

he has fallen apart. Okonkwo has no future since there is no future for his tribe. He has lost his identity and death is his only alternative.

Religion and education as colonizing agents also dominate the text of *Weep Not, child,* by Ngugi wa Thiong'o. The protagonist, Njoroge, also completely accepts Western education and religion. The novel is a Bildungsroman for Njoroge, an innocent child with a dream to go to an English school and complete faith in "the righteousness of God" (49). Njoroge symbolizes the Gikuyu people. He has a dream of a "bright future" in which he will "have a shirt and shorts for the first time" (3-4). He believes himself to be a saviour or religious leader for the Gikuyu: "His task of comforting people had begun" (95). This notion supports an allusion to Jomo Kenyatta, previously discussed in Vassanji's novel, the leader of the Mau Mau and president of Kenya. The people believed that Jomo would save them and their country. But when Jomo became president, eventually the government became corrupt. Njoroge's dreams are also broken and lost in the illusion of the coloniser: "'The sun will rise tomorrow,' he said triumphantly, looking at her as if he would tell her that he would never lose faith, knowing as he did that God had a secret plan" (106). Njoroge's dream, like the Kenyan people's dream, is shattered at the end of the novel by a corrupt government still economically dependent upon the West.

This benevolent gift of Western religion and education proves to be an elaborate deception. Njoroge walks through the woods with his teacher, a Gikuyu who has now re-identified himself as Isaka, while "discussing the saving power of Christ" (101). White soldiers stop them and murder Isaka after accusing him of being a terrorist. Then white men take Njoroge from his school and beat him so badly that he falls into a coma. Soldiers torture and castrate Ngotho, his father, who dies from the torture. After so much tragedy, life itself becomes "a big lie" for Njoroge (126). While ironically recalling his lost faith,

Njoroge considers his religious belief and Western ideals:

> O, God But why did he call on God? God meant little to him now. For Njoroge had now lost faith in all the things he had earlier believed in, like wealth, power, education, religion. Even love, his last hope, had fled from him. (134)

Njoroge realizes that this Western charitable deception would ultimately lead to his pacification. He now understands that as soon as he would have become educated and developed his own voice, any hope of power or wealth would have been taken away: "I know that my tomorrow was an illusion" (132). His identity as defined by Western religion and education and as imposed by colonialism was an empty illusion.

Ngugi chooses a protagonist who symbolizes innocence and total acceptance of colonial conformity. Since Njoroge is a child his life is comparatively easy to disrupt and overwhelm with a new self-identity. He is easy to deceive and once his fragile identity is erased, he has nothing to fall back on. On the other hand, Okonkwo has a more fully formed sense of self and will not accept defeat; but because Okonkwo is a lone voice with no other men from the tribe supporting him, his voice will not be heard. It is clear with all both characters that their loss of self-identity is complete. They are unable to return to any past religion, education or cultural definition of themselves through their clans or alone.

Therefore the mask of Western identity is an illusion. This idea is clearly supported by the texts. Western education, religion, and language simply do not function for Njoroge, Okonkwo, and Vik. Moreover, once the colonizer has left, the enormity of the remaining void is so overwhelming that each character either contemplates or commits suicide. There is literally nothing left to live for when the illusion and deception of a Western identity is revealed.

Specifically Okonkwo's clan no longer supports him, rather they support the Western intruders; his son no longer practices the indigenous religion and has been given a Christian name; and Okonkwo sees no future since he refuses to accept colonial domination. Okonkwo hangs himself even though suicide "is an abomination. ...[and] his body is evil, and only strangers may touch it" (Achebe 147). However, his clan pays him a final, clarifying tribute: "That man was one of the greatest men in Umuofia. You drove him to kill himself; and now he will be buried like a dog" (147).

Njoroge also contemplates suicide and sits holding a rope with which he hopes to hang himself at nightfall. He hears an evil voice urging him to "*Go on!*" and kill himself (Ngugi 135). He laughs while contemplating his action. It is futile to attempt to go against the Western colonizers. However, Njoroge does not commit suicide:

> His mother was looking for him. For a time he stood irresolute. Then courage failed him. He went towards her, still trembling. And now he again seemed to fear meeting her. He saw the light she was carrying and falteringly went towards it. It was a glowing piece of wood which she carried to light the way. (135)

While carrying a burning candle, his mother brings him back to the clan. The only place Njoroge can establish and create a new identity is with his own people joining their struggle to survive.

At the end of *The In-Between World of Vikram Lall*, Vik also sees a glow from a fire. It is surrounding a man who calls to Vik from the bottom of a staircase, attempting to save his life. However, Vik chooses to run away from the glow and kill himself. Ultimately Vik cannot forget his betrayal of his people.

The symbolism of re-weaving and re-creating a connection with one's tribe can be seen in Achebe's novel. Immediately after hearing her mother tell a folk story about a Tortoise falling from the sky and smashing into pieces, symbolising the fall of the British, Ezinma, Okonkwo's daughter, is called by the oracle. Chielo specifically calls upon and addresses her prophecy to Ezinma, the symbol of African hope: "Chielo never ceased in her chanting. She greeted her god in a multitude of names the owner of the future, the messenger of earth" (Achebe 75). Ezinma's womanhood is of interest since Okonkwo is "specially fond of Ezinma" (32), and in fact, "never stopped regretting that Ezinma was a girl" (122). Since Okonkwo represents the past and the traditional values of the clan, he cannot appreciate Ezinma because of her womanhood; but he does appreciate her value. She symbolizes rebirth and the future of the clan. Immediately after Ezinma listens to the allegorical folk tale, she begins a journey to a cave on Chielo's back. As the priestess carries the girl into the night, Ezinma redefines her social identity by submitting to a dangerous ordeal, a liminal phase, prior to reintegrating with her family and clan. The future will be found in the union of native people sharing their struggle, courageous enough to create new religion, language, and educational systems.

A void is left with the disappearance of the colonial power; the economic and political power structure is gone, and each individual is bereft of a definition of himself. Neo-colonialism maintains the relationship with the colonizer rendering the people once again devoid of an identity. The process of community organization is the essential step in the process of re-identification of both the individual and the state. The people's struggle is where the new identity is born:

> We believe that the conscious and organized undertaking by a colonized people to re-establish the sovereignty of that nation constitutes the most complete and obvious cultural manifestation that exists. . . . The struggle for freedom does not give back to the national culture its former value and shapes; this struggle which aims at a fundamentally different set of relations between men

27

cannot leave intact either the form or the content of the people's culture. After the conflict there is not only the disappearance of colonialism but also the disappearance of the colonized man. (Fanon 245-6)

Fanon's focus is on the genesis of national culture and thereby of the discovery of a separate and unique personality. Nation-building as a process not only emerges when the colonizer is in power, but continues in the postcolonial period and creates the new identity. While the colonial erasure of identity appears a permanent condition, by allowing the re-emerging state and individual to define new selves, the culture will be reborn. Fanon defines this re-emergence of identity as a people's revolution placing great importance on individuals organizing at the community level and emphasizing the assistance of the native intellectual in the form of a writer and artist. He also places importance on appreciating the individual citizen and the individual state as unique entities, not as oversimplified concepts. Therefore Nigeria and Kenya are not merely anonymous postcolonial states containing indistinctive postcolonial men and women; they are regions with ancient historical backgrounds that contain, in the present, unique human beings who are re-creating their political, cultural, linguistic, and religious identities. Not only must new selves be re-created, but neo-colonial interference based upon economic greed must be eliminated.

2

A Kehinde

Coetzee

A CENTURY of European (British and French mainly, but also Portuguese, German, Italian and Spanish) colonization left behind an African continent dazed, bewildered and confused. This is why modern African writers see the need for and admit a commitment to the restoration of African values. In fact, the Western world equates knowledge, modernity, modernization, civilization, progress and development to itself, while it views the Third-World from the perspective of the antithesis of the positive qualities ascribed to itself.[1] Such negative stereotypes are perpetrated by a system of education, which encourages all the errors and falsehoods about Africa/Africans. Writing on the jaundiced portrayal of Africa/Africans in Western canonical works, Edward Wilmot Blyden asserted over a hundred years ago that:

---

[1] See: Ngugi, wa Thiong'o. "Europhonism, Universities and the Magic Fountain: The Future of African Literature and Scholarship." *Research in African Literatures*". 31.1, (2000): 2

> All our traditions and experiences are connected with a foreign race – we have no poetry but that of our taskmasters. The songs which live in our ears and are often on our lips are the songs we heard sung by those who shouted while we groaned and lamented. They sang of their history, which was the history of our degradation. They recited their triumphs, which contained the records of our humiliation. To our great misfortune, we learned their prejudices and their passions, and thought we had their aspirations and their power. (91)

Africa and Africans are given negative images in Western books of geography, travels, novels, history and in Hollywood films about the continent. In these texts and records, Africans are misrepresented; they are portrayed as caricatures. Unfortunately, Africans themselves are obliged to study such pernicious teachings. Reacting to this mistake, Chinua Achebe declares that if he were God, he would "regard as the very worst our acceptance, for whatever reason, of racial inferiority" (32). He further comments that his role as a writer is that of an educator who seeks to help his society regain belief in itself and put away the complexes of the years of vilification and self-denigration.

Homi Bhabha also declares that Western newspapers and quasi-scientific works are replete with a wide range of stereotypes (17). In similar fashion, Andrew Milner and Jeff Browitt dwell on the inscriptions of stereotypes of Africa/Africans in Western religious canonical texts (the Bible in particular). To them, canonical texts are:

> those Christian religious texts considered divinely inspired by the Church. In secular aesthetics, literary and other texts accorded a privileged status, within some

version or another of a 'great tradition', as embodying the core values of a culture. (225)

In expansion of Milner and Browitt, Dennis Walder asserts that the Western-associated canons of texts are dotted with a whole complex of conservative, authoritarian attitudes, which supposedly buttress the liberal-democratic (bourgeois) states of Europe and North Africa (74).

Actually the colonization of Africa is explicit in the physical domination and control of its vast geographical territory by the colonial world and its cronies. However this physical presence, domination and control of Africa by the colonizer is sustained by a series or range of concepts implicitly constructed in the minds of the colonized. Therefore more than the power of the cannon, it is canonical knowledge that establishes the power of the colonizer "I" over the colonized "Other" (Foucault 174). It should also be stressed that the available records of Africa's history handed down by the Europeans, far from being a disinterested account of Africa, are interested constructs of European representational narratives. This view is supported by Ania Loomba: "the vast new world (Africa inclusive) encountered by European travelers were interpreted by them through ideological filters, or ways of seeing, provided by their own culture" (71).

The English novel is the "terra firma" where the self-consolidating project of the West is launched, and *Robinson Crusoe* is an inaugural text in the English novel tradition. It is also an early eighteenth-century testament to the superiority of rational civilization over nature and savagery, a text that foregrounds the developing British Empire's self-representation through encounters with its colonial Others. Crusoe, the eponymous hero of the novel, anticipates the Hegelian Master. A postcolonial reading of the novel, however, reveals that Defoe discloses –however unwittingly– some deeper ideological operations: Western colonialism is not content with pillaging human and material resources to sustain and consolidate its power over its colonies; it has to destroy the indigenous cultures and values (religion, language, dressing codes, etc) and supplant them with distorted and totally ambivalent versions. As Frantz Fanon asserts:

> Colonialism is not satisfied merely with holding a people in its grip and emptying the native's brain of all form and content. By a kind perverted logic, it turns to the past of the oppressed people, and distorts, disfigures and destroys it. This work of devaluing pre-colonial history takes on a dialectical significance today. (168)

By distorting the history and culture of Africa, the colonizer has created a new set of values for the African. Consequently, just the subject fashioned by Orientalism, the African has equally become a creation by the West.

On his 'island' Crusoe attempts to subjugate all of nature, including Friday, his manservant. The founding principle of subjugation is force, as he uses his gun to save Friday from his captors (and to silently threaten Friday into obedience). He then begins a programme of imposing cultural imperialism. The first method in this programme is a linguistic one. Crusoe gives Friday his new name without bothering to enquire about his real name. He instructs Friday to call him "Master." He thus initiates Friday into the rites of English with a view to making him just an incipient bilingual subject. He teaches him just the aspects of the English language needed for the master-servant relationship – to make Friday useful, handy and dependent. The master-servant orders suggest how Africans and other 'natives' have been tabulated and classified by the West throughout colonial (and neocolonial) history. The second method is 'theological.' Crusoe's attitude to Friday's religion is akin to the later imperialist missionaries' attitude to the indigenous religions they encountered on African soil. Crusoe sees African traditional religion as blindly ignorant pagan creed. He believes that his own (Western) God is the true God, and that he is doing Friday an invaluable service by converting him. As constructed moral and cultural inferiors, then, indigenous people are 'naturally' suited to work for Westerners; when Crusoe wants to build a boat, for instance, he assigns Friday and his father the dirty and difficult tasks, while the Spaniard is merely to supervise. Perhaps to justify such incipient tyranny, Crusoe sees all natives as savages (marked most of all by their cannibalism) and constantly refers to them as such:

> All my apprehensions were buried in the thoughts of such a pitch of inhuman, hellish brutality, and the horror of the degeneracy of human nature, which though I had heard of often, yet I never had so near a view of before; in short, I turned away my face from the horrid spectacle. (163)

With tongue, pen, gun and Bible, Crusoe is able to prove and assert his superiority and assume a new mantle of power. He is a 'Master' who controls and thus can exploit his environment, a budding imperialist conveniently furnished with an inferior Other to reflect, even constitute, the superior Self. James Joyce also identifies some prototypes of colonial experience in *Robinson Crusoe* in forms of colonization, subjugation, exploitation and Christianization of the colonized:

> The true symbol of the British conquest is Robinson Crusoe, who cast away on a desert island, in his pocket a knife and a

33

pipe, becomes an architect, a carpenter, a knife grinder, an astronomer, a baker, a shipwright, a potter, a saddler, a farmer, a tailor, an umbrella maker and a clergyman. He is the true prototype of the British colonist, as Friday (the trusty savage who arrives on an unlucky day) is the symbol of the subject races. (qtd. in Susan Gallagher 170)

Throughout *Robinson Crusoe* the protagonist embodies Western mercantile capitalism, grounded in a colonial economy, through his money-making schemes (engaging in the slave trade, investing profits, hoarding gold on the island) and his moral lapses (most notably, selling the Moorish boy with whom he escaped from the Turkish pirates for sixty pieces of silver). On the other hand, the natives, represented by Friday, are depicted as careless self-indulgent individuals who lack forethought or reflections. This is why the white man who has a life of reason, introspection and faith, intervenes, like the Almighty God, to civilize the savage Other.

Although Friday is described specifically as not black, and as possessing non-Negroid features, he represents the Black Africans in *Robinson Crusoe* even more than he represents Amerindians (which he presumably is). The novel is set on a New World island; British colonialism at that time was centered in the Caribbean and its slave-based plantation economy. As most native Caribs, Arawaks and Tainos had been annihilated through war and disease, slaves were supplied from Africa.

The triangular trade itself blurred spatial boundaries and, by importing a new 'native Other' to replace the old 'native Other,' blurred ethnic distinctions as well. Every one who is not white becomes 'black.' It is precisely this developing Manichean dichotomy, a direct consequence of the myth of civilization based on repression, that Robinson Crusoe records.

In Defoe's *Robinson Crusoe*, Crusoe the Western European self is equated with futurity, vision, civilization, rationality, language and light. Conversely, the depiction of the non-European (the Amerindian and the African) in the text is an absolute negation of the Other. The black is associated with pre-history, savagery, cannibalism, unconsciousness, silence and darkness. Crusoe, the archetypal Western man, assumes the posture of a king, a prince, a governor, a general, and a field marshal. He is worried by the sense of his self-assumed greatness. He suffers the pang of delusions of grandeur, seeing himself as some kind of God. This temper is reflected in his unconscious (his dreams) most especially, in which he rescues a savage from his enemies. The so-called savage kneels down to Crusoe as a sign of reverence, praying him for assistance.

To a great extent, Crusoe has the passion of racial consciousness. In fact, he is "an unlikable man for [a] hero" (Palmer 10), an egoist who has little interest in anyone but himself. In his portrayal of Africa/Africans/Amerindians, Defoe was expressing an opinion common to his contemporaries. *Robinson Crusoe* articulates the European attitude about the peoples of Africa and America that structured an expanding imperialist venture.

Once considered a model for alternative Rousseauean concepts of education and growing up, the 'Robinsonade' and its protagonist (Crusoe) have had to face harsh criticism. In fact, Crusoe, his kith and kin, and Defoe, the author, are guilty of ethnocentrism, logocentrism, proto-imperialism, and even megalomania. Crusoe is not a role model in this multicultural, pluralistic world of ours. Instead, he plays a role that begs to be rewritten – thus the existence of alternative versions of the Robinson myth in post-colonial fiction, including Coetzee's *Foe.*

Countering Misrepresentation: Post-Colonial Literature in Dialogue with Western Canonical Works

What is today known as colonial discourse, post-colonial theory or postcolonialism is an offshoot of the anti-colonial activism and writings of such nationalists as Leopold Sedar Senghor, Frantz Fanon and Amilcar Cabral (Bill et al 63; Schipper 82; Zukogi 17). The early writings of the nationalists set the tone, pace and character of the debate in the field today. The publication of four key texts whose views many Africans largely share also energized the tempo of counter-discourse in Africa. These texts are Fanon's *The Wretched of the Earth* (originally published posthumously in 1961); Walter Rodney's *How Europe Underdeveloped Africa* (1972); Said's Orientalism (originally published in 1978); and Chinweizu, et al's *Toward the Decolonization of African Literature* (1980). These counter-hegemonic texts decentered, even undermined the intellectual heritage of the Western Academy while questioning the foundational assumptions behind the Western colonial /imperial /neocolonial project.

Similarly, African writers notably Achebe, Ngugi, Salih, Armah and Kane critique European imperialism. The fact that a significant portion of contemporary African literature is preoccupied with reworking Western canonical works is a logical and natural – rather than a misplaced and belated – response. This is because Africa's contact with Europe has impacted greatly on its socio-cultural, political, economic and psychological well-being. The 'dislocation', psychic and physical debilitation that this contact has created, is so enormous that it rarely escapes the critical attention of African writers, and more recently, of the post-colonial discourse analyst. As Ime Ikiddeh claims in his Foreword to

Ngugi's *Homecoming*:

> There can be no end to the discussion of African encounter
> with Europe because the wounds inflicted touched the very
> springs of life and have remained unhealed because they are
> constantly being gashed open again with more subtle, more lethal
> weapon. (xii)

African literature's fundamental engagement is with the
colonial presence in Africa, dismantling its dehumanizing
assumptions and resisting its pernicious consequences. The African
novel, in particular, reflects an evolving consciousness at once
historical, cultural, and political. It strives to counter the negative
picture of Africa and Africans promulgated by some European
writers, including Joyce Cary, Graham Greene, Joseph Conrad,
Ryder Haggard, Daniel Defoe, William Shakespeare and the like.
Even as African novelists seek to interrogate and modify European
racism and exploitation[2] in literature as well as in practice, they use
their writings to 'bridge' the cultural gap between 'Blacks' and
'Whites.' Their reactions to precursor colonial canonical works
emphasize their own difference and unique qualities. They claim
their own culture, aesthetics, history and essence. This nationalist
temper is also reflected in many movements (like Pan-Africanism,
the Black Renaissance, Negritude, Black Consciousness) that
search for African roots and black traditions. In Schipper 's words:

> The medium of the novel proved very suitable to the needs of
> African writers who wanted to address colonial reality as they
> have experienced it. In their work, the novelists uprooted the

---

[2]Schipper, Minneke. *Imaginning Insiders: Africa and the Question of
Belonging*. (New York: Cassell, 1999): 34.

37

myth that riches and power make the white man superior.(37-38)

African writers see the need to tell their people's and continent's stories themselves. According to Ernest Emenyonu, any attempt to relinquish this God-given right would "allow foolish foresters stray in and mistake the middle of a mighty African baobab for an African tree trunk" (4). The idea that only one group of privileged people (in this case, Europeans) is qualified to interpret the world should be interrogated. For instance, Achebe, in *Things Fall Apart* (1958) and his other polemical writings, claims that the missionaries and explorers have lied about Africa. He argues that the depictions of the human and political landscapes of Africa enshrined in Western canonical works are biased and ignorant. Achebe thereby assumes the task of retelling the African *stories* and asserting the primacy of African culture. To Achebe, the ultimate service of African writers to their people is to make African society regain belief in itself and put away the complexities of years of denigration and self-abasement (165).

Inheriting Achebe's legacy, contemporary African critics and writers are required to act with integrity and dedication. This is because the colonial discourses about Africa/Africans need to be subjected to further reworking with a view to correcting erroneous notions about Africa and her peoples. In the words of Walder, "these works require a new sense of their place in the changing world of today, if they are to retain their freshness and relevance" (4). Whether these reworkings take the form of 'national allegories', as Fredric Jameson suggests (85), or appear as inversions of black/white or center/periphery binaries or question binary structures of thought themselves[3] they must keep responding not only to the burdens of the past but also to the exigencies of the

---

[3]See: Bill Ashcroft et al, *The Empire Writes Back: Theory and Practice in*

present and the challenges of the future.

Salman Rushdie in his much quoted statement, "The Empire writes back with a vengeance" to the imperial "centre" admits that postcolonial writing is imbued with nationalist assertion which involves the "Other" claiming itself as central and self-determining by questioning the basis of European and British metaphysics (336). The postcolonial writers therefore challenge the world-view that can polarize centre and periphery in the first place. On his part, Fanon sees the dichotomy (colonizer/colonized) as a product of a 'manichaeism delirium', the result of which condition is a radical division into paired oppositions such as good-evil, true-false, and white-black (81). This dichotomy is absolutely privileged in the discourse of the colonial relationship. Thus the colonial discourse needs new liberating narratives to free the colonized from this disabling position. Therefore the central 'postcolonialist' argument is that "postcolonial culture has entailed a revolt of the margin against the metropolis, the periphery against the centre, in which experience has become 'uncentred', pluralistic and nefarious" (Ashcroft et al 12).

In his "Representing the Colonized", Said prioritizes narratives which take the Third-World seriously by placing what it has to say on equal terms with its own explanations ("Representing the Colonized" 206). Gayatri Spivak is also highly critical of the current intellectual enterprise of constituting the colonial subject as Other in her "Can the Subaltern Speak?" (68). No place is created for the subaltern (raced) to speak, as colonialism's narrativization of African culture effaces all traces of black voice. She believes that postcolonial critics should concentrate on articulating the margins and gaining control of the way in which the marginalized

Postcolonial Literatures. (New York: Routledge, 1989): 63, and Homi Bhabha, *The Location of Culture* (London: Routledge, 1994): 31.

are represented; the postcolonial intellectual should also break with the paradigms of representation that promote antagonism between the First and Third Worlds.

J.M. Coetzee's *Foe* and the Debunking of Racial and Patriarchal Egoism in Defoe's *Robinson Crusoe*

Chinua Achebe, J.M. Coetzee, Wilson Harris, George Lamming, Patrick White, Margaret Atwood, Jean Rhys and other postcolonial writers have rewritten particular works from the English canon "with a view to restructuring European 'realities' in postcolonial terms, not simply by reversing the hierarchical order, but by interrogating the philosophical assumptions on which that order was based" (Ashcroft 33). The African story continues to be (re)told by postcolonial writers. When Coetzee's *Foe* was published in 1986, it added to the growing corpus of counter-discursive writings in postcolonial literature. Although Coetzee is among the most critically revered of world writers, he is also one of the most misunderstood and misrepresented African writers. At least, this is the opinion of critics like Kwaku Korang and Andre Viola, who observe that a problem in Coetzee's fiction is the difficulty of reconciling a liberal humanist approach with the reality of the oppressive power hegemonies in South Africa, which negate such a vision. However, a careful consideration of the various systems of oppression with which Coetzee's novels contend provides a powerful antidote to viewing him as an 'apolitical' relativist. The critic of Coetzee's fiction should be less concerned with the fiction's absolute or historical truth than with its fictional truth as embodied in the narrative. His works engage with a vast literary heritage and question authority invested in literary discourse, as well as investigate power dynamics and political oppression and ethical responsibility.

Foe takes up some central postcolonial issues, which include the following: who will write? (that is, who takes up the position of power, pen, in hand?); who will remain silent? (the issues of silencing and speech); how do colonial regimes distribute and exercise power? (and, in consequence, create zones of powerlessness). Attempting to demythologize a dominant knowledge about empire, *Foe* is imbued with a 'fresh' paradigm; its textual universe is tailored towards not only revisiting but also retracting the long line of epistemic violence foisted on the psyche and intellect of the Other. The text seeks to uncover the silence and oppression at the heart of Defoe's classic novel to suggest the power of anti-colonial as well as colonial discourse.

Coetzee slips through the operations of various critical unfoldings of the Defoe's canonical text and sets up another text as a relatively autonomous but supplementary interlocutor, which seems to add to and substitute the original at the same time. According to David Attwell, it might be true that his novels are "nourished by their relationship with canonical Western literature" but it is equally true that "through his complicated postcoloniality he brings that situation to light and finds fictional forms wherein it can be objectified, named and questioned"(4-5). His works engage with a vast literary heritage and question the authority invested in precursor discourse, as well as investigate power dynamics, political oppression and ethical responsibility.

Coetzee does this by recasting both Defoe (the author) and his protagonist (Crusoe) as minor characters within a woman-centred narrative, thereby distorting and twisting the 'truths' that the reader assumes from Defoe's original. A character omitted from and silenced by Defoe's account (the female) is foregrounded in Coetzee's version through the narrator Susan, an English woman marooned for a year on the island with Cruso and Friday. The optimistic Robinson Crusoe, in *Foe*, becomes Cruso, a weak-minded mountain of insecurity who, unlike the original protagonist, lives sullenly on a desolate island with only a few tools, no gun, no Bible, no writing utensils, and no records. He labors every day to construct gigantic terraces, walled by stone, which stand empty and barren, for he has nothing to plant. In Cruso's island (as opposed to Crusoe's island), there are no providential seeds, spiritual or and natural. Such meaningless construction also symbolizes the hollowness at the core of Empire-building. Cruso as colonist manqué is not only impotent but also ludicrous.

Perhaps most significantly, Friday becomes an eccentric mute with whom the real secrets of the story exist. Further, Coetzee demystifies the racial slippage surrounding Friday. Coetzee has stated that in Robinson Crusoe, "Friday is a handsome Carib youth with near European features. In Foe, he is an African" (463). By transforming the light-skinned, delicately-featured Amerindian into a wooly-haired, thick-lipped, dark complexioned Negro, Coetzee makes visible the racist subtext that drives Defoe's novel, colonialism in the Caribbean, and imperialism in Africa. Reading *Foe* allegorically, then, suggests a reaction against imperialism and white supremacy. As Derek Attridge maintains, *Foe* represents

> a mode of fiction that explores the ideological basis of canonization, that draws attention to the existing canon, that thematizes the role of race, class, and gender in the process of cultural acceptance and exclusion, and that, while speaking from a marginal location, addresses the question of marginality such a mode of fiction would have to be seen as engaged in an attempt to break the silence in which so many are caught, even if it does so by literary means that have traditionally been celebrated as

characterizing canonic art. (217)

While *Foe* re-writes a canonical text from marginal perspectives, it still demonstrates the power of the original to command the desire for imitation; it also exposes the silences and contradictions of the precursor text. Foe privileges the intersection or partial overlap between the postmodern and the postcolonial in contemporary cultures, with reference to its resistance to the monologic meta-narratives of modernism and realism (in arts), to Orientalism (in cultural anthropology), to colonialism and racism (in geopolitical history, fundamentalism and nativism) and to patriarchy (in gender relations). The novel's stylistic and ideological strategies challenge established ways of writing about race. For instance, the resolution of the plot action is an ideologically sensitive site for this challenge. It contradicts the typical ending of the colonial texts, which asserts that choice is over and that the growth of character or the capacity for defining action has ceased.

The core of Coetzee's *Foe* lies in the deconstruction of established literary styles and conventional roles assigned to blacks and women – beginning, as Silvia Nagy-Zekmi has explained in reference to feminist and postcolonial theory, "by simply subverting images of existing hierarchies (gender /class /culture /race) in a patriarchal or colonial setting"(1). *Foe* reworks *Robinson Crusoe*'s representation of black identity in general and female identity in particular, of the values of the colonizer and those of the colonized, and of the forces of patriarchy against those who try to free themselves from it. Friday (the archetypal black man, the oppressed race) and Susan (the womenfolk) in *Foe* transgress social taboos, as part of Coetzee's depiction of colonized/female resistance to colonial/patriarchal power.

Although Friday seems to be an object of colonial knowledge

43

due to his tonguelessness, he – like the black world – has his own story to tell, even if a monocultural, metropolitan discourse cannot hear it. He may seem to be an embodiment of the world of self-absorption, without self-consciousness, without the Cartesian split of self and other, without a desire; yet his silence is not an ontological state but a social condition imposed upon him by those in power. He therefore represents all human beings who have been silenced because of their race, gender and class. The apparent inaccessibility of his world to the Europeans in the story is an artist's devastating judgement of the crippling anti-humanist consequences of colonialism and racism on the self-confident white world. To Dick Penner, "Friday's muteness can be read as a symbol of the inexpressible psychic damage absorbed by blacks under racist conditions" (124). Yet his speechlessness, through negative inversion, becomes a symbol of a pre-capitalist Africa where history was transmitted and lived with full articulation, authenticity, and authority.

Further, Friday's muteness marks Coetzee's rejection of the canon, that is, its limited authority; this rejection takes partial shape in formal innovations and subversions of generic expectations. Throughout the novel, Friday's silence and enigmatic presence gain in power until they overwhelm the narrator at the end. Friday's detachment causes the hole in Susan's narrative, and this is the primary cause of Susan's uncertain narrative voice. In the third and final sections of the novel, Friday/the black world gains in stature as the site of a shimmering, indeterminate potency that has the power to engulf and cancel Susan's narrative and, ultimately, Coetzee's novel itself. This is an instance of the problem of closure. Friday, the radical black man, possesses the key to the ideological sensitive site of the narrative. He cannot give voice to this key, and no external discourse could adequately represent his knowledge. Coetzee does not allow Susan to assume the authority to construct the racial difference. Therefore, Susan's discourse as well as the novel's discourse, cannot appropriate the image of Africa/Africans. In frustration, Susan comments, "I do not know how these matters can be written of in a book" (120). Precisely, in relationship to lack of speech (Friday) and collapses of narrative voice (Susan), it is writing – specifically, writing books that challenge the literary canon – that is at stake in *Foe*.

Friday's own writing, that is, his marks on the slate, shows him to be the "wholly Other" (Spivak, "Theory in the Margin" 20); his trademark is the foot (the recontextualized foot from *Robinson Crusoe* and every Robinsonade). Writing is a means for him to prove that he is a human being and not an ordinary thing. For instance, Friday once installs himself at Foe's desk, assuming the position of authorship with a quill pen in hand. The embarrassed Susan intervenes and tells Foe, "he will foul your papers" (151), but Foe replies, "my papers are fouled enough, he can make them no worse" (151). This interchange upsets expectations of mastery (the white man, the white literary canon), and it has been precipitated by Friday's silent, subversive assumption of 'Western' prerogatives.

Such subversive assumptions become points of 'education' for Susan, who now believes that all races are equal: "We are all alive, we are all substantial, we are all in the same world" (152). Thus, *Foe* like much post-colonial literature rests upon one ethico-discursive principle – the right of formerly un-or misrepresented human groups to speak for and represent themselves in domains defined, politically and intellectually, as normally excluding them, usurping their signifying and representing functions, and over-riding their historical reality. The mystery surrounding Friday's silence as well as the silence surrounding Friday must be unravelled in order to allow Susan to see into the 'eyes' of the island. Friday has the ability to override both Susan's desire for authorization and Foe's ability to grant it. Friday possesses the history that Susan is unable to tell, and it will not be heard until there is a means of giving voice to Friday. This is to suggest that the world's harmony and true 'progress' will improve if there is mutual respect and cross-fertilization of ideas. Friday's voice, to wit, the black world's voice, will liberate not only himself/itself but also Susan (and, we assume, Foe the archetypal European, in other words the European world), for her story is dependent upon Friday's and the black world's meaning. Therefore, in *Foe*, the reader witnesses a gradual development towards and a concern for giving voice to the Other so long silenced in literary history. Consequently, the "subaltern has spoken, and his readings of the colonial text recover a native voice" (Spivak, "Theory" 110). In *Foe*, Coetzee uses a strategy of reading/writing that will "speak to", as distinct from "speaking for" the historically subaltern (wo)man. Although this involves an act of the imagination, it is a profoundly viable vision.

Coetzee has shifted the emphasis from the ostensibly unmediated narrative of *Robinson Crusoe* to the informing intelligence of multiple points of view. Foe wants to control the story of Susan and Friday; he is more interested in what will sell than the truth of the story. He finds the story lacking in exotic circumstances – for instance, a threat of cannibals landing on the island, as found in the original text. Susan, in her feminist temper, retorts: "What I saw, I wrote. I saw no cannibals; and if they came after nightfall and fled before the dawn, they left no footprint behind" (54). Foe, the fictional meta-author, would have preferred a replication of the story as it occurs in Defoe's text. In addition, as a racist and a misogynist, Foe wants to write the significance and meaning of Friday's (black world's) life and determine Susan's story. This is to suggest that authorship and authority are equivalent. Throughout much of the novel, however, Susan resists Foe's authority and insists on telling her own story. If stories give people their identities, and people are written by others, Susan wonders, do people really exist for themselves?

The concluding image of the novel envisions a future when people exist as full individuals and when an equal exchange will be possible among races. Susan lies face-to-face with Friday underwater, and feels "a slow stream, without breath, without interruption" (157) coming from inside him and beating against her eyelids, against the skin of her face. This is Coetzee's articulation of a strong desire for reciprocal speech from the victims of colonization, a cross-cultural dialogue. This image positively reinforces the ironic thesis developed throughout *Foe*, that African history did not begin with the continent's contact and subsequent destruction by the European colonialists. Rather than being the beginning of African history, the colonial period signals the end of the beauty, communality and reciprocity characteristic of African culture. In the post-colonial era, it is the task of African literature to reclaim that which has been misappropriated and to reconstruct that which was been damaged, even destroyed. In fact, the tone and the narrative voice of the novel invest it with the authority to function as a counter-discourse.

Conclusion

Coetzee's *Foe* serves as a counter-text to the dominant discourse of representation in general, and to Defoe's *Robinson Crusoe* in particular. Such counter-discourse is quite justifiable because knowledge about the Other, whether seen as Oriental, as African, as Caribbean, or aboriginal, is neatly packaged and

47

disseminated through the medium of Western literature and travelogue. Consequently, one strong reason for the emergence of postcolonial theory has been to re-think the European representations of non-Europeans and their cultures. To this end, what Coetzee – like other postcolonial African writers – has done in *Foe* is to undermine dominant notions of history by contradicting, challenging, or disrupting the prevailing discourse (Said xxiv). Yet beyond the foisted haze, the Africa that Coetzee depicts in the novel is whole, a community at peace with itself and whose pristine values are crystallized in the beauty of relationship, community and, above all, reciprocity.

Textuality should cease to be a 'battle ground' for orchestrating and illuminating the binary opposition between the colonizer and the colonized. Rather, canonical and non-canonical texts should be a means of promoting racial harmony, equality, and concord. This is in alliance with Bhabha's opinion that textuality should have more to offer in the way of hope for the oppressed. In his words:

> Must we always polarize in order to polemicise? Are we trapped in a politics of struggle where the representation of social antagonisms and social contradictions can take no other form than a binary of theory versus politics? Can the aim of freedom or knowledge be the simple inversion of the relation of oppressor and oppressed, margin and periphery, negative image and positive image? (5)

What is needed in this millennium is the ability of disparate races and ethnic groups to come together to confront the challenges posed by globalization. Contemporary writers, scholars and critics need to articulate alternatives based on inclusivity and the full diversity of experiences. People of all ages, backgrounds and races would have a space to exercise their creativity, leadership acumen and imagination if there is an enduring racial harmony. In this way, we would be able to work collaboratively and strategically to create a world where many visions can co-exist.

3

B Weiss

Andreas, Head, Vera

WOMEN'S voice-throwing in Southern Africa is not a new phenomenon as such. It has always existed, but in varied intensities and restricted spheres. Sometimes !Kung women celebrated their womanhood with verve (*Nisa: The Life and Words of a !Kung Woman*, 2001); sometimes women subverted and ridiculed gender myths in oral storytelling. What is new, though, is that women have crossed the borderline of restricted spheres and have thrown their voices for everyone to hear. Their voice is accusing and sexually daring as Jennifer's, the female protagonist in Dianne Case's *Toasted Penis and Cheese* (1999), who sarcastically dedicates her confessions to the perfect man "James Bond." Their voice is mocking as the one of a young Tswana woman's who, when repeatedly battered and abused by her husband, claims that she one day "got his finger and just chewed it" (*Stories* 51) or as Dorothy's, a prostitute in

Virgina Phiri's collection of short stories entitled *Desperate* (2002), who takes revenge on her husband's lover by "chewing her ear until a piece of it came off in [...her] mouth" (31) and then triumphantly swallowing it, but not before displaying the piece in front of her humiliator and the community. Their voice is shocking as Nonceba's in Yvonne Vera's *The Stone Virgins* (2002), who describes her rape and her face being cut into pieces:

> [T]he moment is painless [...] then a piercing pain expands, [...] my body motionless [...]. He cut. Smoothly [..] quickly. Each part memorised [...]. My mouth a wound, [...] torn, pulled apart. A final cut, not slow, skilfully quick, the memory of it is the blood in my bones. (99)

And sometimes, women deliberately choose to refuse to throw their voice. They, in the true sense of the word, decide to be voiceless, yet as a means of subversion as depicted in Neshani Andreas's novel *The Purple Violet of Oshaantu* (2001) where Kauna defies convention by rejecting to speak at her husband's funeral. Not having a mouth – in this case deliberately – does not mean not to communicate because according to the basic law of communication: one cannot *not* communicate.[1] Every behaviour bears a message and Kauna's behaviour, for everyone to be registered, is very clear to a most shocking degree.

This chapter deals with selected passages taken from novels written by Neshani Andreas, Bessie Head, and Yvonne Vera. Their work mark a departure from the mere notion that women *react* or *write back*, arguments that have often been overemphasised in literary criticism. In fact there is more to that: women *act*, that is to

---

[1] Basic law of communication was introduced by psychologist and linguist Paul Watzlawick in the 1960s.

say, they take action, against their limited position by engaging in a discursive, dismantling, subverting, partly ironic, and deconstructing confrontation with androcentric texts not only of written material, but also, in a broader sense, of socio-cultural constructs and of texts written on the body. Reacting or writing back, in comparison, resembles a mimetic behaviour pattern,[2] too constricting and much less active than when taking action. Taking action refers to a woman's obligation to write down her own story, to enlarge the vision, and to unmake stereotyped allusions. She creates herself by exploring ambiguous multi-layered meanings which helps her to surpass the boundaries of agony and repression, to restore her mutilated body and mind – a prerequisite for authoring herselfhood.[3]

"Shades of Utter(ing) Silences" delves on the idea of women's potential to unveil constricting gender and racial laws by uttering silence, or as the title of the essay also suggests, by being enveloped in utter silence. This voicelessness, however, a cloister into the emotional space, is chosen deliberately and therefore distances itself from the mere notion of the Beti proverb of Cameroon: "Women have no mouth".

The printed dash or the empty page does not necessarily stand for absence and lack, but for gaps and blanks which set great store by what is left untold. The power of the uncommunicated lies in its speculation and interpretation. Silence is not always merely a helpless gesture or a capitulation, but can also be a resource as in Bessie Head's *Maru* (1971) or a reinforcement – in the sense of reinforcing a taboo, and thereby embodying the unspeakable, or a

---

[2]In the sense of imitating, copying the line of arguments; a counter-argumentation in the form of a one to one reflection.

[3]Or to use Hélène Cixous's words who writes from the French context: to "give [.. them] back [... their] bodily territories which have been kept under seal" (351).

platform for finding a new voice as no "mouth can carry a sight such as that" (Vera, *Nehanda* 23). To keep silent, to actively decide on being voiceless, as one encounters in *The Purple Violet of Oshaantu* (2001), may also be used as an instrument in order to subvert patriarchal traditions. As such, silence in all its facets and "as a will not to say or a will to unsay and as a language of its own has barely been explored" (Trinh 416).

In Southern African women's writing, silence can be traced as an option to overcome oppression, violation, and traumatic experiences. A case in point may be found in above mentioned novels and their protagonists: Kauna, an Owambo woman from the village Oshaantu in the northern part of Namibia, Margaret, a Masarwa woman from Dilepe in Botswana, and Zhizha, a young Shona girl from Zimbabwe. These women, though their cultural and geographical background are quite different, all have one thing in common: they suffer severely and in a moment of utmost distress they fall into utter silence.

Going against Expected Voicing

In *The Purple Violet of Oshaantu*, (2001)[4] Kauna is degraded by her husband's frequent infidelity and battering. Her suffering is immense and she has all the reasons in the world to poison her husband, Shange, who one day drops dead in the living room of their house. Rumours spread that she had bewitched or poisoned him an accusation which proves to be untrue as it is later revealed he died of a heart attack. In the turmoil of death's revelation, Kauna goes mad for a couple of hours. She is hysterical and tries to convince everybody that her husband has just come home, did not touch his food, and that there was no evidence of her having

---

[4]For easy reference, the following abbreviation is used: *PV*.

bewitched or poisoned him. The news that she had gone mad proved more sensational than the news of her husband's death. It is not Kauna herself who tells her story, but her best friend Ali. On the day of Shange's death, she is described as hysterical, with a dazed look in her eyes, and having the air of the village's mentally disturbed women (*PV* 11-12). After the first day, as Ali observes, she sleeps intensely, is uninterested in the preparation of the funeral, and does not shed a tear −sadness is totally lacking. Her behaviour is indifferent, partly mocking, partly good-humoured, but it is also considered as estranging, insulting, and outrageous by family and community.

The oshiWambo proverb "a woman is the house," which stands for the notion that the wife is the closest person to her husband (100), is applied by Shange's relatives to force Kauna to confess where her husband's wealth is safely kept. Kauna refuses to designate someone to give a speech on behalf of the widow on the day of the funeral (137-140). The speech on behalf of the widow is given by a person who is very close to the widow and who will say some favourable words about the deceased. The words, however, have either been told to the speaker or written down by the widow herself and must reflect her personal sentiments. This is the custom and to disregard this tradition is taboo. Kauna disobeys this custom by applying a behaviour pattern which is normally favoured by the patriarchal society − a woman's silence.

The church service program lists all the 'on behalf' speeches followed by the speaker's name. The 'on behalf of the widow' speech only shows a blank space which tells a lot by what is left untold (158). Suppressed excitement is in the air when the woman in charge of the funeral program repeatedly calls for a voluntary speaker. Nobody moves, Ali is perspiring heavily, and Kauna is described as "[n]ot giving a damn in the least" (159).

By exporting the law of women's silence into a realm of publicly expected voicing, Kauna beats patriarchy with its own weapons. This outrage is sketched rather grotesquely in the appearance of Kuku Peetu, her favourite uncle. He spontaneously decides to hold the speech. It is less his words, but rather his clothes, described as "navy-blue wrinkled blazer, pink shirt and yellow pants [... and] a lime-green handkerchief [...]" (159-160), which contrast with the mourning scene. He looks like a parrot parodying the expected words on behalf of the widow. Though this is not a victory for the fact of not having given a speech on behalf of the widow, it is a moral victory for Kauna as she could carry through her will of uttering silence and hence making the unspeakable visible: her year-long disgrace and oppression.

Deep Pool of Creativity and Power

The late African-American Audre Lorde once described women's inner silent spaces as "the home of great potential":

> Silence [...] is a site not only of resistance but of transformation, the home from which new dreams and visions are born. [... S]ilences [.. are] deep pools where "each one of us holds an incredible reserve of creativity and power, of unexamined and unrecorded emotion and feeling." (qtd. in Stone 20)

In *Maru* (1971), Margaret Cadmore is such a woman. She is an orphan who is categorised by the derogative term Masarwa or Bushman and is treated like an outcast. Her namesake and foster mother Margaret Cadmore brings her up with love and dignity, which does not, however, shield her from society's vicious racial stereotyping. In Botswana, Masarwa people are considered "untouchable[s] to the local people [...]" (*Maru* 13) and the remote village Dilepe is a stronghold of the most powerful chiefs where Masarwa are held as slaves. As a teacher at Leseding in Dilepe, Margaret passes as Coloured, but she insists on enlightening people about her true identity. She tells everyone that she is a Masarwa and as a consequence faces severe mobbing and hostility. She is threatened with dismissal from school and suffers from loneliness. Her suffering is intensified by her unfulfilled love for Moleka, a Tswana and a son of a tribal chief, and, as Margaret sees it, by the indifference of Maru, the eldest Tswana son of a paramount chief and Moleka's best friend.

Besides school and the hours spent with Maru's sister, Dikeledi, Margaret is surrounded by an inner quietness when she is by herself:

> Her own heart was so peaceful. She stood where she was, empty-handed, but something down there belonged to her in a way that triumphed over all barriers [...]. It was continuous, like the endless stretch of earth and sky, [...] as though her heart said: 'Wait and that will grow in its own time. Wait and you will grow in your own time, but slowly, like eternity.' [...] [S]he sat down and stared deep into her own, peaceful heart. (99)

The house where Margaret is staying is an abandoned old library – books are missing. The metaphorical lack of letters is a suitable environment where Margaret in her solitude and silence finds a source for her creativity and power. She has visions and dreams which she expresses in drawings. Her dear friend Dikeledi supplies her with crayons, oils, drawing ink, water colours, paper, and brushes and orders Margaret to, as she calls it, "experiment with everything" (100) she has brought along. Margaret's state of quietness, which one may regard as a well of inner peacefulness, now experiences a new rhythm which is slowly increasing into days and nights of feverish painting.

On her quest Margaret discovers her unexamined and unrecorded emotions about which Audre Lorde spoke. Her body becomes a "power machine of production" (101) which she cannot control. These emotions, visions, and dreams are not expressed by words, but by decisive and powerful strokes mediated through crayons, water colours, and oils. Three of these drawings form a mosaic: a house in the dark with bright windows; heavy, dark clouds hanging in the sky are contrasted by a field of bright-yellow daisies; and a path running along the field of daisies with a black couple embracing at the end of this path, one of which Dikeledi identifies as Maru (103-104).

Maru, whose name stands for the seTswana word "the elements" (Vigne 104), proves to be the sole supporter of Margaret's visions; he calls himself a dreamer, he has the dreams as Margaret, and he is creative in his ideas – a trait normally assigned to women and less to men. He is the one who makes his dreams come true. It is Margaret's foster mother – the visionary same – who professed to Margaret in her early childhood that she will help her people one day, and it is the three drawings which anticipate Margaret's vision and dreams of transcending the racial discrimination between the Tswana and Masarwa people.

Silence not only resided in Margaret, but also dominated Maru's and Margaret's relationship, and only Margaret's paintings mediated their bond which brought "the wind of freedom" to the Masarwa and "some kind of strange, sweet music you could hear over and over again" to Margaret (*Maru* 124, 127).

Platform for a New Language

Silence and giving voice in *Under the Tongue* (1996)[5] has been mainly considered under the aspect of "the role of language as a medium of healing from trauma" (Samuelson, "Grandmother" 2) or the necessity of breaking silence.[6] The following section will focus on the role of silence as a necessary platform for finding a new language which, as it is argued, gives silence an enlarged, productive dimension.

In reading Yvonne Vera's *Under the Tongue* one is reminded of what Lisa F. Signori calls, in reference to the French author Marguerite Duras, a *livre brûlé*. The story of Duras's experimental novel *La pluie d'été* (1990) presents an image of a *livre brûlé* which has a burned hole in the middle making the text of the book unreadable. The words are destroyed, similar to Zoë Wicomb's *David's Story* (2000) where the letters of David's story flow out of the computer due to a bullet which has destroyed the monitor. The notion that the present, dominant language can satisfactorily narrate all experience is subverted by these incidents. As suggested by Signori, "meaning must be inferred from the remaining, charred words that surround the hole, and must ultimately be recovered in the blank, in the hole left behind" (121). What serves for Duras is also applicable in a figurative sense for Vera's *Under the Tongue*: language is pushed "to the limit and delves into the silence at the heart of language, into the hole, the vide out of which a new beginning is possible" (Signori 121).

By listening to her inner monologue, a speaking from within the body, one follows Zhiza's story of repeated raping by her father, while her mother Runyararo was among the women who

---

[5]For easy reference, the following abbreviation is used: *UT*.

[6]Also cf. Samuelson, "*A River in my Mouth*," 15-24.

had fought beside men during the war. The story of *Under the Tongue* begins and ends with the incestuous rape act which gives the story a cyclical structure, a structure which might hint at the recurring drama of rape in the microcosm of the family and, in a metaphorical sense, in the macrocosm of society where the exploitation of a woman's body is closely linked to the conquering and exploitation of land.[7]

The taboo of incestuous rape resides in Zhiza's mouth, buried like a stone under her tongue. Zhiza's mother, Runyararo, her name stands emblematic for "quietness" (Eppel 13), loses no words, when she comes to know of her husband's rape act. She kills him – the unspeakable is made public in an unspoken performance, in an

---

[7]Vera's works suggest a reading which establishes an affinity between a woman's body, the land and the nation. Whereas *Nehanda* displays the conquering of land and her subsequent killing with imperialist domination, "Independence Day" leads a discourse around men metaphorically equating the taking over of land with their sexual exploitation of women's bodies, and civil war fighters raping and torturing women's bodies as a metaphor for their war in shifting political power relations in *The Stone Virgins, Without a Name* and *Under the Tongue*, as discussed in Meg Samuelson's essay "Re-membering the Body," "can be read on the allegorical level as using rape to signify [the psychological scars of] colonial invasions into the land occupied by the Shona, and the [anticipated] post-independence betrayal of Zimbabweans by a national government [in which women are the main losers]" (93).

And as Samuelson argues in an earlier essay "Reclaiming the Body": "The rape from within the family in *Under the Tongue* issues searing attack on the betrayal of post-independence governance and shatters the familial trope of nation" (2). Vera opposes national discourses that claim to purify and restore the abused female body/land; the symbol of the Nation 'Mother Africa' is not re-establish. To back up her study, Samuelson cites Gayatri C. Spivak's résumé: "for the subaltern, and especially the subaltern woman, 'Empire' and 'Nation' are interchangeable names, however hard it might be for us to imagine it" ("Reclaiming the Body" 2).

act of murder and her subsequent imprisonment. She remains silent as the act of rape is too horrible to speak of, and can only be answered by another taboo: a wife killing her husband. When Runyararo is confronted by her mother after having killed her husband, the words of anger and bewilderment lay astray on the floor, unsuitable to name what has to be named. The scattered words are futile and leave both women in "[t]heir waiting [which] is silent with no words to accompany it" (*UT* 32).

It can be suggested that for Zhizha incestuous rape is more than an "unsayable word" (6) as Stephen Gray puts it. It is an unspeakable word, a taboo, which she keeps under her tongue.[8] Zhiza remains silent, but not as a means to retreat as a victim, but as a Signorian delving into silence, into the hole, the *vide* out of which a new beginning is possible. She is anxious to

> listen to Grandmother, to discover her places of silence. [... She knows that] there is a wide lake in her memory, a lake in which ripples grow to the edges of the sky, a lake in which all our grief is hidden [where grandmother's ..] word rests at the bottom of silent lakes, (70)

the word which will ultimately be given to her. In one of her tormented nights one learns that she "listen[s] to the softness in the silence [... and] remember[s] [.. her] scar" (21). Nightmares and her fragmentary inner monologue replace her outward silence. The traumatic rape experience leads to the loss of language. Her voice, as she puts it, is "pulled from its roots [...], empty and forgotten" (3).

The voice, it can be argued, is forced to die and it is necessary to plunge into silence, and – to borrow Signori's words – into "the

---

[8]The unspeakable refers to a taboo whereas the unsayable only indicates the inability to be said (Mills and Smith 2).

hole, the *vide*" (121) as there is no place to speak about this horrific tale, as there is "no mouth left" (86) as Mazvita, the protagonist of another of Vera's novels entitled *Without a Name*, (1994) determines. Though, Zhizha is aware that her "tongue *is* a river," but for the time being it "is heavy with sleep" (*UT* 1, emphasis added). The tongue, in order to speak, has to be a river, it has to be filled with water like a riverbed after heavy rains. Pulling at the root, the origins, as grandmother does, is closely connected with water: river, lake, rain, and tears. There is a link to the Shona mythology of lakes and rivers being the source of life (Baumann 221), and it is grandmother who is said to be a river, whose body harbours the river. She is said to be the source of life who has "placed it there before [Zhizha] was born, before [Zhizha's] mother was born" (1). Yet, the river remains in a silent waiting, to be remembered, for Zhizha will only find the source of life/being, that is, she will only heal, if she does allow herself to go into the river, or, as she puts it, to be "inside Grandmother," "[... to be] Grandmother" (2).

Enveloped in this silence, one witnesses Zhizha's gradual "awakening" (1). Only a murmur, coming from her grandmother and observed through quiet body movements, Zhizha sees her grandmother's "eyes pull this root from inside her [...] her lips tremble, her arms so silent, her voice departed, her elbows bare [...] she waits [...]" (1-2). Zhizha acknowledges her knowing that grandmother's "waiting is also her giving" (1-2). They all wait: Zhizha, her grandmother, and Runyararo, her mother. Grandmother waits for her voice to find "the forgotten, the departed, who wait[s] to be remembered" and Runyararo and Zhiza wait for the healing of grandmother's voice-throwing to the moon when darkness falls (9, 11).[9] They all wait for the same: finding a new language to

---

[9]Darkness is associated with horror, destruction, and taboo; the moon,

speak the unspeakable; and all this waiting holds an element of tense quietness. Being confronted with the unspeakable and trying to find a new language to unveil the taboo also breaks open old scars. A nightmare perpetuates another nightmare and Zhizha fearfully waits for the horrifying sound indicating grandmother's death (*UT* 12).[10] She describes her body parts as dissolving, enlarging, and as discovering "their own ability for silence" (12-13).

It may be argued that she could most probably not overcome her emotional scarring on her own as the parent-child relationship is a significant factor in a child's traumatic experience. In addition, in therapeutic intervention the mother as a co-therapist plays a significant role in mastering the trauma (Leibowitz et al. 104, 106-107). In fact, Zhizha's healing is possible with the help of her mother in form of flashback fantasies which emerge into a dreamlike awakening (*UT* 80-82, 95, 97). The play between mother and child of repeating, reading, and writing the syllables "a e i o u" initiate a new phase of life, a new beginning which Zhizha replays in front of the mirror:

> I watch myself through the mirror, [...] till tears fall down my cheeks. [...] I sit up straight like my mother [...] and sternly say repeat after me a e i o u, then I change into me, and I say a e i o u. [...] I have turned into mother, and she laughs, because she has become me. (81-82)

The presence of the mother, though, is not real, but is

---

similar to the metaphor water, as a place of rebirth and closely connected with women.

[10]Zhiza's anxiety about grandmother's death may suggest her dread of the impossibility of finding a new language to describe the unspeakable.

constituted by Zhiza's intermingled fantasies, flashbacks, and dreams. Grandmother's words calming her down: "sh sh sh you only have a fever you will soon be well" (95) and Zhizha's wishful longing: "I wish my mother would stay, but I meet her in dream" (97) refer to these phantasmic encounters.

It is quite obvious that Zhiza's mother is sentenced for life and will not return home as women's offences are treated differently before the court than men's. As one is told in the short stories of Bessie Head, in contrast to a man who is only sentenced for a few years for killing his wife which is considered as "a crime of passion" or, in the worst case, as a "mess and foolishness" ("Life" 46), a woman who kills her husband will be sentenced to life imprisonment as she has been charged with "Man-slaughter" ("Collector" 88).

Zhizha's healing is also, and especially, possible with the help of her grandmother who takes the place of her absent mother. Interestingly, the grandmother has no name – a suggestion that she may be an epitome of the Grand-Mother of maternal voice, a voice or a new language which Meg Samuelson justifiably asserts as "*feminising culture* as the opposition between nature (mother) and culture (language) is broken down [...]. Language is returned to the realm of the body" ("Grandmother" 30-31). Yet, it is also Zhizha who plays a major part in overpowering the horror: In the act of naming, Zhizha is her mother and her mother is Zhizha's grandmother (*UT* 14-15).

The cyclical corporeality displays the mutually endured pains and the travelling through these "territories of pain" (Veit-Wild 346) results in a re-membering which leaves the grandmother with empty eyes and arms, an emptiness which is a burden too heavy to carry. This emptiness, this silence has to be filled with new dreams, and new dreams are only possible if the unspeakable is aired.

To air the unspeakable, in turn, necessitates a new language.[11] Zhizha sets great effort in helping grandmother to find this new language by metaphorically placing a basket which is waiting as it is being described "with words to be shelled and tossed, waiting with words to be chosen, cast aside, separated, dismissed" into grandmother's arms:

> I [Zhizha] look at the basket and know that the best words are those that are shared and embraced, those that give birth to other words more fruitful than themselves, stronger than themselves. [...]
>
> I move my feet toward the tarnished wall and reach for the basket. The basket is far above my head but the rope is nearer so I pull hard at the rope which holds the basket to the wall and the basket falls into my waiting arms. There is a basket in my arms. I carry the basket across the silent room. I notice that my feet are my feet and I have also found my arms. I give the basket to Grandmother. I place it safely under her embrace. She touches my arms with hopeful caress.
>
> She moves her right hand inside the basket to gather something she has recently discovered, something that she has lost while gathering words. (*UT* 16)

Zhizha needs her grandmother just as she needs her mother, and her mother needs her and grandmother just as grandmother needs Zhizha and Runyararo. This symbiotic support is where women come together, where they re-member, where their tears form a river, and where the river forms a tongue where voices hide

---

[11]As Rosi Braidotti asserts in her essay "Mothers, Monsters, and Machines," "[a]dequate representations of female experience [...] cannot easily be fitted within the parameters of phallogocentric language" (60).

65

and where, as Zhiza observes, a "healing silence" presides; it is in silence, she asserts, a dream will germinate, grow, and will not be lost (*UT* 41).

In fact, this reading of *Under the Tongue* carefully suggests that there are two types of silence: the one which paralyses and the one which helps to re-member, to heal. It is a silence which offers a platform for a new language which starts with "the word" that grandmother has given to Zhizha and which she has to recollect.[12] The maternal voice gives the word to a woman who gives it back or hands it over to another. The word is "a place where women harvest" (54).

Throwing voicelessness is, as the above examples have shown, a further means to go against oppression, exploitation, and distress. It serves the women as an instrument to rebel against patriarchal conventions, to find the necessary power to go against racist practices, and to find a new language to overcome traumatic experience of male induced violence. This essay is especially interesting as silence has, to the best of my knowledge, only been regarded in the context of silencing women or women falling into silence as passive victims. *The Purple Violet of Oshaantu, Maru,* and *Under the Tongue* impressively depict that silence can be read in a quite different and liberating way.

---

[12]As to this repeated reference cf. *UT* 5, 12, 20, 21, 30, 41, 53, 54, 61. According to Adrienne Rich, 'speaking silence' can be a mode of healing and may form the beginning of a narrative, of finding a voice for one's experience (qtd. in Hoogestraat 27).

4

A Lewis

Achebe, Dangarembga

POSTCOLONIAL literatures embody a dynamic of perpetually writing back in order to move forward, challenging misconceptions entrenched in and perpetuated by previous texts, whether on the basis of race, nationality, or gender, and opening fertile ground for future elaboration and discussion. In an attempt to forge an ever-widening space within the major critical discourses in the humanities, postcolonial literatures and theories engage in unlocking unspoken, unheard or silenced pasts (of individuals, communities, genders, nations) thus expanding the scope of possibility for culturally and politically viable presents and futures. Postcolonialism is primarily concerned with 'voicing'. Fundamentally, postcolonial literatures and theories aspire to the establishment of an ongoing dialogue, aiming to facilitate a "democratic colloquium between the antagonistic inheritors of the colonial aftermath" (Gandhi x). Inclusive rather than merely "nebulous" or "diffuse" (viii), the dialogue of postcolonialism often focuses on regions "whose subjectivity has been constituted in part by the subordinating power of European colonialism" (Adam and Tiffin vii). The dialogue can also, on a wider level, mobilise "a set of discursive practices...[including] resistance to colonialism, colonialist ideologies" and their insidious contemporary forms and "subjectificatory legacies" (vii). Indeed, this dialogue, or ongoing process of 'writing back', while situated in the symbolic and literary, is firmly engaged in the process of eliciting positive (and necessary) change in the real world. The explosion of Eurocentric notions of canonicity, literature, and language facilitates a 'decolonisation of the mind' of both African reading audiences and their white neo-colonial counterparts.

This dynamic of writing back (and thus moving forward) is clearly visible in Chinua Achebe's *Things Fall Apart* (1958) and Tsitsi Dangarembga's *Nervous Conditions* (1988). In this literary conversation, or argument, Joseph Conrad's Africanist images in *Heart of Darkness* (1917) provoke an impassioned response from Achebe, who in turn prompts Dangarembga to raise her voice. Dangarembga suggests that, in protesting the reductive 'othering' of the black African as 'savage' by skilfully portraying a rich and vivid pre-colonial Ibo existence, Achebe has effectively 'othered', or repressed the voices of, African women. The politics of writing in English, as well as the complex interplay between traditional and colonial forms of patriarchal oppression, will be explored as, departing from Spivak, it becomes apparent that it is not the case that 'the subaltern cannot speak', nor need the "babel" of subaltern voices be "unpleasant" or "confusing" (Gandhi 3). Rather, postcolonial texts such as *Things Fall Apart* and *Nervous Conditions* might most fruitfully be seen as speaking clearly and building with and upon each other in a process of self-assertion and self-empowerment, seeking not to have the definitive last word but rather to contribute to a multiplicity of voices, opinions and culturally-specific realities.

Achebe and Dangarembga speak to Nigerian, Zimbabwean, African and global audiences of past and present experiences (both positive and negative, 'traditional' and colonial) and thus pave the way, through greater awareness and respect for difference, to a positive future in an increasingly postcolonial world.

Set in much the same chronological period as *Heart of Darkness* (the late nineteenth century), *Things Fall Apart*, Achebe's response to Conrad's text, is an "object lesson" (Thieme 19) in how to achieve much-needed redefinition (and expression) of African subjectivities. Constructing an alternative fictional historiography of the incursion of European colonial society in West Africa, Achebe replaces the limited and reductive Eurocentric gaze with the deeper insights of an Ibo point of view. Achebe refrains from answering perceived racism with racism: his European characters, although heavily overlaid with ironic or symbolic commentary regarding white ignorance, are more three-dimensional than Conrad's 'natives', with the Reverend Smith's Manichaean worldview, where "black was evil", contrasted to his predecessor Mr Brown's more accommodating approach (TF 162). However, he presents the close-knit communities of Umuofia, and each of the Ibo individuals therein, as possessed of far greater agency, insight and interest than mere 'black shapes crouching' (HD 34). Ibo society is shown to be vibrant and complex. Fundamentally, Achebe deals the smug self-importance of empire a savage (harsh and calculated, not unthinkingly 'primitive'!) blow by displacing white missionaries, soldiers and government to the margins of the text. Their fatal imposition is registered, but it is only *part* of the text of African cultural history, with the first appearance of the colonialists, denaturalised through Ibo eyes as "albino" men (TF 121), not occurring until Chapter 15, a substantial way through the work.

In this sense, while Innes has claimed that Achebe "rarely lets his reader forget the otherness of the Igbo culture" (34), it is rather the case that the Western reader is 'othered' by the Ibo traditions and words which, while often explained in the glossary present in most editions, if not the text itself, act as a firm reminder that not all experience can be contained by the English language or the corresponding prevailing European worldview. From the Ibo perspective, cross-cultural encounters render the invaders ludicrous and lacking intelligence (rather than the reverse), a people who, in translation, seem unable to master the difference between "myself" and "my buttocks" (126). As Obierika bitterly observes, it is unlikely that the white man will "understand our custom about land" when he "does not even speak our tongue" (155). The dangers of cultural blindness and the self-legitimating superiority of the 'centre' are made starkly apparent in the sudden shift of perspective to the "the distant eyes of an outsider" (Harris 108) at the novel's close, where the striking juxtaposition in tone and insight betray the utter inadequacy of the uninvited, self-reflexive commentaries of the "student of primitive customs" (TF 182). The tragic hero Okonkwo (who, despite the masculinist orientation of his *chi,* or personal spirit, the reader has come to admire) is, in the District Commissioner's blinkered frame, nothing more than a limp body hanging from a tree: pacified, rather than staunchly resisting. The Commissioner concedes that the death of "one of the greatest men in Umuofia" is "interesting" enough to warrant "a reasonable paragraph" in his upcoming Africanist manual (183). Achebe's work, as "Ur-text" of post-colonial African literary tradition, undermines this "rhetoric of lack" (Gikandi 8) by drawing attention to the need for whole books, by suitably qualified authors: Obierika would be such a spokesperson, had he not, like Okonkwo, "choked" (TF 183) on his words in anger and frustration. As Huggan has suggested, while one of the greatest achievements of Achebe's "self-consciously hybrid" work is its success in attaching a local, largely ancestral, orally transmitted body of knowledge to an "imported sensibility, the modern European novel", he also manages to turn "the language of Western evolutionist anthropology against itself" (43). Not only does Achebe write back to a particular English canonical text, he also parodies "the whole of the discursive field" (Tiffin 23) within which such texts continue to operate, suggesting that, regardless of how "much thought" (TF 183) we devote to the critical enterprise, as long as a false sense of cultural superiority and Western self-definition against a 'primitive other' is maintained, the understandings produced will be fundamentally flawed.

Literary production is, for Achebe, a highly political act. In his view, art is not "pure," or removed from the context of its creation and reception, but should be actively "applied" to society in order to achieve positive "education" and change (qtd. in Osei-Nyame 148). Importantly, Achebe addresses an intended audience not only of white but, primarily, Nigerian readers, aiming to "teach…that their past…was not one long night of savagery from which the first Europeans acting on God's behalf delivered them" (148), and thus to restore a stolen "dignity" (qtd. in Ogungbesan 37) to the African postcolonial self-image.

Achebe asserts that the "world language…forced down our throats" by the history of colonisation (and continuing cultural imperialism) can be used, with skilful appropriation, as a "weapon of great strength" ("African" 63): one with the potential to impact upon a wide reading audience. Although he hopes that the two hundred Nigerian mother tongues will continue to flourish (Rowell 262), Achebe envisages the gradual creation of "a new English" that can be made to "carry the weight of…African experience" ("African" 65), an idea which mirrors Bakhtin's conception of words being not only constrained by the traces of previous usages, but also open to the layering of new meanings that fit and validate different social and geographical demands and contexts (Harrow 27). In *Things Fall*

71

Apart, Achebe succeeds in forging a written style that echoes oral story-telling, with an abundance of proverbs, "the palm-oil with which words are eaten" (6), facilitating a heteroglossic orchestra of community voices that traverses past and present. The Yeatsian title and epigraph, appropriated from the Western canon, point to the devastation wreaked by empire-building practices as the imperial "knife" attacks the core values of its colonial peripheries, "the things that held us together" (156); exposing, on another level, the fact that the 'heart of darkness', of human cruelty and despair, is not culturally specific but exists wherever "The best lack all conviction, while the worst/ Are full of passionate intensity."

However, African intertextualities and resonances are privileged in the text. As such the "straightforward act of bearing witness cracks" (Harrow 66), necessitating a slightly different mode of reading. Achebe paints a paradoxical portrait of a protagonist who is at once a 'typical' Ibo man (even an emblem or allegory of his entire society) and a selfish individualist (Nnoromele 152) who transgresses community values, transforming himself, in death, into an extended proverb or "warning…against taking too-rigid stances" (Harrow 67). As Okhamafe has observed, things begin to fall apart in the nine Umuofian villages long before white missionaries arrive (134), and the civil order crumbles largely because of internal stresses that lead the marginalised (including mothers of twins and osu (outcasts)) to "find relief outside" existing structures (Wren 35). This is not a simplistic acceptance of the "historical inevitability of modernization" on a linear frame à la Hegel (Booker 76) but a complex realisation of the "seemingly contradictory need for both tradition and transformation" (Harris 109), which can be applied with great effect to the contemporary setting, and the need to fashion an inclusive postcolonial order. We need to avoid equating 'tradition' with stasis, non-change, or fixity.

As the world changes, and different voices jostle for attention, the process of writing back will necessarily be ongoing. Despite Achebe's successful illumination, subversion and explosion of the racial stereotypes of paradigmatic colonial texts, it has been suggested that, "for the modern woman writer in Africa," Achebe's (male) 'author-ity' must seem "as difficult to challenge as [was] the district commissioner's voice" in Achebe's time (Cobham 178). Much as Conrad repressed the perspectives of women excluding Kurtz's European 'Intended' from the domain of masculine reality and further sidelining his African mistress to the river bank several feminist critics contend that Achebe has relegated women to the margins, obscuring a valorisation of patriarchal domination beneath "the rhetoric of racial and cultural retrieval" (Nzenza 216). In particular, Florence Stratton has urged female African authors to refute, or refuse, Achebe's gendered framework. Her essay "How Could Things Fall Apart For Whom They Were Not Together?" points to the systematic exclusion of women from all non-domestic aspects of community power in the novel. Following Stratton, the argument that Achebe's gendered depiction of Ibo life is historically 'accurate' can be challenged on the basis that he "could have done more to question those relations" (Booker 73). Although Traoré has called such readings "culturally illiterate" (66), drawing attention to the manner in which the imposed values of Western feminism might be a form, albeit well-intentioned, of cultural imperialism, it is clear that the "reactionary masculinity" (Hogan 125) embodied by Okonkwo (driven to despise everything his father loved, he rejects 'effeminate' gentleness along with laziness) is also rife in his wider society. As Traoré concedes, Okonkwo's suicide is in many ways "a direct result of the …attempt to displace the *Nneka* principle in his private and public life" (50), and it is notable that, while Achebe is consciously concerned with enforcing a sense of the need for societal equilibrium,

73

the overriding proverbial wisdom that 'mother is supreme' never translates from the symbolic to the level of literal or personal experience. Okonkwo's mother remains nameless in the text, alluded to only in reference to the silliness of her stories (TF 66). Even the hospitality of his motherland Mbanta is experienced as a form of punishment for a lesser, that is, female, crime.

Champion wrestler Okonkwo's misogynist tendencies are certainly heightened beyond the cultural norm, with his insistence upon the retelling and reenactment of "masculine stories of violence and bloodshed" (47) contrasted to the compassionate Nwoye's respect, even preference, for women's wisdom. Similarly, Okonkwo's participation in the killing of adopted son Ikemefuna, stemming from his own (feminine) fear of "failure and weakness" (12), is condemned as unnecessary and undesirable by Obierika. However, the general economy of Umuofia also rests on gendered distinctions. Not only was "Yam, the king of crops...a man's crop" (21), but yam ownership was a greater status symbol than marriage: Okoye is lauded as having "a large barn full of yams" and "three wives" (6), in that order. *Agbala*, the word for "woman," is "also used of a man who has taken no title" ('Glossary'): both, then, are implicitly insulting. Women, as property, are subjected to violence, and it is significant that the earth goddess Ani does not punish Okonkwo for the act of beating Ojiugo (his anger at her having gone to plait her hair instead of cooking was, the narrator decrees, "justifiable" (25)), but merely for doing so during the Week of Peace. The narrative "backs away" (Stratton 28) from fertile gaps or spaces in which these inequalities might be questioned, as do the female characters. The Chielo-Ezinma-Ekwefi encounter might be read as a woman-centered paradigm of resistance: three strong females enacting powerful roles priestess, child, courageous mother in a situation where Okonkwo's "machete, the symbol of his male aggression, is of no use at all" (Davies 247).

Intriguingly, the priestess interrupts Ezinma just as she is on the cusp of relating how Tortoise and Cat "went to wrestle against Yams" (88), that dominant male symbol, with the unresolved ending of the fable a potential site of disruption. Such possibilities, however, are subsumed within the prevailing phallocentric story. The feisty Ezinma, who might have figured more in Achebe's narrative, as in Okonkwo's affections, had she been a boy, is, after all, merely one of those infantilised women who, instinctively, "took to their heels" (79) when the (male) egwugwu appeared, fleeing submissively from the centre of political and religious authority. Tellingly, although Achebe does not romanticise Ibo life, the implied male narrator fails to question the injustice suffered by women, and for the most part, the female victims endure with minimal complaint, even silence. Stratton warns that, published at a time when political power was being transferred from the colonial regime to a "Nigerian male elite" (27), such fictional representations risk legitimating the exclusion of women from contemporary public affairs. Indeed, just as the first "nationalist" authors "had to rewrite and reinvent a *presence* that colonialist discourse, in its arrogance, imposture, and triumphalism, had theorized as absence," so too have female writers been motivated to recover the "submerged female traditions" of artistic expression in order to rise above the seemingly "inevitable, natural *sexism*" (Jeyifo 190, 183) often perpetuated by male writers. In taking the pen into their own hands, female writers are becoming an increasingly powerful force, asserting rightful demands for respect, recognition and participation in the formation of a range of positive postcolonial futures.

Challenging the reductive representation of women and advocating improvement in their social and material conditions is a major feminist concern, but, in the 'Third World', women's existence is "strung between traditionalism and modernity in ways that make it

75

extremely difficult for them to attain personal freedoms without severe sacrifices or compromises" (Quayson 103-4), a struggle illustrated to great effect in *Nervous Conditions*. As Mohanty has argued in "Under Western Eyes: Feminist Scholarship and Colonial Discourses," some feminist writers "discursively colonize" by imagining a composite, singular, "third-world woman" (qtd. in Quayson 104). This may explain why "the role of 'Africa' in 'post-colonial theory' is different from the role of 'post-colonial theory' in Africa" (McClintock 260): the former often dangerously symbolic, the latter, so far removed from material reality as to be irrelevant, even counterproductive.

Dangarembga's work, the first novel by a black Zimbabwean woman to be published in English (Vizzard 205), is so important to postcolonial understandings (in Africa and in the West) because it displays the vast differences, in aspirations and approaches, both within and between class and generational groupings of Zimbabwean women. Each of the women Tambudzai and her cousin Nyasha, Ma'Shingayi (Tambu's mother) and Maiguru, Lucia, Anne the servant, Tambudzai's grandmother, even the "family patriarch" (NC 142-3) Tete Gladys are aware of the patriarchal incursions upon their lives; but they negotiate very different paths through the complex matrix of "triple" (Ashcroft 23) colonisation or oppression. These women experience "the poverty of blackness on one side," with the effects of white colonial rule in 1960s Rhodesia, as well as "the weight of womanhood on the other" (NC 16), with ramifications in both traditional and European frames that compound and intensify as they coincide. In addition, they deal with the fraught fusion of emancipatory strategies in a desired "genuine post-colonial feminism" (Ashcroft 33), rather than merely an Anglo-American or French body of theory transplanted onto the very different actualities of the former colonies. All of the characters, including the men, are linked in the text to nerves, frustration, powerlessness and anxiety, but the confusion resulting from colliding cultural and gender norms is most palpably apparent in the experience of Nyasha, her body providing "testimony" (Suleri 341) to her psychic disruption as she expels that which she cannot digest, or reconcile. The combination of sadza and foreign sweets and biscuits, along with all they represent, is indeed disturbing; but, unlike Tambu, who can eventually "question things and refuse to be brainwashed" (NC 204) by both imported ideals and imposed inferiorities, asserting the independent will to education and change within the overarching "rules of their community's paradigms" (Kalu 153), Nyasha experiences a kind of homelessness, and emptiness, of self and intellect. Nyasha's socialisation in England may have taught her of her right to stand up for what she believes in (which in turn inspires Tambudzai to look beyond the edges of what she knows), but, alienated from Shona language and norms, she is left without a firm belief for which to fight, only a paralysing sense of the looming problems. Shredding the one-sided history books "between her teeth" (NC 201), Nyasha feels "trapped" by the "Englishness" against which Tambudzai's mother has warned, but she is simultaneously constrained by her father's inability to see his family's, and society's, pre-existing and perpetuated problems of gender inequality, "punching him in the eye" after he calls her a "whore" (114-5). As Tambudzai observes, "the victimization" is, in many ways, "universal. It didn't depend on poverty, on lack of education, or on tradition…Men took it everywhere with them", such that, at base, all "conflicts came back to this question of femaleness," and presumed inferiority (115-6).

It has been suggested that Orientalism (and Africanism) are fantasies built upon sexual difference, with the phallocentric discourse of colonialism inscribing the landscape and population of the exotic 'other' as weak, inferior, yielding and feminine (Yegenoglu

11-12). *Nervous Conditions,* without suppressing "an ounce of its legitimate anger at the misogyny of African men" (Sugnet 36), shows clearly the manner in which those men may themselves be the emasculated products, and puppets, of a colonial hierarchy. The title and epigraph point to Sartre's introduction to Fanon's *The Wretched of the Earth,* which asserts that "the status of 'native' is a nervous condition introduced and maintained by the settler among colonized people *with their consent*" (qtd in Booker 191), a kind of psychological subordination. Although Dangarembga's main concern is with "feminizing Fanon's findings on colonial cultural alienation" (Boehmer 228), the male characters are portrayed as having been bewitched by colonialism. Split between loyalty to tradition and the desire to share the perceived material benefits of 'modern' culture, they are led to "accept their own inferiority" (Booker 191), thus cooperating in their subjugation, with both Tambudzai's father and brother suffering "painfully under the evil wizards' spell" (NC 50). Jeremiah, a parody of the 'shiftless native', brandishes an imaginary spear while becoming reliant on the generosity of his Western-educated brother, while Babamukuru, kept "busy" (102) between the demands of life as a surrogate Englishman and traditional obligations to his extended family, is haunted by the sense that, created by the British colonial system to serve its purposes, his power is illusory. At the Sacred Heart Convent school he, like Tambu, is a mere black face, an (inferior, segregated, undifferentiated) "African" (194). Even Mr Matimba, in order to assist Tambu sell maize to fund her schooling, is forced to perform a subservient and compliant role with white people, speaking "in the softest, slipperiest voice I had ever heard him use" (27). These curtailments and false reshaping of self are spiritually stunting, even fatal: Tambu's brother Nhamo dies, if indirectly, because of his attempt to transcend altogether the 'dirty', cumbersome realities of

African communal life. While Tambu herself acknowledges, and for a time even succumbs to, the seductions of a clean, clear-cut white world, Dangarembga ingeniously demonstrates that what colonial discourse defines as 'African' is often really "the debased form of indigenous ways *after* colonialism has disrupted them" (Sugnet 44). The apparently straightforward symbolism of hygiene at first seems clearly arranged in favour of English customs, but Tambu soon reverses her conviction that "the further we left the old ways behind the closer we came to progress" (NC 147). There may be "reproductive odors", children with "upset bowels" and strong "aromas of productive labour" (1) on the slow Umtali bus, but the sparkling white porcelain of Maiguru's bathroom actually suppresses normal bodily functions (making Tambu's menstrual blood seem "nasty and nauseating" (95)), and masks the pathological. The filthiness of the pit toilet is as much a symptom of colonial disease as is Nyasha's vomit: in the "early days" before Tambu's mother 'lost' her children to a new way of life, along with her pride and reason for living, the latrine "had never smelt and its pink plaster walls had remained a healthy pink" (123). Much as an 'unadapted' English vocabulary might be inadequate to convey African realities, so too do housing structures derived from English circumstances have difficulty coping with the African "dust" (71) which, creeping pervasively in, widens existing class and gender inequalities. Although Maiguru has been educated overseas like her husband, her wages are subsumed within his; her point of view goes largely unacknowledged; and, although she breaks free of her baby-talk to leave his reign for a few days, she ultimately returns to serve at table, and maintain, with the help of servant Anne, the deceptively shiny surfaces of their existence, scrubbing at doubts with an ammonia cleaner which was "efficient but chapped your hands much more roughly than ash dissolved in water from Nyamarira ever did" (67).

It appears Dangarembga sets the novel "back in history in order to blame the colonizers, rather than Mugabe's government, for the plight of women in Zimbabwe" (Sugnet 46), but it is evident that, in writing about "the things that move" (Veit-Wild 29), affect, enrage and inspire women, traditional African patriarchy does not escape unscathed. Dangarembga has spoken of the need to stop subsuming women's issues, which have not yet received "proper attention or the right kind of analysis", within the "national question" (qtd in Osei-Nyame Jnr 55), and *Nervous Conditions* demonstrates the complicity between colonialism and patriarchy, with pre-colonial forms of oppression merely transplanted onto and exacerbated by Western culture. The narrative achieves a "defamiliarization" (Skinner 116) of gender norms by showing them through 8-year-old Tambu's eye to be (like the concept of racial inferiority) mere cultural constructs. The preferential treatments of sons, and the gendered division of housework, labour and authority in traditional society, are magnified in the context of colonial education: the male role as family breadwinner makes Nhamo the 'natural' choice for further schooling, increasing his privileges exponentially. Tambu's "callousness" to his death (which is also her window of opportunity) is necessary if she is to "escape" the patterns of "entrapment" (NC 1) she sees around her. Convinced of her own worth, Tambu sees the "injustice" (12) of her mother's acquiescence to learning, "the earlier the better," what "sacrifices" (16) will be necessary. The text enters fully into the "woman-centered spaces" (Aegerter 231) the cooking and sleeping areas as well as the mental and emotional terrain mapped therein providing detailed insights denied to the reader in Achebe's male-centered work. As a result, it becomes clear that modes of female resistance from within a tradition-based contemporary African culture are possible. In an echo back to the village elders' adjudication of Mgbafo's marital dispute in *Things Fall Apart* (77-83), where women are excluded simultaneously from proceedings and from readerly view, the perspective of "we, the women and children" becomes the focus in *Nervous Conditions,* making way for the expression of an attitude of "quite violent…opposition to the system" (137) while the *dare* or male meeting regarding Lucia's sexual transgression is conducted. Determining that "she should be there to defend herself" (137), Lucia storms into the house, eyes glittering, and, tweaking Takesure by the ears, demands some "sense" and honesty. Tambu is later unsure whether the "patriarchy" shared her (disrespectful) "laughter" (144), and is herself racked with physical reaction to the wedding which makes a mockery of her parents' existence, as of her own, but the spirit of the moment resonates throughout the work, and beyond the last page.

Just as Tambu questions the success of Nyasha's "rebellion" (1), the reader may fear that the freedom she claims for herself and Lucia is illusory. Notably, Lucia's declaration that Grade One has made her mind "think more efficiently" (160) is overshadowed by both the colonial ideologies undeniably inherent in the pre-independence syllabus, and the necessity of her "grovelling" to (200) (or, "like a man herself" (171), skilfully manipulating) Babamukuru for assistance. However, Tambu manages to retain positive contact with the spiritual life of the African landscape and her body, immersing herself in "the old deep places" (4) as sources of strength and orientation (rather than succumbing to a reductive identification of the singular subject position, unthinking 'woman', with land and the national identity, able to be raped and lost forever). So too there is a sense that she might be able to break down the "Englishness" (203) to manageable pieces, choosing to consume (rather than be consumed by) some aspects, and rejecting or protesting against others. The young Tambu, fearing that it was "unwise to think too deeply" (39) about sexism lest dissatisfaction "interfere with the business of living", soon learns that to "bury" (50) thoughts and desires for self-fulfilment is to enact a stifling live burial (much as the burial of the voices of female characters in other texts might have contributed to the social and political stasis of their female readers). To truly know "myself," Tambu must speak the "knotted" complex issues that characterise her experience of being African, and being female. Although, like her education at the mission and boarding schools, her self-authorship involves the use of the colonial language, her decision is ultimately an empowering one, and she achieves the authoritative status of "interpreter" (Uwakweh 78), rather than the paraphrased or unheard interpreted subject of knowledge. Dangarembga, like other postcolonial women writers, in her "double...perspective of ethnicity and gender" turns "absence into presence" (Begum 27) by giving voice to a multiplicity of previously silenced or marginalised female viewpoints. While there will always be "another volume" (NC 204) to be filled, and new or altered perspectives from which to write back, this text alone has made important inroads into breaking free of the reductive and stereotypical presentation of African women in literature, thus inspiring positive changes in life.

Appiah has stated that "postcoloniality is the condition...of a relatively small, Western-style, Western-trained, group of writers and thinkers" who have "invented" (149) an Africa for their own use. Such a view might prove as disabling as the notion that 'the subaltern cannot speak', or that self-expression in the once 'colonial' language, English, undermines authenticity: put together, not only would postcolonial writers by definition not be able to communicate but, even if they could, the rest of the world would be too self-absorbed to hear them. Rather, as Darby refreshingly suggests, we may need to alter our mode of approach, so that, instead of becoming caught up in the self-referential requirements of an "often resistant body of theory", we should give much more weight to the "problems", and authors, of the so-called 'Third World': in this respect, "Achebe is a better guide than either Derrida or Foucault" (17). Social responsibility, as well as forming the self-professed motivation of the creative work of authors such as Achebe and Dangarembga, "must be the basis of any theorizing on postcolonial literature" (Katrak 157), necessitating a "good-faith effort" to cultivate "readerly tact" (Linton 29, 43) and responsiveness as non-African readers respectfully approach and seek to understand (but not assimilate to their own Eurocentric perspective) different African "ways of knowing" (Kalu xv). *Things Fall Apart* and *Nervous Conditions*, in dialogue with each other and with texts from the Western 'canon' such as that purveyor of Africanist myths, Conrad's *Heart of Darkness*, provide a positive "way forward" (Dodgson 101) in both the literary and socio-cultural-political domains, encouraging readers to approach the multiplicity of voices they contain in light of the knowledge that, as Achebe has remarked, postcolonial "travellers with closed minds can tell us little except about themselves" ("Image" 791).

5

LN Nwokora

Oyono,
wa Thiongó

IN HIS work on Chinua Achebe's novels, entitled "Chinua Achebe and the Tragedy of History,"[1] Thomas Melone says that the content of literature ought to be judged as "a portion of his destiny" (12). Explaining his reasons, the Cameroonian critic says that every authentic literature should be a "carrier of humanity" ("porteuse d'humanite"), since it should, whether it be African or European, "witness for man and his destiny"; because, continues the critic, "men are first of all men ... , their identity is fundamental, and their destiny human" (12).

More than any other form of literary criticism or appreciation, comparative literature highlights this universality of even' creative

---

[1]This book is actually published in French, under the title, "Chinua Achebe et la tragedies de I' Histoire." The English version, both of the title and the quotations from the book, are author's own translation.

literary art. Universality, however, does not mean that one must necessarily compare authors from different countries or different cultural backgrounds. It is possible to compare and contrast two or more writers from the same country, from the same village, even from the same family, and finally, an author can be compared to himself. One comes up with interesting findings in comparing, for example, the Achebe of *No Longer at Ease* with the Achebe of *Arrow of God*. The young graduate returning from England, unable to find his feet in his former home, and the village of Umuaro no longer the same under sweeping religious attacks on the gods that had hitherto guaranteed its security and unity, both are witnesses each in its own way to the same cracking society under the invasion of foreign culture. Does it mean that the celebrated Nigerian novelist has said everything when he published his famous *Things Fall Apart*, and that thereafter is only repeating himself? Far from it! The novelist is comparable to a surveyor, whose field is the human society; in each novel he observes society from a particular point of view. The product of his artistic (here literary) creation is a "portion" of man's struggle with life, i.e., with his destiny, and this "odyssey" reproduces, *mutatis mutandis*, similar characteristics, whether it talks of Achilles, of Antigone, of Hamlet, of Obi Okonkwo or Ezeulu.

The above considerations help us to better appreciate Ime Ikiddeh's definition of a novel as "fiction based on an historical event recreated in human terms" (xii). The particular point of focus of the two authors we are studying is the child in his relation to given certain "historical events recreated in human terms" in two different countries and at nearly ten years' interval in time. Before comparing these historical events viewed as recreated fiction, we should first of all ascertain why the two authors chose each a child to be his hero.

Why the Child as hero?

Childhood is the only poetic state, says Melone. This is probably because poetry is best appreciated, not by reasoning, but by feeling, i.e. by entering into the ecstatic sentiments of the poet at his moment of writing. The poetic verse aims, therefore, at arousing these sentiments in the reader, and not at a logical understanding of the passage. Whereas prose may receive one clear interpretation or explanation, no one interpretation can ever exhaust the wealth of meaning couched in a few poetic verses. If it is true that a piece of literary work escapes its author once it is set down on paper, it is even truer of poetry than of any other form of creative writing. There are certain experiences in life which, in order to retain one's mental health, were better felt than reasoned about. By his age, nature, and psychological make up, the child feels things and does not reason about them, at least in the cut and dry syllogism of the adult. The child's innocence, his openness to every instinct and desire his connivance with nature, his instinctive intransigence for purity and truth... are among the qualities that make Melone believe that the only poetic state is childhood; in the sense where the poetic state or condition may be interpreted to mean the ideal state of paradise lost. The first aim, therefore, of a novelist whose hero is a child could be the desire, conscious or not, to travel back along the slippery steps to his lost Garden of Eden.

The second reason – and this is nearer to the two authors we are studying – is that the unreasoning attitude of the child, with whom the author often identifies himself, helps to rub off the sharp edge of the cruel experiences narrated in the book. The child is by temperament elastic, his own idealism is not the dangerously stiff rigidity of an Okonkwo who commits suicide in order not to witness what Melone calls 'the glorious funerals of a dying Africa' (77). Oyono's 'house boy', Toundi, suffers series of humiliations, but does not commit

87

suicide (he is actually killed by the whites while attempting to run for his life), and Ngugi's Njoroge is recalled from his suicide attempt by the voice of his mother. Okonkwo's adult pride stung him beyond recall; he had to die.

The third and final advantage of the child-hero is that, thanks to his naivety and undiluted reproduction of events, what he narrates is nobody's exclusive property. The author can therefore use him and (how apt at the hands of Oyono and Ngugi!) hide perfectly behind his translucid frankness to relate whatever happens. Who can accuse the child of fomenting trouble, or of inciting one particular political party or ethnic group against another? Does he even feel the pinch and sting of discrimination and racism as adults do? At best he feels shocked, and registers his shock like the faithful photographic paper that he is. The most salutary aspect of the child's character is that he is completely absorbed by the present, does not ruminate on the past as adults do, and has a carefree attitude about the future (i.e. when this even dawns on his consciousness).

It is true that the heroes of *Houseboy* and *Weep Not, child* oscillate between infancy and adolescence, but their age and experiences in the two novels are still completely characterized, on their part, by innocence and naivety of childhood.

Toundi and Njoroge

Some of the points raised here above, about the artistic benefits of the child-hero, do not apply to the two novels under consideration. While one could describe Camara Laye's *African Child* as an unbroken chaplet of one nostalgic childhood memory after another, it would be almost impossible to imagine any atom of nostalgia in Oyono's mind, or Ngugi's either, when they bend over the creation of their Toundi and Njoroge respectively. For while *The African Child* affords the Guinean undergraduate in Paris a salutary fight into fancy from the cold, indifferent, lonely and capitalist atmosphere of the French capital – exactly as Louis Guilloux's 'Pain des Reves'[2] does for the novelist from Brittany in Nazi-occupied France of 1942 – the two novels being studied evoke rather the same bitter taste in the reader's mouth as Mongo Beti's *Remember Ruben*. If nostalgia there was, it is rather for a childhood that never existed, or rather that is not allowed to exist as it should. Toundi and Njoroge belong to the generation of African children who never had any childhood – a model of which one reads in the Edenic memories recounted by the hero of *The African Child*; they rather resemble the generation of those European children born in the late thirties, and whose childhood was spent in concentration camps or in cities terrorised consistently by Nazi brutality. A Sigmund Freud would have summed up all that has been said here above in one short phrase: that sort of childhood is just a "reve manque" – a lost dream – if not a nightmare, like that of Morzamba in *Remember Ruben*. And who likes to recall a nightmare? Except, of course, for some very serious reasons best known to the author. These reasons already form the subject-matter of several commentaries on Oyono and Ngugi, and will only be very briefly dealt with here. We shall now examine and compare the nightmarish experiences of the two child heroes.

Resemblances

For purpose of clarity, examining the areas of resemblance or similarity between Toundi's fate and that of Njoroge will be quite in

---

[2]*Le Pain des Reves*, (*Bread of the Imagination*) [1942], a semi autobiographical novel, was like a bridge which the author, Louis Guilloux, built between the horror of 1942 France and his childhood in Brittany during Second World War. Guilloux was born in Saint-Brieue in 1899 and died in 1980.

order. The two heroes are both children, not just from the titles of the novels, but from indications about their age. Toundi, the personage-cum-narrator of *Houseboy* speaks about his age at the very beginning of his "dairy," explaining what – according to his own understanding– was his true reason for leaving his parental home.

> In fact I just wanted to get close to the white man with hair like the beard on a maize cub who dressed in women's clothes and give little black boys' sugar lumps. I was in a gang of heathen boys who followed the missionary about as he went from hut to hut....(9)

As for Njoroge in *Weep not, child*, his age is indicated right from the opening of the very first chapter of the book where his mother, Nyokabi, asks him "would you like to go to school?" (3).

Most Africans know the relative age of any child about to start school – exceptions being made for adult education. Later on, in flashback chronology, the author, explaining how Ngotho (Njoroge's father) had become a "Muhoi", says among other things: "Njoroge had never come to understand how his father had become a 'Muhoi.' Maybe a child did not know such matters. They were too deep for him" (13).

The two child-heroes grew in a precarious atmosphere of colonial oppression and exploitation. Need it be stressed that this point is at the very core of the two novels under study? *Houseboy* is set in the French Cameroons of between 1921 and 1939, i.e., between the placement of the former German protectorate (1884-1914) under French mandate, after the Allies had occupied it from 1914 to 1916. We have indications of this in the novel, first from the only direct allusion to "the War" by Mekongo, "the army veteran" (Oyono 57), and then indirectly from the cook shocked by the boldness and unhealthy inquisitiveness of "youngsters of today" who pry into the secrets of the white man. Says the cook to Toundi: 'I don't understand you, you youngsters of today. In the time of the Germans we took no interest in the affairs of the whites'(Oyono 61).

Ngugi's *Weep not, child* is set in a Kenya where the indigenes return from the white man's wars of 1914-1916, and 1939-45 to find their land gone: the white settlers now own all their land. The unsuccessful attempts to recover the lost land lead eventually to the terrorist underground movement called the "Mau-Mau." We are therefore in the Kenya of the fifties, of the liberation struggles by Jomo Kenyatta, in a Kenya as mercilessly exploited as the French Cameroon of Oyono's *Houseboy*. As a fitting explanation for the predatory appetite of the white settlers of this period, Ngugi explains, in a flashback, the genesis of the passionate love of Mr Howlands for the land (in Kenya) his almost sensual attachment to this "shamba" (29). And the reason is that,

> He (Mr. Howlands) was a product of the First World War. After years of security at home, he had been suddenly called to arms and he had gone to the war. With the fire of youth he imagines war a glory. Bur after four years of blood and terrible destruction, like many other young men he was utterly disillusioned by the 'peace.' He had to escape. East Africa was a good place. Here was a big trace of wild country to conquer. (30)

The theme of economic exploitation in the colonies has been the most common among African writers, especially in this pre-independence era. And Mr. Howlands is presented to us as one among many who, "disillusioned by the 'peace'... had to escape." They were no longer coming as mere colonialists just to keep order and levy taxes for the Imperial Crown; they had emigrated in search of a new permanent home. And what better place than this unprotected "wild country," which was a prey "to conquer"? One is not surprised

91

therefore to hear Mr. Howlands declare peremptorily to the despoiled Ngotho (father of the child-hero): "my home is here"(32). Ngotho tries gradually, and on several occasions to explain to little Njoroge how the land that was formerly their family property had passed into the hands of Mr. Howlands, and how he, Ngotho, had become a "Muhoi" (a sort of a vassal in feudal times) on his own land (26).

But the best summary of the sad story of expropriation is given by Kiarie, one of the speakers at the rally in support of the strike embarked upon by the despoiled Kenyans:

> All the land belonged to the people black people. They had been given it by God. For every race had their country ... Later, our fathers were taken captives in the first Big war to help in a war whose course they never knew. And when they came back? 'Their land had been taken away for a settlement of the white soldiers.... . Our people were taken and forced to work for these settlers.... When people rose to demand their rights they were shot down... When the second Big War came, we were taken to fight Hitler - Hitler who had not wronged us. We were killed, we shed blood to save the British Empire from defeat and collapse. (58)

But now that "there was a man sent by God whose name was Jomo" (note the biblical language verbatim with the fourth Gospel), they "have gathered ... to tell the British... The time has come. Let my people go... We want back our land! Now!" (58)

Did they get it? The "Mau Mau" was the answer.

In Oyono's *Houseboy* the tragic experience of exploited Africans is, like everything else in this fundamentally satirical novel, presented in a rather ludicrous fashion. Since the "narrator" is Toundi himself, we are hemmed in with him in his little world of a child: we only see what he sees, and experience what he experiences. But childish and of little consequence as Toundi's experiences may be seen, they are nevertheless pointers to a similar spirit of merciless exploitation.

The first instance of this which we meet in the novel is Toundi's joy at finding himself the boy of a white man (a rare privilege at the time), and, what is more, one whom the white man has taught how to read and write. What did it matter to the child so raised in his expectations if he was paid no wages?

> I am his boy, a boy who can read and write, serve Mass, lay a table, sweep out his room and make his bed. I don't earn any money. Now and then he gives me an old shirt or an old pair of trousers. (15)

Exploitation of child labour? And by a missionary? Father Gilbert is only being true to a generally prevalent mentality towards Africans at the period. The second is the symbolic episode of the nightly raids on indigenes' quarters by the chief of police, nicknamed the "Gullet" ("Gosier D' Oiseau" in the original French text) because of "his long flexible neck like a tickbird's neck" (24). Toundi narrates one such visit to the house of his brother-in-law with whom he lived.

> The door gave way before I could open it. Into the tiny house charged four Ful'be constables followed by Gullet. I slipped behind the door while my brother-inlaw and sister, half dead with fear, watched Gullet ... and his men overturning the bits of furniture ... . Gullet kicked a water jug that shattered into pieces. He told one of his men to turn over a pile of banana bunches.
> He pulled off a banana and gobbled it down.... . he picked another banana and began to eat it. My sister's eyes grew round. I began to be afraid again. Gullet turned, bent his long neck and went out. The noise of the engines died away and then there was silence. (24-25)

The above clearly depicts the condition of the African terrorised by armed white settlers who destroy or appropriate his belongings.

Our third and last example comes to show what easily becomes of the salary of paid African workers who have the misfortune to damage anything while on duty. Mrs. Decazy, the wife of the commandant, like any other unfaithful wife (or husband) is ever jittery and her domestics naturally bear the brunt of her cantankerous mood. If they broke any plate or dish their salary would go in compensation out of all proportion. In one of these moods, "she carried out in inspection and found a broken decanter. She fixed a price and deducted it from the cook's wages and mine. It came to half our month's earnings" (74). Toundi is lucky this time to be paid any wage at all, and he and all the other domestics are warned that "that's only a beginning... only a beginning" (74). It is the litany of similar humiliations, which, *mutatis mutandis*, provoke the ill-fated strike in *Weep not, child*. Jacobo's ignoble role in the latter novel is comparable, in its meanness, greed and treachery to a similar role by Toundi's repugnant uncle in *Houseboy*. Unable to resist his greed for the delicious porcupine prepared by Toundi's mother, the greedy uncle advises his brother (the hero's father) against Toundi's childish misdemeanour, saving, "if you want to make him obedient... take away his food.... This porcupine is really delicious" (12). Hence the hero, reduced to "peering through the cracks in the mud wall" of his parental hut at his father and uncle gulping down greedily his own share of the evening meal (12), is a symbol of Africans despoiled of their lawful rights through the instrumentality of those fellow Africans who are supposed to protect and defend them. They are just like the Kenyans of *Weep not, child*, who through the treacherous puppetry of chief Jacobo (himself an indigene), become 'Muhoi' on their very ancestral lands.

The last important point of resemblance in the two novels is the use of child innocence and naivety to puncture the myth of white racial superiority. Oyono's naive Toundi leaves no aspect untouched, his symbolic "broom" sweeping through not only the official residence of the commandant and discovering Madam Decazy's contraceptives... but also through the church and the prisons where hypocrisy equally held sway. Beneath the facade of a mythical racial superiority, Toundi finds the same lying, cowardly and unimaginative brutes as one could find anywhere. Madam Decazy is the highest lady of the land being the wife of the highest white official. Was her nymphomania not exactly the same as that of the professional African prostitute, Kalisa? The latter had at least the honesty to accept her place and keep it. Such a sacrilegious scrutiny could not go unpunished, and Toundi paid for it with his life.

In *Weep not, child*, Njoroge and Stephen Howlands meet at an inter-schools' sports to discover to their mutual surprise that they had each secretly wanted to befriend the other, but were held back by this mysterious "electric tension in the air..." which is nothing but racial prejudice and induced xenophobia:

> 'I used to hide near the road. I wanted to speak with some of you.'
> Stephen was losing his shyness.
> Why didn't you?'
> 'I was afraid.'
>
> …
>
> 'I am sorry I ran away from you. I too was afraid.'
> 'Afraid?' It was Stephen's turn to wonder.
> 'Yes. I too was afraid of you.'
> 'Strange'
> 'Yes. It's strange how you do fear something because your heart is already prepared to fear because may be you were brought up to fear something, or simply because you found others fearing..."
> (110)

95

And thanks to their world of children, which "stood somewhere outside petty prejudice, hatred and class differences," they felt "close together, united by a common experience of insecurity and fear. no one could escape" (88, 111). "No one" neither black nor white. This momentary freedom from the inhibitions of social and racial prejudices helps these two children (one white the other black) experience what is inescapably fundamental to every human being in circumstances such as the Kenya of Mau Mau terrorism, a common experience of insecurity and fear no one could escape. Imprisoned hitherto in his ghetto-mentality, the black would have thought that the "superior" race should also be "superior" to feelings of fear and insecurity. After this discovery, they are never the same again, just like Toundi who, having discovered to his utter amazement that "a great chief like the Commandant (is) uncircumcised ... was relieved by this discovery," because "it killed something inside (him)": fear. "I knew I should never be frightened of the Commandant again" (28).

Differences

From the above points which still do not exhaust all the aspects of resemblance, it is clear that there is much in common between *Houseboy* and *Weep not, child*. Let us examine the divergences in the experiences of the two child-heroes, because no mater how much destinies resemble, each is still unique in its own way. The fact that *Houseboy* is an English translation from the original French text, *Une vie de boy*, hardly merits any mention, except to stress the different colonial backgrounds in which the two novels are written. If, according to an American proverb, "the first hour is the rudder of the day" we can hardly find a better way to start a study of the divergences in these two destinies than to go back to their origin, i.e. to their family background.

While Toundi evolves as an orphan, Njoroge, is all along surrounded and protected by the warmth of his parental home. It is quite true that at the opening pages of *Houseboy* we find Toundi surrounded, like Njoroge, by the warmth of a family. But, like the "predestined personage" of Marthe Robert's *Family Novel*, Toundi is not destined to "spend his childhood days with his parents, in the warmth of their common love" (Robert 52). Because his father did not love (him) as a father ought to love his son, he had his mother's "blessing" for fleeing his parental home for good (13). A little further on, he writes: "My parents are dead. I have never been back to the village" (14). We shall see the disastrous consequences of this on his destiny at the end, when compared especially with that of Njoroge. The latter, as we have said, spent all his childhood with his parents.

Njoroge inherits his parents' lifelong ambition: to recover their lost land which, to his father, Ngotho, was "a spiritual loss" as well (74). It is mainly for this reason that he was sent to school, for, as Ngotho himself says, "education was good only because it would lead to the recovery of the lost lands" (39). Right from the start therefore, Njoroge feels weighing on his young fragile shoulders the onerous task of playing a messianic role:

> Njoroge listened to his father. He instinctively, knew that an indefinable demand was being made on him, even though he was so young. He knew that for him education would be the fulfilment of a wider and more significant vision a vision that embraced the demand made on him (...). He saw himself destined for something big, and this made his heart glow. (39)

Little by little he comes to believe that God may have chosen him to be the "instrument of His Divine Service" (94). Hence this prayer on hearing that he is going to go to High School: "Give me more and more learning and make me the instrument of Thy Light and Peace"

(104). The budding Moses was confirmed in this vision of his national messianic role on the occasion of his departure for High School:

> Somehow the Gikuyu people always saw their deliverance as embodied in education. When the time for Njoroge to leave came near, many people contributed money so that he could go.
>
> He was no longer the son of Ngotho but the son of the land (...). Njoroge had now a new feeling of pride and power for at last his way seemed clear. The land needed him and God had given him an opening so that he might come back and save his family and the whole country. (104-105)

The reader knows the disaster that put a tragic end to these dreams. The laconic manner in which the embittered child sums up his sad story: "I have now lost all my education, my faith and my family .... I, alone, am left" (131). His dreams now behind him, "life seemed (to him) like a big lie where people bargained with forces that one could not see " (126).

The hero of *Houseboy*, Toundi, for his part, is a blind victim of these invisible forces from the very beginning of the novel. Unlike Njoroge, all his "schooling" consists of learning how to read and write which the white missionary taught him with the sole aim of making him more useful as a houseboy: "Father Gilbert says I can read and write fluently. Now I can keep a diary like he does" (9). We know that this "diary" is actually the novel, *Houseboy*. Naive and imprudent, inexperienced and deaf to reason, Toundi commits one blunder after another, believing stupidly all the time that he enjoys the powerful protection of the commandant. Wasn't he "the dog of the king," and hence the "king" among his fellow "dogs"? Who would dare to harm the "chief European's boy?" (20).

Unlike Njoroge's, all his ambition for the future is a purely self-

98

centred vague seeking to become like the white man he serves, without knowing too well how to go about it. When, one day, the commandant's wife advises him "to buy a wife" – flattering him that "as the commandant's house boy he is an attractive match he answers: "Perhaps, madam, but my wife and children will never be able to eat and dress like madam or like white children" (56).

Having severed the umbilical chord that links him with his ancestral "primitive" origin, he wants to become a white man with black skin. Subconsciously, he thinks he has become a member of the Decazy family hence "(he) could do what (he) like(d)" (73). Even though he discovers the secret of the myth of the white man's "racial superiority complex": hypocrisy, he still aspires to resemble him. This infantile megalomania as madam Decazy points out to him (56), coupled with his incurable naive confidence in the commandant's all-powerful protection, blinds him to the fact the he could one day fall victim to this hypocrisy, whose universally recognized stock in trade is treachery and betrayal.

This brings us to the last point of difference between Toundi and Njoroge, the last and in the fact the greatest, as it is a matter of life and death, a question of to be or not be. "If water is polluted at its very source..." begins in Igbo proverb, Toundi's "source" [destiny] is vitiated right from his earliest childhood. Forced by the punitive brutality of an iron-fisted father to flee his parental home, he becomes literally a prisoner of his greed which attaches him irresistibly to the world of the white man. He grows deaf to all advice and warning to flee the residence "when the water [was] still only up to the knees," i.e., before the river swallows [him] up altogether – according to the time-tested saying of our ancestors (100). A few days after this warning, to which he paid a deaf ear, he is shot and killed at the Spanish Guinea frontier in a belated attempt to escape from his fate. He had left his destiny in the hands of the white man and the latter had disposed of it as his colonialist predatory greed dictated.

Njoroge, as we have seen, goes from an optimistic vision of bright "tomorrow" to a bitter disappointment which finds him in a situation, "to which 'tomorrow' was no longer an answer " (122). In such a bleak predicament, he has only just one ray of hope: in love. In his love for Nwihaki, he begs the latter to escape with him from the wicked reality of their country – a disguised form of suicide. He has lost all hope in any future; but Nwihaki opposes this cowardly escapism. "She sat there, a lone tree defying darkness, trying to instil new life in him. But he did not want to live. Not this kind of life" (133).

When Nwihaki bluntly refuses to yield to his own type of "life," his last hope vanishes with the dying steps of the retreating girl, symbolised by the last rays of "the sun (that) was sinking" (134). He sinks into total despair. Pessimism and nihilism take control of him, and his attempted suicide is not a surprise in such circumstances. But he is timely saved from putting his neck in the noose by the voice of mother, Nyokabi, calling to him out of the darkness... (135-136).

Suicide is the worst form of escapism, the last and final surrender of a coward before the challenge of living is the only irreparable failure in life. Njoroge therefore feels a strange relief to have been saved in extremis, and as he humbly accompanies his mother home, he feels ashamed of his triple failure:

> He followed her, saying nothing. He was only conscious that he had failed her and the last word of his father, when he had told him to look after the women.
>
> He had failed the voice of Nwihaki that had asked him to wait for a new day. (... He) felt only guilt, the guilt of a man who had avoided his responsibility for which he had prepared himself since childhood. (136)

100

Having accepted the challenge to live, he behaves true to a very wise saying of the Igbo: *Kama aga amu ozum amu, si mua uzo msi gba oso* (which paraphrased in English means: better a living coward than a dead hero). He therefore ignores the "voice" rebuking him for being "a coward" (since he had also "failed" this "voice" too, by not committing suicide). He therefore accepts being a coward, "and ran home and opened the door for his two mothers" (136).

Conclusion

So much in common, and yet how dissimilar in the end or, are they really? All the differences between Toundi and Njoroge can be traced back to one that is fundamental: Toundi's deafness to advice and his escape from his parental home. He was like a young plant plucked from its roots and thrown on a rough river; how and where can such a plant ever take roots again? Both he and Njoroge represent Africa exploited and tortured in its infancy (we are in the pre-independence era). For this we agree with the German philosopher, Nietzsche, who says that man's tragedy is that he was once a child, i.e., the last-comer to the adult world of scrambling humanity, and hence the victim of others' predatory greed.

But Toundi and Njoroge represent two faces of the same child Africa; one that imprudently breaks with all tradition in a naïve and blind chase after the white man's "better" way of life (this is tantamount to cultural suicide, symbolised by Toundi's death at. cross-roads between two countries); the other which while holding solidly to tradition, seeks to acquire the white man's secret of domineering power: education. Njoroge's deliverance in extremis by his mother's voice is a ray of hope; telling a suffering and weeping Africa that "hope of a better day was the only comfort (one) could give to a weeping child" (111). Did that "better day" come with the era of independence?

Although Oyono and Ngugi each wrote in different countries, in different languages, and in slightly different, historical circumstances, and did not know (or have to know) each other's existence, they still gave to the child, Africa, the same message in tragically different ways. This comparative study shows that *Houseboy* and *Weep not, child* are two complementary novels and could, with great benefits, be studied as such. There is no limit to what may be discovered by undertaking such a study of any authors or even the same author.

6

Lopes

N Iloh

HENRI Lopes is a Congolese writer who has severally been a minister in his country. He represents his country at UNESCO till date as a permanent delegate and Extraordinary and Plenipotentiary Ambassador in France. He is equally reputed for his Feminist commitment especially in the concern for the total emancipation of African womanhood. This chapter looks at Lopes' portraiture of free, liberated and sophisticated African womanhood through the trajectories of the ndoumba women in Congoland. The word 'ndoumba', originally spelt as 'ndumba', appears for the first time in Henri Lopes' *Tribaliques* (1971). Among the seven novels, the word 'ndoumba' is used in four, viz: *Sans Tam-Tam* (1977), *Le Chercheur d'Afriques* (1990), *Sur l'autre Rive* (1992), and *Le Lys et le Flamboyant* (1997). The other three novels where the word is not used are *La Nouvelle Romance* (1976), *Le Pleurer-rire* (1982) and *Dossier classé* (2002). Before going into the main discussion, it will be necessary to ask some salient and pertinent questions as: what is 'ndoumba'? what are the characteristic traits that serve as indices for its identification? who are the 'ndoumbas' in the novels studied? And even where the word 'ndoumba' is not used in some novels, how can it be identified and recognized in some of the characters? Also, of what importance is ndoumba in the author's works and what role does it play?

The Concept of Ndoumba

Apart from Didier Gondala and Zanzi et al who studied this phenomenon, there has been few studies on ndoumba. However, it is a common term in Congolese songs. In Lope's writing, Le Chercheur d'Afriques, the word 'ndoumba' is explained at the bottom of the page as a "free woman in Lingala, manner of a courtesan who lives on lovers she freely chooses" (240). *Tribaliques* defines it at the bottom of the page also as "courtesan or hetaerae" (5). 'Hétaïre', originally used by the author, is an archaic word which in *Petit Robert* means "courtesan of a special class of women valued as highly cultured companion" (926). Literarily, in the same dictionary, the word in ancient Greece simply means 'prostitute'. In *Sans Tam-tam*, the author has a glossary at the end of the book where 'ndoumba' is explained as "luxury chick, without a pimp" (125). In *Le Lys et le Flamboyant*, the author speaks of 'big ndoumba' without a precise definition. By implication, there are categories of ndoumbas. *Sur l'autre rive* shows that "the word ndoumba cannot be translated by a lone word" (151). However, the narrator explains it this way: "If you talk to one of these ladies or to one of these gentlemen in the civil service here; without hesitation, they will translate ndoumba as "prostitute" or, something slightly better, like "luxury chick" (64).

Following the narrator's explanation that "it is a notion peculiar with the Congolese society" (151), it is therefore pertinent to glance through the perception of this Congolese society's notion. Congolese music is a good example where the usage of the word is found. Didier Gondala, in his article 'Amours, passions et ruptures dans l'âge d'or de la chanson congolaise' published in *Afrique Culture*, traces the origin of 'ndoumba' to the 1950s and 70s where the Congolese music celebrated "moving love, a vacillating love, ephemeral, tributary of good grace and caprices" in the ndoumba, the 'free woman', or "the mammy water, the seductive siren (who) …reinvents the rules of the love game" (1). This was the predominant musical genre of the times filled with amorous complaints. With regard to another musical text, "Reward soap", Blaise quotes Mere Eve in an article on *Congopage* that Lingala lexis comprises also the word 'ndoumba'. He explains two prefixes that precede the word 'ndoumba':

> The prefix BO is at times replaced indiscriminately by the prefix KI. The latter is in fact borrowed from Kituba (another Congolese language). Hence bondoumba becomes kindoumba as in the song "TU VOIS" (aka Mamu) by LUAMBO MAKIADI. Whoever engages in kindoumba is an ndoumba. But the ndoumba is not a prostitute in the French sense of the word. It is an unfaithful woman who at times goes out with other men in exchange for a number of material gains. (In the song), MAMU is an ndoumba because she settles comfortably in Brussels while her husband works to death in Kinshasa so as to send her money orders. She is not moved by her jumping from left to right in search for more money. In Lingala, a prostitute in the French sense of the word is called 'ntoungué'. (1)

According to Zanzi et al in their article entitled 'Des particularités lexicales et des emprunts dans l'œuvre romanesque de Zamenga Batukezanga', "ndoumbas are women who live on commercial sex and free themselves from all forms of morality linked with modesty" (120). Blaise writing to Sonia on *Congopage* notes that the Congolese like every other person competes for ingenuity: "I even have a male friend who calls his darling "ndoumballa" from the word "Ndoumba" and it is more of a "litigious" term. Ndoumba equally means: young girl, beautiful girl and prostitute" (1). In Lingala/French bilingual dictionary, ndoumba means 'single girl' or 'public woman'. Ndoumba therefore is a term that generates a lot of controversy. The concept of ndoumba will be better understood if the characteristic traits are considered in relation with two facts. First is their reinvention of love game rules – rules which distinguish them categorically from prostitutes. Second is the case of infidelity which does not differ very much from masculine infidelity. What is interesting about this notion is the fact that the Congolese society does not consider an ndoumba a prostitute in the French sense of the word since 'prostitute' has its Lingala equivalence as 'ntoungué.' The character and trajectories of these ndoumbas will throw more light on the complexity surrounding them.

Characteristics of Ndoumba

In *Sur l'autre rive*, "ndoumbas are in fact big ladies, concerned about their liberty and consider marriage as a cemetery of love" (64). In *Tribaliques*, ndoumbas are "the big militants of women emancipation" (4) who can read and write. They speak and write about the emancipation of the African women. They are not married, so they mock at married women who imagine they can keep their husbands to themselves alone. They are city women. They are free and independent and according to the narrator of *Le Lys et le Flamboyant*:

Ndoumbas are not women who you whistle at simply by

exhibiting some bank notes. They choose their preys themselves, set them up when they decide, bend them at will, make them succumb, then command and lead them to their taste and fantasies... . (335)

These African women do not want to languish as housewives, the mode of living by married women considered by the narrator as "faithful wives, all honourable and respectable" (336). By this juxtaposition, the narrator pitches married women against ndoumbas. The latter by contrast, are unmarried and if married, they are "unfaithful", "dishonorable" and "despicable" wives. Their traits include their mode and style of life: they are charming, beautiful, coquettish but insolent. They have numerous lovers. Gondala thinks that Congolese music, what Biaya, cited by Gondala, describes as "the idol of modern music and the centre of the audience" (355), has contributed in the description of *ndoumba* as "free woman or courtesan". Often, if they decide to have children (a decision which is not common among them), the fathers of the children are severally different. An example is Monette in *Le Lys et le Flamboyant* and Gigi in *Dossier classé*.

One can therefore ask what 'ndoumba' symbolizes in Henri Lopes' novels. Can one really call them prostitutes? Why does the author avoid the use of the word 'prostitute' in most instances?

Since they do not depend entirely on prostitution for a living Henri Lopes does not consider his ndoumba women prostitutes. Rather, Lopes uses the word 'prostitutes' for other female characters who fit the description more appropriately. In 'Monsieur le député' of *Tribaliques*, for instance, Marie Thérèse is clearly described as a prostitute. *Dossier classé*, also describes the escapades of other prostitutes. In *La Nouvelle Romance* (1976), Elise's status is left at the discretion of the reader. From the definition and explanation given by the author it is obvious that there is a distinction between the two because the word 'ndoumba' "is translated as something better than a prostitute" although few some still translate it as prostitute. Sometimes this can lead to confusion as to which term is appropriate. One might be tempted to conclude that 'ndoumba' is untranslatable since 'ntoungué' is the proper translation of 'prostitute'. However, a panoramic view of the lives of ndoumbas will aid the comprehension of the word, concept, characteristic traits and their identification.

The Life of Ndoumba

Having recognized the traits and characteristics of some of these women, ndoumbas can henceforth be typified by their itinerary or trajectories. Elise in *La Nouvelle Romance* is single and beautiful. She has a certain level of education. The narrator confirms her life as that of a courtesan (63). Elise boasts of her acquisitions when she tells her friends, Awa and Wali:

> But take a look at me. No husband, a house that none of you can boast of, T.V, lovers who kneel before me, clothe me better than any husband could have done, the pleasure of going out many evenings in a week... I am the eternal fiancée. (64)

It is Wali who asks Awa if "girls like Elise look like brothels" (65). That is to say, by implication, that Elise is a brothel. The word 'brothel' is an infamous title that describes a wretched woman of easy virtue. A brothel is a house of prostitution or a house where people pay to have sex with prostitutes and by extension, in Lopesian Congolese vocabulary, a prostitute; hence Elise is a prostitute. According to Awa, "if prostitution is the sale of one's body for money, it is exactly what Elise is doing" (65). For Elise, she thinks that she is not more of a brothel than the married woman and according to her friend, Wali, "the only difference resides simply in this fact that the married woman chooses her life partner and not partners" (68). And Elise, defending herself, affirms: "I choose my partners! It is not he that wishes to sleep with Elise but he that is able to" (66). She is revolutionary and proclaims herself "a polygamous woman", that is, polyandry. She reinvents the rules of the game to suit herself because she is in charge of herself. By so doing, she does not condemn polygamy. She asks her friends: "Do you think you can keep your husbands to yourselves alone? What then do we live on? It is because we have not had the luck to obtain certificates to enable us earn a living" (67).

The difference between Elise and her friend Awa is that the latter is not a 'brothel'; however, they are both single. It is their life style that distinguishes them from other women who lead a normal life. Elise is a seamstress who depends on her lovers financially and for material gain as she often boasts. Traditionally a prostitute does not have any other professional career or handiwork. It is sometimes tempting to ask what is the difference between Elise who is a seamstress and Gigi who owes a bar/ restaurant? Can one distinguish them from Kolélé, the heroin of *Le Lys et le Flamboyant* who is a self proclaimed ndoumba by her liberty to choose her partners at will?

In *Dossier classé*, Gigi is called "old layer". She is not only single but a single mother. She has four children from different fathers, yet, she is known to have married none of them. She was the mistress of several men including Ngandalouka, Goma, Mambo and many politicians who frequent her bar/restaurant. From the description of an ndoumba, Gigi can be considered one. She is a tall "Massai figure" (152) of a light complexion due to miraculous cream. She owes her own bar/restaurant known as "Aunty Gigi's." One can say that the author is concerned about the presence of bonafide prostitutes in the novels. Motherhood distinguishes an ndoumba from a prostitute who normally does not have the time to bear and rear children.

In *Le Chercheur d'Afriques*, the narrator, André Leclerc sees himself as a "son of ndoumba" (240) because his mother, Marie Ngalaha, is regarded as a brothel. Ngalaha had several lovers after the departure of Commandant Leclerc with whom she cohabited. According to the young narrator:

> With all these *makangous* who take turns during the days of the week...it is not for her to defend her honour each time I am regarded as a son of *ndoumba*. I had been beaten already in the quarters because one kid treated Ngalaha as a brothel. (240)

The word 'makangou' is a Lingala word meaning 'lover' and is explained at the bottom of the page (240). Does the narrator and, by implication, the author, exchange the word ndoumba with brothel? Ngalaha has several lovers. She rejects all the suitors who come until finally deciding to marry Veloso. The narrator-son complains several times that he is forced to change surnames in order to accommodate his mother's many lovers. It is important to note that Ngalaha finally gets married to Joseph Veloso. As he (the narrator) puts it, "first, André Leclerc, later Okana. Now Okana André. Tomorrow Veloso?" (242). Ngalaha resembles Monette in *Le Lys et le Flamboyant* who is always changing partners. Ngalaha is the only ndoumba in Lopes' work that can neither read nor write. Prostitutes are never housewives. They are rather contented more with the gains of commercial sex.

Monette is the pet name of Simone Fragonard, alias Kolélé, the heroine of *Le Lys et le Flamboyant*. Congolese colonial history has produced mixed bloods such as Monette. The narrator, by comparing

Monette with his cinema star, Wali, explains that the latter is a mother of five, fathered by different men (336). Monette is a mother of three, all fathered by different men just like Gigi in *Dossier classé*. The narrator, Victor-Augagneur Houang, expounds the theory of ndoumba thus: Monette is a brothel (369); she marries François Lomata with whom she has a boy called Léon. The marriage does not work. She moves in with Jean Batestti, and later Mr. Sergent with whom she has had a daughter, Maud. With Mr Sergent's departure, she moves in with a Caribbean, Dr Sallustre, with whom she has another boy, Charles. Finally she relocates to France, thanks to her marriage, with Jeannot Boucheron.

Monette's life is already complicated with these five different men. In France she undergoes a transformation which changes her life: she becomes a well known singer, joins African politics and moves from place to place in the company of African leaders and soon becomes notorious as a brothel. A rumour from the enemy party has it that:

> Kolélé was a brothel. She was mistress, successively and simultaneously to Sekou Touré and Kwame Nkrumah. She had been seduced by Lumumba then by Gizenga and Mulélé, who, tired of her, had all rejected her before she slipped into Tomboka's bed. (369)

The rumour turns out to be true when her compatriot Marie-Chinois confirms her life of "luxury brothel". In her story to the narrator, she reveals that Monette had proclaimed herself "willing to share and a fanatical partisan of free love" (378). Since Monette has several lovers, is a free and independent woman (236), and a singer in a night club, the link between her and a call-girl is very narrow. According to her, "Me, I sort out. I keep at distance men I do not want and I choose my preys myself" (238).

Henri Lopes seems to model his star/heroine after the ndoumbas of his time. Because he does not want to call Monette an ndoumba, he leaves the judgment to the reader. Monette is licentious, coquettish and charming. One notes the personalities of a socially elevated class with which she associates and who are her lovers. If Lopes succeeds in presenting ndoumbas as free women, and often singles, he shows another perspective in *Le Pleurer-rire* with married women like Ma Mireille and Soukali.

In *Le Pleurer-rire*, Soukali Djamboriyessa is wife of the Inspector of Customs but she is unfaithful and adulterous because she maintains a few lovers. She is beautiful, has been compared to a thief and sorcerer and is also considered by the narrator as a great lady. She refuses to be addressed as a "street girl" (191). Speaking to the narrator, who is one of her lovers, she asks him: "Do you take me for a street girl?" (192); another time she tells him: "Me, I do not cease to think of you. You men, it is only to fuck, fuck, fuck. As if I were a street girl..." (191). She is educated and works with the Bulgarian Embassy. She has a certificate in secretarial work or something in the same genre. She ends up being arrested on charges of conspiracy and, thanks to the lady President, is released and sent to her hometown. Can she be called a prostitute?

Ma Mireille is the beautiful lover of the president, Hannibal Ideloy Bwakamabé Na Sakkadé. She becomes the wife of the president but keeps the narrator as her lover. While the President flirts with young girls, what is considered as normal with men, the narrator who boasts of his flirtation and prostitution with big ladies in the society neither condemns them nor is he condemned by others. Women who are neglected by their husbands are reproved by the society. Can men be accused of being the cause of female infidelity? Or can women be condemned for their situation? The narrator exonerates himself by saying "I should have nourished some remorse for caressing another man's wife. But if your maize farm is far from your house, is it not normal for birds to peck on it? (23).

The President and the Inspector General of Customs are so engaged with their jobs that they do not think of the sexual needs of their wives who are left to cater for the children and housework. They are bored. For instance, as soon as Soukali can no longer bear it, she engages herself in the search of a job which she finds at the Bulgarian Embassy. Once, she imposes herself on the Inspector in order to travel with him abroad leaving the children behind. The narrator profits from the Inspector's negligence by accusing Soukali of daring to leave her children behind. Professional prostitutes do not have time for motherhood but Soukali is a mother and Mireille mother of the nation. Mireille's biological children are never mentioned. She demonstrates this national motherhood during the arrest of Soukali and Malaïka who are accused of plotting against the government. She employs the tactics of sex and hunger strike just to get the two imprisoned women released. She succeeds eventually as the two women were not killed.

In *Sur l'autre rive*, the three ndoumbas are, in reality, three great female characters in the novel. They are Marie-Eve, the narrator, and her two friends, Clarisse Obiang and Félicité. The three are married but infertility problems and sexual dissatisfaction cause their separation and divorce with their husbands. The question of infidelity in the African woman, her culpability and punishment, are gender discriminations in African customs and traditions which these ndoumbas revolt against. Marie-Eve disappears leaving not only her husband but her family, town, country and continent behind. Clarisse leaves her husband, Obiang, to be with her lover, popularly known as "during the holidays".

It is the meeting between the narrator and Clarisse that necessitates the story in the novel. Félicité is an intimate friend of the

113

narrator. She convinces Marie-Eve to participate at the international conference where the latter meets Femi Olayode, the source of her marital infidelity. Félicité and Marie-Eve are both interpreters having studied English. Félicité is a mother. Her husband, Côme, was a politician compromised in a coup plot and executed, thus rendering her a widow. Her activities during the International conference were not hidden. Marie-Eve is a painter, photographer, singer, and hence a rare phenomenon in Africa. Marie-Eve, who is also known as Madeleine, has had a bad marriage as a result of infertility. After her affair with the Nigerian delegate, further sexual relation with her husband deteriorates; she burns every trace of her existence and crosses the borders to start a new life in the Caribbean islands. A common and striking point about these women therefore is their willingness to marry first and foremost.

In 'Monsieur le député', from *Tribaliques*, (a collection of stories), Marguerite is a young widow of reputable beauty. She is well sought after and since she cannot satisfy everyone at the same time, she offers some of her cousins to her customers. It is a case of professional prostitution which does not seem to attract the author's Lopes' endorsement. Thus one wonders exactly what Henri Lopes' mission with these ndoumbas is.

Lopes and Female Emancipation

Henri Lopes emphasizes on the importance of female liberation and not prostitution as would many chauvinistic writers who criticize prostitutes and prostitution directly. In *Tribaliques*, 'ndoumbas' are presented as "the great militants of women emancipation" (4) who can read and write. They speak and write about women emancipation in Africa. Lopes seems very interested in the personalities of his female characters, with female sexuality as an important theme.

In *Le Pleurer-rire*, Ma Mireille exhibits a great influence on all offers of employment and government positions despite her less than moral lifestyle. She becomes the head of protocol, in charge of members of the entourage who accompany the President to France (28). She is also in charge of women associations in the country. It is evident that Lopes identifies with the ascension of African women in positions of public influence. Osazuwa, citing Ridahalgh, affirms the importance that Henri Lopes attaches to the social position of women and the exploration of female sexuality in *La Nouvelle Romance*. Also explaining the reciprocal eroticism in *Le Pleurer-rire*, Osazuwa notes that the novel *Le Pleurer-rire* "is somewhat in the vanguard, in the sense that Soukali and Ma Mireille are too sophisticated to be authentic African wives of our times" (35). Both texts lay emphasis on personalities and their achievement in day to day life; they unmask as well as demystify the morality issue and traditions which complicate feminine conditions. For Houque, what Lopes shows in his novels concerning female adultery is to show sexual equality between a man and a woman. Lopes wants to show that African women have equal rights, as men do, when it comes to sexual life. Therefore the woman also has a right to choose motherhood without necessarily being under a man's domination.

This is the case with the ndoumbas in *Le Pleurer-rire*, *Sur l'autre rive*, *Le Lys et le Flamboyant* and *Dossier classé*. Monette, as a great politician in her time, is often found in the company of presidents of African countries. It is also inspiring to see her among Lumumba's guerrilla fighters. Here Lopes is quite eager to show the pioneer social emancipatory commitment of the character Monette. Her life and personality are more pertinent than her life as courtesan. She is a good singer, quite alright, but also a great spy (espionage), interpreter and nationalist.

Marie-Eve is a further example of the great African ndoumba. As a painter, singer and photographer, Marie-Eve is an embodiment of a true female artist – a rare theme in African novels. Since sexual independence for African women occupies a preponderant place in the entire work, Lopes is therefore not wrong in his presentation of Monette and Marie-Eve as ndoumbas.

As to the distinction between a prostitute and ndoumba and, if there is no difference, why the author avoids using the word 'prostitute' for these women, Jennifer James thinks that big prostitutes have always been competent dancers and singers. The old socioeconomic dependency of women has been reversed and here women no longer occupy an inferior position in relation to the men in society. Her traditional status as an inferior, restricted and uncertain specie is not the case in Henri Lopes' feminist obligation. Lopes can be compared to the Senegalese writer and film maker Ousmane Sembène in their positive presentation of African women as free and independent characters. In *God's Bits of Wood*, for instance, Penda, despite her life of prostitution, is able to lead the women's protest march. This is not a case of writers trying to justify prostitution or to even find the cause. As prostitution is a scourge long in existence, the novelist must go beyond the level of criticism to that of advancing the development of the individuals concerned. It is in this light that Lopes' Monette is a considerable figure in her role as a great ndoumba not only of the Republic of Congo but of the whole of Africa.

Thus Lopes' choice to look at the positive aspect of 'ndoumba' lies in his Feminist commitment which finds its climax in the sexuality, sexual life and feminine world view of his characters independent of moral considerations. He uses ndoumba to repudiate societal norms which do not allow women to live out their sexuality and motherhood outside of marriage. It seems a proper conclusion that Lopes is committed to the arrival of independent female characters on the literary scene in spite of their behaviour and faults.

Judith Sinanga Ohlmann declares in her article, 'La femme chez Calixthe Beyala et Henri Lopes: Objectivation et Sublimation du corps' that "in Lopes' work, the woman, even when she is unfaithful, a prostitute or a raging woman, remains a sublime creature" (270). In Lopes' work, Ndoumbas prove to be the epitome of erotic and modern womanhood. Since they are, after all, human beings with faults like every other, Lopes' characterisation of them dwells rather on their contribution to society than their idiosyncrasies, the message being that African societies must rise beyond inhibiting norms in order to achieve the emancipation of African womanhood in all its ramifications.

7

DM Toko

<h1 style="text-align:right;">Laye,
Ce</h1>

CAMARA Laye's The *Dark Child* (DC)[1] and Chin Ce's *Children of Koloko* (COK), respectively set in the Guinean and Nigerian societies, present African traditional values as the foundation stone of child education. These traditions, though some may be discarded, are a springboard to the African child's mastery of western technology and science. In Laye's novel, the tension between the traditional caste system, the Koranic and French schools is resolved by the parents' and the community's deep reverence for cultural values. In Ce's novel, although the capitalist unbridled craze for money and power has perverted postcolonial Koloko, Yoyo attains growth due to his attachment to traditional African wisdom and value which he successfully blends with western education. In the two works, the main protagonists thus opt for what Amanda Grants calls "a middle

---

[1]*The African Child* was the first translation of the original title *L'enfant noir* of Camara Laye's novel. The edition used in this work is entitled *The Dark Child*.

course"[2] signifying that tenuous balance between two polarities or extremities which westernisation and traditionalism represent in contemporary African societies.

Western Colonisation and the African Writer

Colonization, leading to the hybridization of African societies has generated heated debates on the type of education that should be imparted to the African child. In his article "Hegel on Education," Allen W. Wood notes that education, "has to do with the activities of school, their pupils, teachers or tutors (including parents) and their students, whether they are children or adolescents" (20). Wood's analysis that examines the various meanings of the Hegelian "Bildung" focuses on the key components of education: the learning of specific skills, the imparting of knowledge, good judgment and wisdom, as well as the imparting of culture from generation to generation. Education is thus a tripartite process that involves the environment (natural and social environments), the trainer (educator) and the child (the trainee).

This truism carries great weight today in most African societies where African traditions are more than ever before, jeopardized by globalization and the challenges of western culture. This phenomenon thus raises many questions: What is the responsibility of African parents and societies in child education? What type of education should be imparted to the African child today in a twenty-first century world marked by a flood of mass media and hi-tech that tends to standardize cultures? In *Homecoming*, Ngugi wa Thiong'o

---

[2] In "Memory, Transition and Dialogue: The Cyclic Order of Chin Ce's Oeuvres," Amanda Grants notes that "the three ways: left, right and middle signify three choices involving two extremes and a middle course, an important element in Chin Ce's oeuvres (JALC 11).

holds that:

> The real snake was surely monopoly capitalism, whose very
> condition of growth is cut-throat competition, inequality and
> oppression of one group by another. It was capitalism and its
> external manifestations, imperialism, colonialism, neo-
> colonialism, that had disfigured the African past. (45)

Continuing the argument, Ngugi further professes:

> ...in order that one group, one race, one class (and mostly a
> minority) can exploit another group, race or class (mostly the
> majority), it must not only steal its body, batter and barter it for
> thirty pieces of silver, but must steal its mind and soul as
> well...Through the school system, he can soothe the fears of the
> colonized, or make them at least connive at the rationale behind
> capitalist exploitation. (45)

If monopoly capitalism disfigured the African past, generated
egocentrism and an exacerbated quest for wealth, today, this quest
overrules the key precept of communal good that underpins
education in traditional African communities. Kashim Ibrahim Tala
points out that "pre-capitalist African society subsists on the social
philosophy of the greatest good of the greatest number. In other
words, collective responsibility is the very essence of ancestral
authority" (Moto 158). Incorporating this precept, the ideological
matrix that prevailed in pre-colonial Africa guaranteed a symbiosis
between the individual and the group. Consequently, from this golden
rule, derived a whole pedagogy, which, using African folklore, taught
the child sound values such as communal good, compassion, mutual
aid, truthfulness, the sense of right and wrong, spontaneity, and love
of man and nature. Before the Negritude movement, this ideological
matrix was celebrated in *Adventures of Huckleberry Finn*, Mark
Twain's nineteenth-century masterpiece where Huck Finn, the white

teenager, wholeheartedly espouses Jim's (the African slave's) ideology rooted in the above-cited values. Thus, earlier than Chinua Achebe's *Things Fall Apart*, and Camara Laye's *The Dark Child*, *Adventures of Huckleberry Finn* was already in the nineteenth century, a strong advocate of African cultural values.

In African literature, the celebration of he untainted African traditions reverberates in the bildungsroman or the coming of age story. Jerome Buckley, explaining the German origin of the bildungsromane in *Seasons of Youth*, argues that while "roman" means novel, "bildung" connotes "portrait," "picture," "shaping," and "formation," which all converge to the idea of development or creation. "The development of the child can also be seen as the creation of the man" (13-14). The bildungsromane thus revolves around childhood, a recurrent theme in African literature. Maxwell Okolie posits that "childhood, like the past with which it is associated, occupies a prominent psychological part of African literature." In his words,

> the evocation of individual childhood, calls up as a corollary the evocation of Africa's 'childhood' itself, which, in effect, is an indirect apology and illustration of its splendour before the advent of colonization. ... Rediscovering this glory is in a way an indirect exhortation to the Africans engrossed in the pursuit of Westernization and its allurements, to retrace their steps back to the honourable values they are inclined to despise thus re-equipping themselves with the pride of their worth and the psychological reassurance vital to their existence and rejuvenation. (35)

Like Ngugi, Okolie points an accusing finger at western culture and its impingement on African traditions. Both Ngugi's and Okolie's statements will lay the foundations of this analysis which seeks to prove that despite the prevalent cult of Westernization in modern

African societies, African genuine and positive cultural values are the stepping stone of a successful African child education.

The Dark Child and *Children of Koloko* are possibly two bildungsromane that retrace the lives of two protagonists from childhood to maturity. Far from being mere evocations of childhood experiences, both works pose the crucial problem of the African child's growth in the contemporary global village. They bring to the limelight the encroachments of western civilization on African traditions and their impact on the African trainee. Comparing the two, this study shows analogies and differences in the protagonists, their training and growth. It focuses on the three main factors of child education: the society (the settings of the novels), the training (the way education is imparted) and the trainee (the impact of education on the protagonists and their subsequent response and growth).

Traditional Education in *The Dark Child*

The Dark Child, an autobiographical novel, furthers the Negritude aim to uphold African values that were jettisoned under slavery and colonization. The novel outlines the conflict between African traditions and Western culture imposed by colonization. Though Camara Laye from his country of exile (he was writing from France) revives the memory of the mythological Africa, he overtly presents himself as the prototype of the modern African who hovers between the black tradition and the white civilization. In contrast to Deicy Jiménez who argues that Laye's work "shows the African struggle and search for an identity in colonial times" (CASA), this reading asserts that the struggle and search for identity in the work is a contemporary quest in postcolonial African societies.

Laye's autobiographical novel is divided into three main sections that show the protagonist's development from childhood to maturity.

The first section that may be titled "Childhood," covers the first five chapters (1-5). This part of the book depicts the family's compound at Kouroussa where the child comes into contact with the family totem. The totem is a small black snake, the guiding spirit of the family. As the father enlightens the boy on the small snake, the clash between traditional education and the colonial school already looms: "I fear, I very much fear, little one, that you are not often enough in my company. You are all day at school, and one day you will depart from that school for a greater one. You will leave me, little one…" (27). This statement uncovers the parent's fear: the father, a famous goldsmith knows that he will pass to his elder son neither the totemic tradition, nor the profession of his caste. Even at Tindican (the mother's village) where the child spends his holiday among a loving grandmother and innumerable kind playmates, the young boy does not really feel part of the village community. He will not therefore inherit his mother's magic power and her crocodile totem despite his rite of passage that is carried on in the second section. The second section of the autobiography "Years of Initiation" (Chapters 6-8), recalls the boy's experiences both in the Koranic and the French schools which are the first steps of the protagonist's initiation.

The trek to the sacred place (a prelude to circumcision), the enormous baobab tree at the junction of the Komoni River, and the mysterious Konden Diara stratagem instill fear and at the same time teach the Guinean young men to overcome their fright. The protagonist's initiation is then achieved through a long journey in the forest. However, even at the apex of this initiation rite, the reader perceives the narrator's fear that one day, the white culture will annihilate this traditional practice that gives rise to a village feast, to a community communion. During the dancing ceremony, the new men are presented objects, symbols of their allegiance to their fathers' castes (professions). Unlike other boys who are shown articles that are related to their fathers' professions, the protagonist is shown an exercise-book and a fountain pen, embodiments of the white culture. Here, once more, the boy is gradually taken away from his tradition. He is on his way to exile which the final section of the book concretizes. The last part of the text "Exile" (Chapters 9-12), depicts two different types of departure: the journey to Conakry after the narrator has been admitted into the technical high school and the longer journey to France where he will learn engineering.

In this bildungsroman, the family is the bedrock of the boy's education. The young boy's "relationship with his parents is the link between the child and his African roots" (CASA). Both the mother and the father assume responsibility by monitoring the son's education. They see to it that the boy imbibes the fundamental values of African culture: the sense of community and solidarity that characterize social relations in African communities. John Mbiti holds that in the traditional African community, an individual only exists as an element of a group. Joining Mbiti, Kange Ewane, a Cameroonian historian, argues that in the African context, animate and inanimate beings commune in the same unit of life and participation. Within such a context, solidarity is not assistance with a taint of condescension: it is rather a vital necessity; it becomes co-possession and co-utilization (*Semence et moisson* 62). The protagonist's father thus teaches the son this principle by example. He is himself a good model to the youth: "I have nothing which other men have not also, and even that I have less than others, since I give everything away, and would even give away the last thing I had, the shirt on my back" (*DC* 25). The father has been given the totem, the guiding spirit because he is "the most worthy" member of his tribe (25). Being "the most worthy" implies possessing and respecting everlasting values such as the sense of solidarity, compassion, spontaneity, and the precept of communal good inherent in African culture.

The father and the mother thus teach the young boy the powers of the natural world. They introduce him to the small snake, the totem of the family which embeds customs, beliefs, morals and discipline handed over from one generation to the other. In fact in the novel, the family and the society at large are conducive to child education. The father instructs his son: "Take care never to deceive anyone. … Be upright in thought and deed. And God will be with you" (182). The hero's education is successfully carried out thanks to three elements that Laye regards as key actors in the education of a child: a stable family (parents), the school, and a viable society. William Plomer notes that "where [Camara] grew up, the sense of community is implicit and inherent. Tradition and long usage have created politeness, correctness, mutual respect, and simple dignity" (*Current Concerns*). The narrator himself highlights this point in his statement: "I lived actually amidst a deeply united family where all domestic quarreling was strictly forbidden" (150). In other terms, this assertion implies that a peaceful environment is a primordial requirement for child education. When the young trainee moves to Conakry, a bigger town, Uncle Mamadou, whom the narrator describes as being "tall and strong, always very correctly dressed, calm and dignified"(150), perpetuates these values. He thus ensures the continuity in the imparting of culture from generation to generation.

After the family and the community at large have laid solid foundations of the child's moral and spiritual education, they can now hand him over to the western school that will teach him science and technology as the father rightly points out:

> Each one follows his own destiny, my son. Men cannot change what is decreed. Your uncles too have had an education…This opportunity is within your reach. You must seize it. You've already seized one, seize this one too, make sure of it. There are still so

many things to be done in our land…. Yes, I want you to go to France. [….] Soon we'll be needing men like you here. (182)

Camara's father and mother understand that though the child may lose some of his traditional cultural values, his mastery of science and technology is useful to the community. Here again, the African traditional principle of "co-possession and co-utilization" underpins the father's decision. When the parent observes that "soon we'll be needing men like you here," he implicitly advises the son not to forget his allegiance and duty to his community. Although this blend may not eradicate the tension that arises from the contrast between African and western cultures, it lessens it and thus validates G. N. Marete's view that there is absence of conflict in the narrator's maturation (93). In effect making a choice is the protagonist's dilemma: "And I was no longer sure whether I ought to continue to attend school or whether I ought to remain in the workshop: I felt unutterably confused" (DC 27). But the narrator's indecision is short-lived as it is quickly resolved by his father's order: "Go now" (27). Later the parent never mentions the little black snake again to the son (28). The male parent's decision portends a choice: the son must attend the western school. This choice releases the tension that reoccurs in the last chapter when the boy is faced with the mother's objection to his departure to France. At the end of the novel, the metro map given to the young traveler by the director (the school headmaster) symbolizes guidance, orientation, knowledge, and conquest. It is a tool that will enable the African child to reach Argenteuil, the new environment where he has to complete his training.

The African community thus monitors the child's education from the opening to the close of the novel, giving the action its linearity. As a result, the narrator's departure to France is not, as Jiménez mentions, "the metaphor of the social and cultural oblivion of his African roots"

127

(CASA). It is rather a symbolic appropriation of western technology and science to the benefit of the African (Guinean) community. When the father punctuates that: "Your uncles too have had an education," he covertly refers to the "middle course" that is neither the abrogation of western culture nor "oblivion" of African roots. Uncle Mamadou, whom the boy "regarded as a saintly personage" (151), successfully imbeds both African and western cultures. By the end of the novel the reader infers that the narrator will follow the same course, thus fulfilling his promise to his male parent: "I will come back" (DC 182). The same promise is reiterated to Marie: "Surely I would be coming back" (188). "Coming back" to Guinea symbolizes a return home (to roots) with the much needed science and technology that may enhance the economic development of Guinea.

Capitalism and Child Education in *Children of Koloko*

Unlike *The Dark Child*, Chin Ce's *Children of Koloko*, written more than three decades after Laye's book, is set in a postcolonial African country (Nigeria). Colonization has given way to neo-colonization, and monopoly capitalism has permeated most of the genuine positive African values depicted in the first novel. *Children of Koloko* thus presents the turbulent community of Koloko where communal good, compassion, mutual aid, truthfulness, the sense of right and wrong, spontaneity, and love of man and nature have been replaced by a monomaniacal pursuit for money and power. Within such a context, Ngugi's statement that "capitalism had disfigured the African past" rightly applies to Ce's novel. The craze for wealth has established corruption, thievery, drunkenness, egocentrism, and violence as commonplace practices. In the second episode, "Coming to Koloko," there is a metaphoric representation not only of postcolonial Nigeria but of most post-independence African

128

countries ridden with disunity and turbulence:

> Koloko was not much like one had thought. The very name which
> sounded to me like the noise of empty gallons falling on dry earth --
> ko-ko-lo-ko-- was now something else beyond my little
> imagination. As we drove past the Market Square, in the heart of the
> town, I saw that the road meandered right through as if splitting the
> town in two. Now who would live in a town split in halves? Koloko
> didn't look good at all. (27)

The town is characterized by division discernible in its various social strata and economic classes: the rich include Dogkiller, Fathead and the numerous unscrupulous businessmen. The poor comprise teachers like Old Bap, and Bap, small workers that are involved in petty jobs, crapulous men and women who spend their time at De Mika's (JJC, Da Kata), and a group of youths whose rascality and crapulousness rival the elders'. Da Aina, head of the women, and the main female social critic in the book, clearly points at the causes of the prevalent depravity of the community: 'The elders have spoiled the village...because they lost the wisdom to teach their young who look up to them' (102). Both old and young people are corrupted by their craze for monetary gratification that undermines their morals and sense of common good. Yesterday, young people used to respect their elders, women used to respect their husbands, and the husbands used to give them their due. But today, women and young people join the elders in off licenses where all indulge in vices. Their inebriety thus reflects their irresponsibility and failure to build stable families and a stable nation. The population of Koloko is thus divided into three groups:

> Koloko had a lot of men whom you didn't get to see except in a
> season like Christmas. There were fat folks whose bulging eyes and
> beefy cheeks probably only served to frighten children. There were

the returnees: young men, polished and dressed to reflect the places they lived and worked. There were those you could see were struggling to make a living and look respectable in their lavish dressing. [...]These were Koloko's children. (130)

Despite the dissimilitude that exists among the members of the various groups, each social stratum imbeds the numerous foibles and deficiencies of the society. The fat folks' "bulging eyes and beefy cheeks" signal affluence and greed. These folks overfeed on the masses' sweat and their ill-gotten wealth and authority separate them from the children they are supposed to educate. The returnees, who experience economic hardships, cover up their misery by lavish dressing, a veneer of wealth that badly conceals their struggle to make a living. As for the bad-tempered youths that harbor "mischievous grins," they have lost the childhood primeval innocence while the elders, a symbol of wisdom and dignity in traditional African societies, no longer typify these values despite their great attempts at dignity. In this perverted environment, as Grants notes:

> three youngsters ... are negotiating their passage into adulthood ... keenly aware of the deficiencies of their environment – and of themselves. [...] They are all participants in a drama of social transition and psychological awareness. The result is a kind of growth. (*JALC* 14)

Koloko contrasts sorely with Kouroussa; it is hardly an appropriate environment for child education; Buff's and Dickie's (the protagonist's friends') education is thus impaired in such a locale. These teenagers acquire neither the perennial moral and spiritual values of African culture, nor the science and technology of the western school. While Buff's failure to get admission into college causes his decision to become a businessman in the North, Dickie's three unsuccessful attempts to go to college lead him to schizophrenia. It is not only the town that is split in halves. Most of the city dwellers, though descendants of the same ancestor, do not share many things in common: "they have fallen apart" in a community where sound values are transformed into a general make-believe. The inhabitants of Koloko are split subjects in quest of an identity in a community whose traditional moral values, guideposts of pre-capitalist African societies, are uprooted.

Dogkiller's complex of superiority, his mansion, his love for lavish titles, and his avoidance of close-ups (35) mask his dwarf-size, wrinkled face and a shallow bogus identity constructed on flimsy foundations. Fathead, an exhibitionist, harangues the crowd by citing his numerous donations to curb a dire need for praise (132). His false modesty aims at rationalizing his profligacy and egocentrism manifest in his fleet of cars and mansion that have engulfed so much money in a town that lacks basic infrastructures. Fathead's 'generosity' is a semblance that does not match the African traditional principle of "co-possession and co-utilization." His 'generosity' is assistance with a taint of condescension; it sharply contrasts Camara's father's generosity in *The Dark Child*. Dickie, the schizophrenic is a split subject par excellence in Ce's novel. His schizophrenia is an outcome of economic and psychological violence that leads to frustration, drug addiction (the smoking of weed), and finally to madness, a sort of retreat from a stifling society. This retreat confers freedom on the schizophrenic as Deleuze and Guattari point out:

> Such a man [the schizo] produces himself as a free man, irresponsible, solitary and joyous, finally able to say and do something simple in his own name, without asking permission; a desire lacking nothing, a flux that overcomes barriers and codes, a name that no longer designates any ego whatever. (131)

Overcoming barriers and codes that engender repression, Dickie can openly chastise his community and party bigwigs in particular:

> All their hidden crimes in community history were revealed to Dickie in regular moments of mystic illumination and he dutifully hollered the secrets to the roof tops and street corners in the wee hours of every morning. (179)

Dickie's violence against his townsmen and bigwigs is a replica of the same violence he has been subjected to during his childhood. His invectives against Koloko's bigwigs are criticisms against a materialistic money-minded upper class that has set numerous barriers that impede the youths' economic and psychological growth. To attain growth, Yoyo has to transcend these barriers. As Grants observes, "while the society records painful imperviousness to change, the pace of psychological growth of the hero predictably outmatches all of his contemporaries" (14). In effect, among the three friends, only Yoyo succeeds in going to college; his success and later maturity are attributable to three factors: the community's ethics at Boko where he was born and spent the early years of his childhood, his family background (Old Bap's presence at Koloko), and his departure to Gamji College. The first episode of the novel, "Last day in Boko," shows Yoyo's feelings about his natal land:

> If I had to break my silver cord with Boko, I thought, then I might as well have the rest of what's left of this morning, feel the sky, feel the ground, re-live every bit of what came to mind about the little province of Boko where I was born and grew before leaving it for good. (17)

Boko, like Kouroussa and Tindican in *The Dark Child*, is a peaceful provincial environment that favors Yoyo's communion with the natural world. He learns to understand the "mysteries" of nature that, in the Emersonian terms, "never wears a mean appearance" (Cain 479). Nature in this sense exemplifies purity, honesty, and truthfulness, values that are transmitted to Yoyo before he goes to Koloko. His relationship with the ants: "I always had a great respect for the ant community…great workaholics!" (COK19) shows his attachment to community life and communal good. He is amazed at the way ants always find their way back home, and he makes it a duty to bring back home blackhead, the wandering ant: "But as I gently picked up the blackhead with the stick and brought it near the dark hole, I knew a home was almost ready for this adventurer and his kind" (22). Providing a home to the ant is both a sign of generosity as well as a metaphor that forecasts Yoyo's later commitment to home at Koloko and to his ancestral roots despite his stay at Gamji College and his internship at the northern Trium Press. At Boko, Yoyo's father stands for authority, discipline and order: "And there stood daddy, whom all of us called Bap, a huge thundering demigod. My legs shrank at the prospect of confronting the violent rage that shook the face and hands of Bap (22). Yoyo is afraid of Bap whenever he misbehaves because Bap represents sanction and the son's bad conscience. Yet Bap can also be gentle and communicative: "Bap said with a fond and gentle pat on my head, 'C'mon son, it's time to pack your things. We are going home. We are going back to Koloko'" (22). Bap thus combines strictness, gentleness and communication, indispensable elements to child education. Before his journey to Koloko, the father's home state, Yoyo has imbibed all the African values necessary to child education. At Boko, Yoyo's playmates Nunu, Ngoo and Tukur resemble the narrator's kind playmates in *The Dark Child*. They lack Buff's and Dickie's precocity and rascality. When he arrives Koloko, Yoyo is constantly with Buff and Dickie who initiate him into drunkenness and teach him some means he can use to know and adapt to his new environment. Yet the boy is more influenced by his grandfather (Old Bap) who becomes his role model. In Koloko's society fraught with immorality, Old Bap is an icon of morality and dignity ('consequency'), while his wife (Old Mam) and her sister (Da Kata) who abuse and fight each other symbolize 'inconsequency'. When the two crones use all sorts of bad names during their quarrels, Old Bap only mutters: "'This inconsequency is becoming too much'" (52). Although he addresses the two querulous old women, Old Bap targets his society where fights are daily issues. As the chairman of the Peace Council, he has to settle innumerable conflicts:

> He seemed to have too much work in his hands for every house in Koloko had a fight, a quarrel and perhaps a curse to settle. The circle revolved viciously seven days a week and even on God's day of rest. (53)

This turbulent setting is diametrically opposed to Tindican, Kourroussa and Uncle Mamadou's home where "all domestic quarreling was strictly forbidden." (150). As his community's peacemaker, Old Bap shows his commitment to the group. In other words, Old Bap has been chosen as Chairman of the Peace Council because, like Camara's father in *The Dark Child*, he is "the most worthy" (25). A former mission school teacher, Old Bap, Bap, his son, and later Yoyo, his grandson, blend African traditions and western education. It is this blend or 'middle course' that explains the hero's positive balance sheet at the end of his education:

> I had begun to consider myself a man of my own world. Afterall my CV was quite impressive I had finished college, done a stint of press work, joined national defence academy, deserted almost immediately and in the few months ahead, I hoped to find my

bearing although I knew not what it would be at present. Did I add I was a father too? (167)

However, this positive balance sheet is somewhat tainted by the protagonist's short-lived jobs. This job instability poses the question of the quality and usefulness of western education dispensed in modern Nigeria and in many other postcolonial African countries since the 1990s. JJC castigates this education when he tells Buff, Dickie and Yoyo that "'You knows it's a rotten system you operate here. Your education is in shambles y' know?'" (65). This statement replicates Ce's argument in "Bards and Tyrants":

> The 1990s Nigeria witnessed the final crumbling of all that constituted its educational heritage...The social impact of degenerate education in Nigeria had taken its toll by the high incidence of unemployed graduates, the collapse of its economy and the erosion of cultural values. (ARI)

Due to its fallen standards and its unsuitability for the present job market in which cutthroat competition obtains, education for many African youths since the 1990s has given rise to bitter critique. In most African countries today, many youths and parents echo De Mika's brother's statement: "'No job anywhere for school-leavers'" (COK 66). Western education is thus open to critique not just because of the youths' awareness of rampant unemployment, but because of its problematic teaching strategies that have supplanted traditional African pedagogy.

Conclusion

In Camara Laye's *The Dark Child* and Chin Ce's *Children of Koloko*, the education of the child starts by the trainee's (the child

135

hero) mastery of the natural environment and his/her African cultural values. Camara Laye's and Ce's protagonists may have been strengthened in nature (vegetation, rivers, animals etc.) through their ritualistic journeys and exposure to folklore and tradition. However, the moral and spiritual values ingrained in African culture are more and more eroded by monopoly capitalism in Ce's *Children of Koloko*. To curtail these deleterious effect of western school and monopoly capitalism on African culture, the African child is taught positive traditions at family and community levels, the "Village meeting" in *Children of Koloko* being a good example. The cognizance of these basic principles of African communal life ensures the child's future mastery and exploitation of modern science and technology skills. In a way, Laye and Ce are saying that Westernization and globalization may threaten African traditions, but genuine traditional values will prevail if they are made the cornerstone in the education of the African child.

8

K Secovnie

Aidoo, Onwueme

AN AFRICAN-American woman's search for her identity in Africa is the theme of Tess Onwueme's drama, *The Missing Face* and Ama Ata Aidoo's *The Dilemma of a Ghost*. In both instances, the protagonist must struggle with an African "been-to" man, educated in the United States and having returned to Africa. In each case, the man fails to adequately help the woman in her search for identity and the community itself, initially hostile to the desires of the African-American woman, comes to her aid, eventually embracing her as one of its own. Thus both plays affirm the simultaneous necessity, and refusal of, cultural translation. In each case, the requirement for cultural translation, which is initially unclear to the African-American women themselves, is obvious to those in West Africa, while it also becomes clear that the designated translator (the African husband/lover) has refused the mantle of translator, leaving the task to other translator figures. Specifically, the "traditional" West

African mother-figures smooth the way of these African-American women into the communities they strive to inhabit. In this way, both authors redefine a Pan-Africanist agenda through a feminist emphasis on community to do the work of joining a diasporic (in this case African-American) community to Africa. Using the theory of cultural translation described by Homi Bhabha and others, then, this essay illustrates the ways that West African dramatists have addressed the question of how to widen the frontiers of their cultures to embrace those of African-Americans and thus provide for a Pan-Africanist framework that is both realistic and effective.

Widening Frontiers?

When we speak of widening frontiers, we must acknowledge both the limits and possibilities of this paradigm. Pan-Africanism as a way to widen what it means to be African has a history that has been aptly analyzed by scholars. The problem for Pan-Africanism is the divide that often erupts between Africans and their diaspora. The reason for this lack of connection among groups in Africa and the diaspora is the unexamined notion that race and a common history of oppression or – in the Afrocentric scheme– a shared worldview, will automatically serve to draw disparate elements within the diaspora to "mother" Africa. This assumption of natural kinship needs to be challenged in order for true and more effective Pan-African connections to be forged and horizons widened. A frank acknowledgement of difference with the accompanying willingness to understand the view of the other and renegotiate identity provides the framework for these burgeoning connections.

The paradigm of cultural translation provides a useful metaphor with which to examine the details of this negotiation. In his article "Translating Culture vs. Cultural Translation" Harish Trivedi describes the evolution of the phrase from its origins in linguistics:

"the unit of translation was no longer a word or a sentence or a paragraph or a page or even a text, but indeed the whole language and culture in which that text was constituted" (3). Thus, as a metaphor, it addresses cultures as if they were different languages, in need of translation in order to be understood. Cultural translation as a construct has been taken up by some critics to theorize about the ways that postcolonial subjects find themselves, in Salman Rushdie's phrase, "translated men" (17). Homi Bhabha defines cultural translation as a process of imitation in which:

> the priority of the original is not reinforced but by the very fact that it *can* be simulated, copied, transferred, transformed, made into a simulacrum and so on: the 'original' is never finished or complete in itself. [Thus,] the 'originary' is always open to translation so that it can never be said to have a totalized prior moment of being or meaning --an essence [. . .] which makes them [cultures] decentred structures--through that displacement or liminality opens up the possibility of articulating different, even incommensurable cultural practices and priorities. (210)

We can easily see how this model relates to the former colonial subject, a subject for whom the "original" is often a nation in Europe. How, though, might the idea of cultural translation work in a situation where the original itself has been identified (in this case by the West) as a copy? This question specifically relates to the African diaspora and its efforts to form a Pan-African identity with Africa as its originary space. If we find, for instance, Black Americans looking for an originary moment in African culture, as opposed to European or American culture, how might the idea of cultural translation change? Or, when the formerly colonized look to the modernity represented by European or American culture as a type of originary model, with African-Americans as a part of that modernity, how does their identity get renegotiated? In light of post-structuralism, a number of theorists have dismissed African American claims for an African-based identity, stating that identity is no longer relevant – we are all hybrids, etc. In the face of this, postcolonial theory and African American critical race theory have seemed as if they were at odds, or at best incompatible. Through the paradigm of cultural translation, however, we can see the ways in which African American identity-based theory and cultural translation and the hybridity that attends it, are not, in fact, incompatible. Indeed, the idea is explored in several pieces of West African dramatic literature which delve into how two disparate cultures (those of African Americans from the United States and those of West Africa, specifically Ghana and Nigeria) can come to understand one another and thus widen their horizons.

Ama Ata Aidoo's *The Dilemma of a Ghost* and Osonye Tess Onwueme's *The Missing Face* demonstrate the process of finding a cultural identity that does not privilege an originary moment, yet provides space for a negotiated Pan-African identity for West Africans and African Americans. Both of these plays deal with the issue of constructing a Pan-African identity through connecting African Americans with West Africans and both highlight the simultaneous necessity for and failure of cultural translation to facilitate that connection. In each play, we find a female protagonist returning to Africa only to find that the connection she initially sought was not naturally *there* just waiting for her. Both women (Eulalie in *Dilemma* and Ida Bee in *Face*) find the need for a cultural translation and each looks to her African "been-to" husband/lover to provide it. In each case, the expected translator fails in his duties. It is left, instead, for the West African communities themselves, led by women, to provide a translation of culture to the two African-American women that will allow them to connect with and embrace their African identity while respecting the cultures that they find in

Africa (rather than the culture that they project onto Africa).

These plays, then, challenge romanticized notions of Pan-African identification through an emphasis on cultural translation and reveal the failure of the male-centered model of translation that would posit the husband as the sole translator for the wife and the "been-to" man as the sole translator for the community. Instead, a feminist agency is exerted by the West African communities in which these plays are set that undoes the western notion of translation as the domain of the male,[1] and moves it into a female-led, democratic process by which the community as a whole makes decisions about how to translate itself to the diasporic culture, thus asserting a kind of indigenous African agency while privileging the role of the female within this agency. At the same time, it allows for the intervention of West African communities into shaping their own identities in new ways.

This reshaping of identity is shown in *The Dilemma of a Ghost,* the story of Eulalie, an African-American woman who has married Ato, a Ghanaian man who had been studying in the United States. The couple moves to Ghana, where Eulalie realizes that Africa is not all that she had anticipated in a homeland. Ato's family, especially his mother Esi, seem rooted in their ways and intolerant of what they see as white people's ways adopted by Eulalie and Ato in their new life in Ghana. The central conflict revolves around the family's expectation that Eulalie will become pregnant and Ato's unwillingness to entertain the idea, while he allows his wife to take the brunt of his family's criticism. When, in the end, the family, led by Esi, finds out

---

[1]Lori Chamberlain remarks on the field of translation studies and its reliance on male-centered metaphors to describe the function of translation, and attempts "to examine what is at stake for gender in the *representation* of translation: the struggle for authority and the politics of originality informing this struggle" (Chamberlain 314-15).

about Ato's treachery, they take Eulalie in as their own, reprimanding Ato for his failure to uphold his values and to translate those values to Eulalie.

This embrace is not automatic, however. Eulalie initially romanticizes the idea of Africa. While still in the U.S. she and Ato have a conversation about moving to Africa where she demonstrates her lack of awareness about her soon-to-be home:

> EU: I'm optimistic, Native Boy. To belong somewhere again....
> Sure, this must be bliss.
> ATO: Poor Sweetie Pie.
> EU: But I will not be poor again, will I? I'll just be 'Sweetie Pie.'
> Waw! The palm trees, the azure sea, the sun and golden beaches...
> (Aidoo 244)

Although Ato initially lets her know that she has a picture out of a "tourist brochure," he also keeps her in the dark by dismissing any questions she has about his family and the new place they will be living (244). When, for instance, Eulalie expresses concern about his family's possible objection to her desire to postpone having children, Ato refuses to even entertain the idea: "Eulalie Rush and Ato Yawson shall be free to love each other, eh? This is all that you understand or should understand about Africa," he assures her (245).

While Aidoo does present Eulalie as a naïve character in some ways, she also presents a side of her that the audience would sympathize with. As Angeletta KM Gourdine points out, Eulalies "epitomizes a double consciousness: she recognizes that part of her is linked to Africa as geographical and cultural space, yet her knowledge is encoded in an Other discourse" ("Slavery" 33). Thus, when Eulalie first arrives in Africa, she speaks to her dead mother, saying, "Ma, I've come to the very source. I've come to Africa and I hope that where'er you are, you sort of know and approve" (Aidoo

254-255). At the same time, we are confronted with her rather ignorant views of Africa, including her idea that it is a barbaric jungle, full of drumming designed to sound the alarm for a witch hunt (255). These contrasting views show how Eulalie is identified with the discourse of the Other through her attitudes about Africa. Thus, she cannot help but cause conflict within her husband's family.

These attitudes get in the way of her forming a relationship with Ato's family in Ghana, as she does not understand their language or their customs and looks at them as rather quaint and backward. At the same time, they see her as very untraditional and cannot understand her drinking alcohol and smoking cigarettes. The central conflict, however, occurs over the issue of children, as Eulalie expected it might. Initially Eulalie wants to wait for a few years to have children and Ato agrees, but when they move to Africa she changes her mind. Ato wants to earn some money first; so he stays with the original plan. The problem comes in when Ato's entire family comes to see him to ask him if they might administer some medicines to cure Eulalie of her barrenness. Instead of telling his relatives about their decision, he chooses to say nothing, allowing his family to see Eulalie as the problem and allowing Eulalie to see his family as hostile and uncivilized.

It is at this juncture that the need for a cultural translator is fully affirmed. It seems that both cultures are at an impasse – each unable to understand or accept the other. Ato is the obvious choice to make these different "languages" understandable, but he seems unwilling to take on the role. For instance, near the end of the play, he and Eulalie fight over his family and she insults them, calling them "bastards" and "stupid, narrow-minded savages" (Aidoo 271). Instead of explaining the reasons behind his family's behavior toward Eulalie as a good translator might, he slaps her across the face, which sends Eulalie running. When he goes to his family's compound to find her, he is forced to admit to his mother and the others that he and Eulalie were using birth control. When his mother Esi discovers this, she confronts him directly:

> Why did you not tell us that you and your wife are gods and you can create your own children when you want them? You do not even tell us about anything and we assemble our medicines together. While all the time your wife laughs at us because we do not understand such things…yes, and she laughs at us because we do not understand such things…and we are angry because we think you are both not doing what is good for yourselves…and yet who can blame her? No stranger ever breaks the law…Hmm…my son. You have not dealt with us well. And you have not dealt with your wife well in this. (274)

Just as Esi is reprimanding Ato, Eulalie arrives and is tenderly taken in by Esi, leaving Ato alone in the courtyard where the play ends.

Critics have variously theorized about why Ato acts the way he does in relation to Eulalie and his family. Vincent Odamtten sees Ato as representative of the "been-to" man or a *sujet-en-soi* who is "a paradox who, for the 'loved ones,' augurs the possibility of surmounting the restrictions and limitations of their neocolonial reality," while for those who do not receive his benefits he is a source of envy and a symbol of their oppression (31). Because Ato is a been-to, he is caught like a ghost between two worlds and his position is always tenuous. Unable to act in either direction, Ato is, in the end, paralyzed and the play ends on an unsettled note, according to Odamtten. Miriam C. Gyimah agrees with Odamtten's approach, noting that the point of depicting the masculine character of Ato as "struggling with this duality" and as "incapable of asserting a position or a reinventing of himself" is to demonstrate the "effects of colonial and masculinist exploitation" in African societies (57, 67).

By contrast, Arlene A. Elder argues that "Ato's downfall is not the frequently posited, inescapable dilemma of being a 'been-to,' but that he fails to communicate the expectations of African culture to Eulalie or of African American culture to the Odumna clan. He is a faulty medium, the failed voice who should have served as intermediary between two cultures" (160). Ada Uzoamaka Azodo also affirms Ato's failure as a "culture bridge" (235).

These readings of Ato and his dilemma are important to understanding aspects of the play and also bear strongly on the idea of how to form a Pan-Africanist discourse that is sustainable and can widen the frontiers of literature and culture. Ato, as the person who knows both cultures, is responsible to serve as a kind of translator for each and yet he is continually reluctant to do so, first in America when Eulalie wants to know more about Africa and about his family, and, then with his own family when they want to know why he is not following their custom of having children after marrying. Rather than explain the ways of one to the other, he ignores the needs of Eulalie and his family and ends up alienated from both.

This situation demonstrates both the possibilities and the limits of a cultural translation between African Americans and West Africans. Aidoo recognizes both the reason for the African American longing for Africa and the lack of knowledge that they possess about the continent itself. She also feels compassion for Ato's family who, having sacrificed to support their son's American education, find him ungratefully looking down upon their traditional ways and not returning what they saw as an investment (262-3). Although the family *seems* unaccepting of Eulalie, it turns out that they are not, in fact, rejecting her, but are responding to the information (or lack thereof) that was given to them by Ato.

What is apparent then is that a translator is required in order for cultural contact to be possible between African Americans and

Africans on the continent. Although Aidoo recognizes this need (and implicitly, its meaning for the linkages that can possibly be made between the two cultures), she is also critical of it and seeks to balance out the gendered aspects of who this translator can be (the been-to) through her affirmation of the power of the matriarch to balance the translator's possible selfish interests. In this case, it is Esi, as Lloyd Brown points out, who assists Eulalie by "recogniz[ing] Eulalie's dilemmas as a displaced black American and as a woman caught between conflicting cultural assumptions about women" (90). Esi not only recognizes her son's failure as a translator, but also fills in that gap through acknowledging the differences between the her culture and Eulalie's. Thus, Esi takes her in out of compassion, as a sort of motherless child in need of help. Indeed, this is acknowledged at the end of the play when Esi states,

> "Yes, and I know they will tell you that before the stranger should dip his finger into the thick palm nut soup, it is a townsman must have told him to. And we must be careful with your wife. You tell us her mother is dead. If she had any tenderness, her ghost must be keeping watch over all which happen to her." (Aidoo 274)

Thus, Esi affirms the role of the mother in protecting her child against the bad advice of the "townsman," in this case, her own son Ato. Ultimately, then, Aidoo does not simply point out the failure of cultural translator in the figure of the been-to man, but also offers an alternative figure to do the work of translation – the African woman and her community. It is the "traditional" woman who sees the problem and steps in to fix the disconnection that has occurred and she holds the power to widen the frontiers of a Pan-African connection.

Like Aidoo's work, Osonye Tess Onwueme's *The Missing Face* very early on alerts the reader to the cultural conflict to come. Based on an earlier play called *Legacies*, *Face* introduces readers to Ida Bee and her son Amaechi, who have come to Africa in search of Amaechi's father Momah. Ida Bee wants her son to know his father, who stayed with her while studying in the U.S., and to embrace his African ancestry, and so they wander into the camp led by Odozi, the elder, and his wife Nebe. The first moment of misrecognition between Ida Bee and her son Amaechi and the Idu community comes when Odozi questions the strangers about who they are and where they are from. When Ida Bee is pressed for information about her lineage, she responds:

> From ... from Idu...from all of Africa. We are the children of Africa...born in the new world. Africa is our land. We do not have to claim any particular land or country because Africa was our nation...before the white man came to divide...disperse us. So why must we limit ourselves to one country...one state. No! The whole of Africa is our nationality. This is our land. We are the children of Africa. We come from here....(Onwueme 10)

After this passionate speech, Odozi responds with laughter and ridicule to the – in his view – ridiculous assertion, one which he ascribes to the "Oyibo," or white man, who "has spoilt our land" (10). He asks what he is supposed to do in the face of such a world torn apart, and Afuzue, the Town Griot, answers "continue to adjust" (11). This adage spurs the old man into thinking through the issue more deeply, recognizing the ways in which the strangers are asking him to change his own worldview: "a stranger has come to tell me that I do not know who I am. [. . .] She has come to make me Hausa, Yoruba, Bini...In my old age, I am now born again?" (11). Thus, Onwueme demonstrates how the African-Americans' quest for identity also forces the West Africans to question their own sense of self.

While Odozi is quite disturbed by this turn of events, he does not blame the strangers for their ignorance of Africa, for, as he says, "You are Oyibo. You cannot understand us"(11). Iniobong Uko notes, "Odozi is convinced that Ida Bee's inablity to comprehend these issues is because she is 'oyibo', a white person, thus signifiying that even though she is black, she is a white person, a stranger, as evident in her ignorance of African traditional values" (Uko 125). By identifying the strangers with the white man – Oyibo – he shows the distance between the two groups and identifies the lack of understanding between them and the West Africans they claim as kin (Onwueme 12).

It is clear, then, that the need for a translator – one who can understand and interpret each side to the other – is imminent. The obvious choice seems to be Momah; unfortunately, rather than serve as a link between the two groups, he is a hindrance to relations. Thus, although the cultural misunderstandings between the two groups are emphasized in the play, the real source of conflict is the failure of Momah to fulfill his role as translator. Odozi attests that this expectation was put upon his son (by leviration) early on, when the village sent him to the white man's world "so that [they could] learn his [the white man's] ways to arm and strengthen [them]selves with better knowledge" (14). While Odozi professes to the strangers that Momah has succeeded in his mission, showing himself a "true son of the soil" and, "having left behind whatever belonged to their world, that would not be good for our land", these last lines reveal an overemphasis on Momah's achievement, given that, although Momah returned many years ago from America, he is only now being initiated into manhood (14). These last lines reveal an overemphasis on Momah's acheivment, given that, although Momah returned many years ago from America, he is only now being initiated into manhood.

This becomes even more apparent later when Nebe asks the strangers to leave the shrine and they do so. Speaking to her husband, who has come to see the truth of Ida Bee's assertion, she says "Go on searching for grains of truth lost in a bag of garri! Go on! I will be the last to fold my arms when strangers come to chase my only son into the claws of the city. Momah has packed his bag ready to run back to the city. And you remember how long it took us to bring him back from the city?" (17). In these scenes, we find that the underlying problem is not so much the challenge that the strangers bring to the Idu sense of identity, but the challenge that their own son Momah brings to them. Thus, Nebe's concern that he will leave gives the lie to Odozi's earlier assertion of his son's fidelity to his clan and calls into question the sturdiness of the identity of the West African peoples themselves.

Onwueme also provides a flashback scene that reveals the Momah's true character and demonstrates his rejection of the mantle of cultural translator that his village has bestowed upon him. Instead, he has fully embraced the culture that those in the West tout as superior, while defensively asserting that Africa will one day adopt it:

> Yes, we strive to turn Africa into modern Europe. [. . .] African ways are so long and burdensome. American ways, so 'cool' and fast! A world of individualism and prosperity [. . .] We must aquire a new form of civilization. Transform the basis of our lives. Step into the 21st century walking tall. Modernize our culture. Americanize our ways. [. . .] Black-out the past. Our ancestors are nothing but archeological specimens for advanced studies on impoverished human species...Black-out the black past, backward in time and space. (29)

The above diatribe is worth quoting at length because it reveals the depths to which Momah has sunk in America. It also reveals, in a larger sense, the potential anxiety the been-to man could have about his own traditional identity in the face of an American or European modernity. This characterization and Momah's continued unwillingness to accept Ida Bee until the very last page of the play belies Uko's characterization of Momah as "the metaphoric bridge between Idu and the New World" since, "Odozi extols him as the one whose responsibility it was to bring to Idu the benefit of the white man's world [. . .and] Momah, as the true son of the soil, fulfills these aspirations" (Uko 126). In contrast to Uko's position, we argue that, although it is true that Momah was expected to be a cultural translator, like Ato in *Dilemma,* he does *not* fulfill his role and, in fact, only makes matters worse for both his community and for Ida Bee. Clearly, there is a vacancy to be filled in the role of cultural translator, and it is Nebe who steps in to fill the gap, initiating Amaechi into the rites of manhood and, in Movement Four, performing the "Ibe ugo onu" ritual with Ida Bee, which, according to Onwueme "is an indication of love and romance from male to female, or as in this case, from any member of the family to a wife married to that family as an indication of the bond between them" (33, 36). Initiating Ida Bee into the fold, she chants, "Welcome! Welcome! Welcome Egbe! Woman…Egbe, woman-bird who does not know a land but journeys there all the same. My fellow woman…and daughter…welcome to our land…" (36). It is at this moment that Momah breaks into the scene, tells his mother to leave and proceeds to exile Ida Bee from the village into the forest of demons.

Momah's action is not without consequences, however, for Nebe later curses him, saying, "I have no son. Never had a son, nor ever will. Our son lost his manhood to woman whose breasts now swell with pride. Henceforth WOMAN shall be my song, for I can see through the eyes of woman today, the contorted brows of the land bearing the burden of tomorrow" (41). It is clear that Nebe has embraced women as the future of her land and she will not rest until

150

she can remedy the situation with her newly-adopted daughter Ida Bee.

At this point in the play, Momah is chided by a Voice (presumably that of his ancestor, Meme) and it seems that he will finally embrace his heritage; it appears that Momah will be redeemed. Juliette Bartlett takes this view, asserting that Momah becomes more authentically African through Ida Bee's challenge to him: "She serves as a catalyst to re-acculturate with his heritage toward the end of the play when she confronts and challenges him to be more authentic" (61). The play, then, serves as a critique of the figure of the been-to man through Ida Bee because she "serves as the reconciler between African Americans and Africans" (71). Although Ida Bee is a catalyst for change, we argue she is unable to reconcile the two groups, since she is implicated in the conflict and, by the end of the story, is not even in her right mind, having been cast into the evil forest by Momah. This is further confirmed as Momah's lecture to his son Amaechi is interrupted by the appearance of the two women. Nebe, who "emerges rather frantically" from the forest with her face showing that "she has been searching for too long" and Ida Bee, seemingly out of her mind from her time in the forest, disrupt the narrative of redemption that might have been offered to Momah (55).

While Nebe desperately tries to bring Ida Bee back from the brink, she also condemns her son openly, saying, "See the destructive handiwork of man! How I wish I knew it would come to this. MOMAH! Oh! It's MOMAH's doing" (56). She then turns her attention to understanding and interpreting Ida Bee's strange actions, eventually realizing that the Ikenga that Ida Bee carries was given to her by her father, having been passed down by their mutual ancestor Meme. The dramatic final scene results in the matching of the two halves of the missing face, one held by Momah, which was apparently left upon the footpath while their great grandfather Meme was being taken captive, and the other provided by Ida Bee. Nebe plays a key role in restoring order after the village recognizes the kinship of these two "strangers" with the community itself and, as Onwueme writes, "Nebe recovers and walks over to the loom. She sits down and begins to weave. Ida Bee slowly disengages herself from Momah. She walks over to join Nebe at the loom. The two women begin weaving together" (59). The scene ends with Amaechi and Momah once again lifting the two pieces of the Ikenga together in the air, symbolizing the joining of the two communities.

The fact that Nebe and Ida Bee end the play weaving together is significant to the thesis of this essay, which sees Nebe as the lead cultural translator in the drama. It is, once again, she who takes the role in solving the mystery of Ida Bee's identity. She also embraces Ida Bee even before she realizes their literal kinship, on the basis of her own realization of the unity of the two women despite the differences in place and time that had separated them. She realizes that the true separating factor is not so much culture as her own son, whom she rejects when she realizes his complicity in destroying the Idu world. Instead of simply falling victim to this fate, however, she steps up and takes the initiative to draw the strangers into the fold of the community, and thus provides an example for her son and others to follow.

Nebe is described in the cast of characters section as "(56 years old): Mother to MOMAH and wife to ODOZI. 'Nebe' – 'We Watch the World' (Onwueme 1). She sees the world, which could be taken to mean the world both within Idu and beyond. This ability to see beyond what others see gives her a leading role as a translator figure for the play, though she also shares it with the community at large. Of Nebe, whose name in the earlier version of *The Missing Face,* is Anene, Mabel Eveirthom writes:

Elozie's [Momah's] mother is a character who stands for the

maintenance of tradition, and this trait makes her stand out in the text. [. . .] Anene's character complements that of her blacksmith husband (by leviration) Baadi [Odozi], who fully accepts the returnees as children of Idu, while she advocates for their expulsion at the initial part of the play. [. . .] One could wager that Anene voices the writer's ideological stand, although one wonders why this role is not adequately developed in the play, and why Anene should be the character for such a purpose. (202)

Anene's characterization remains much the same in the later play and looking at Nebe as a cultural translator helps to answer Eveirthom's query: Nebe not only voices Onwueme's ideological stance, but she *enacts* it, which reveals her purpose in the play – to bring the two cultures together. Thus, like the figure of Esi in *Dilemma*, Nebe, the "watcher of the world" is the person who fulfills the role not taken up by the heir-apparent to the mantle of cultural translator. Through her embrace of the role, she is able to reconcile the two cultures, integrating the African Americans into her own Idu culture through her leadership in the community. Because she is one of the larger African 'traditional' community, and not the worldly been-to that her son is, she is able to access a translation of one culture to another and, through her compassion, rescues the African American woman from the harm her former lover wishes on her.

Although his focus is *Legacies*, Chris Dunton expresses some doubt about what happens after the reconciliation, writing, "there is a failure to establish with any conviction the structure of a society that will maintain its traditions and yet reabsorb the travellers from the West" (106). This concern could also arise in *The Dilemma of a Ghost*, where the play ends without a glimpse of everyday life after the crisis. This essay argues that this concern, however, is one that would ultimately be mitigated with the ascension of the mother as translator figure. Presumably, relations cannot and will not be the same with the taking on of the translator role by the mother figure, rather than the figure of the been-to son, the one who, as Ida Bee puts it earlier in the play is "so undefined" (Onwueme 28). One imagines that the chastised figures of Ato and Momah will continue to struggle with their identities, but that the Esi and Nebe may be better equipped to handle their own struggles, and thus, with understanding, patience, and compassion will continue to serve in their role as cultural translators, easing the otherwise fraught transition of the African American characters into their adopted communities.

These two plays, then, show the way that cultural translation is both a necessity and a danger to Pan-Africanist relationship. In both instances, it is at once required, rejected by what would seem to be the obvious choice (the been-to husband or lover), and taken on by a member of the "traditional" West African community. The fact that in both cases, the mother of the errant son is the leader in taking on this mantle suggests a radical altering in the way that identity is posited in these plays and leaves space for a more feminist community-based identity to flourish. But, one might ask why this particular metaphor might be important to use in describing these relations? Why not some of the other metaphors used to describe this formation of community?

In *The Difference Place Makes*, for instance, Angeletta Gourdine argues that "understanding 'the difference place makes' made a *bridge* the only logical chronotype for the analyses I undertake, [. . .] Functionally, the writers and their writing bridge the Middle Passage (103-104). Gourdine's attention to the metaphors used to describe the relationship is vital, but caution should be used in foregrounding "place" in terms of a physical geography, since it assumes a possible melding with the idea of nation that can be difficult to disengage from. In the work of Aidoo and Onwueme, for instance, the insistence is less on a particular place than on the situation of *time* and its relation to the present. Thus, in both plays we see inquiries into the ancestors of the African American visitors, neither of whom, because of the distance that time has created, can adequately answer the questions. This provides the central conflict around which a redefinition of diasporic identity comes into play, pulling into the equation the need for a cultural translation, and initiating what will be the central motif of each play, which is the radical shift of the figure of translator to that of the "traditional" African woman, who can connect one cultural "language" to another and smooth the way for an integration of the diasporic and the "originary" self.

Gourdine is not the only one to use the metaphor of the bridge, however. As noted earlier, some critics have seen Ato's role in *Dilemma* as being like a bridge. While he could be thought of in terms of a cultural bridge between the two groups, albeit a faulty one, this metaphor lacks applicability in a situation wherein the two cultures are not, in fact, land masses which are static and unmoving, but people who, through time, interaction (both with colonial powers and with one another) have ever-shifting allegiences, situations, and needs. Thus, the bridge metaphor is itself shaky and may be part of the problem with presenting the 'been-to' man in such a manner. Lakoff and Johnson, in *Metaphors We Live By*, suggest that the conceptual metaphors that undelie the way we speak about abstract concepts such as culture help to determine the very way we think about those concepts, since, "much of cultural change arises from the introduction of new metaphorical concepts and the loss of old ones" (145). Our proposition of the metaphor of Esi and Nebe as cultural translators, then, seems to better suit the positions of each side, since it allows each to find in the other a type of moveable source and, in doing so, helps to renegotiate identity to improve the lot of both parties. The fact that both women's sons fail as translator suggest that the role needs to be taken on by characters who are more flexible, more able to "continue to adjust." What this metaphor offers, then, is an open-ended solution to the problem – how does an "Other" look to another "Other" for self-definition? In each case, the two cultures are disparate and yet understandable to one another – but only with the aid of a cultural translator. Aidoo and Onwueme make a radical move in insisting that a new metaphor requires new actors to widen the identity horizons of Africans both in the diaspora and in the Continent.

9

Òsófisan

A Van Weyenberg

THIS chapter focuses on Fémi Òsófisan's reworking of *Antigone*, entitled *Tègònni: an African Antigone* (1994). It first examines Òsófisan's decision to draw on *Antigone* within the context of Nigeria. Then it discusses Antigone's representative value within her "new" surroundings, the (meta)theatrical aesthetics that characterise her cultural translocation and, finally, the political implications of this translocation for Antigone's status as a Western canonical figure.

The popularity of *Antigone* within Western literature, art and thought has been discussed at length, most famously by George Steiner who classifies it as "one of the most enduring and canonic acts in the history of our philosophic, literary, political consciousness" ("Preface"). At the heart of the tragedy is the conflict between Antigone, who sets out to bury her brother, and her uncle King Creon, who has issued a decree forbidding this burial.[1] *Antigone*'s appeal largely derives from this central conflict, a conflict that appears straightforward, but on closer inspection reveals the intricate nature of the various oppositions it explores, such as that between woman and man, individual and state, private and public and the gods and mankind. Not only does this complexity make the conflict between both protagonists tragic to begin with, but it also ensures *Antigone*'s continuing attraction as a source for philosophical and artistic inspiration.

A great number of playwrights have revisited Sophocles' original, but its contemporary popularity is particularly striking on the African stage, where Kamau Brathwaite, Athol Fugard, Fémi Òsófisan and Sylvain Bemba have given *Antigone* post-colonial relevance in a variety of settings.[2] It may seem strange that African playwrights would turn to texts that represent the classical Western canon. After all, Greek tragedy originally came to colonial areas through imported, and forcefully imposed, Western educational systems, and in that sense could be seen to epitomise imperial Europe. In their seminal study on post-colonial drama, Helen Gilbert and Joanne Tompkins clarify that it is precisely this

---

[1] Antigone's brothers Eteocles and Polynices have died fighting over the throne of Thebes. Her uncle Creon becomes king and forbids the burial of Polynices, because he has led an army against the city. Antigone defies Creon's edict and sets out to bury her brother, for which Creon has her locked up in a cage to be executed. The play ends tragically with no less than three suicides: of Antigone, her betrothed and Creon's son Haemon and Creon's wife Eurydice.

[2] Edward Kamau Brathwaite, *Odale's Choice* (1967); Athol Fugard, *The Island* (1973); Fémi Òsófisan, *Tègònni: an African Antigone* (1994); Sylvain Bemba, *Black Wedding Candles for Blessed Antigone* (1990, originally published in French in 1988 under the title *Noces Posthumes de Santigone*). Though Brathwaite is originally Barbadian, his *Odale's Choice* is set in Africa and was first produced in the newly independent Ghana (Gilbert and Tompkins 42-43).

enduring legacy of colonialist education that explains the
"prominent endeavour among colonised writers/artists" to "rework
the European 'classics' in order to invest them with more local
relevance and to divest them of their assumed authority/
authenticity" (16). Still, whether or not African reworkings of
Antigone should be considered counter-narratives to the Western
canon is a question in need of closer investigation, and one that
will be discussed later.

The Choice of Antigone

As Kevin J. Wetmore Jr. explains in his study on African
adpatations of Greek tragedy, Sophocles' *Antigone* is a play that
"can be adapted into any situation in which a group is oppressed,
or in which, in the aftermath of struggle, the forces of community
and social order come into conflict with the forces of personal
liberty" (170-171). Òsófisan's *Tègònni: an African Antigone* well
fits this description. It is set in Nigeria under British colonial rule,
while also referring to the military dictatorships that have held
Nigeria in its grip almost incessantly ever since its independence
from Britain in 1960. *Tègònni* was first produced in 1994 at Emory
University in Atlanta (Georgia, USA), which Òsófisan was visiting
during one of the most chaotic periods in Nigerian history,
following the military junta's violent intervention and annulment of
the presidential elections of 1993.[3] In the production notes
Òsófisan explains that *Tègònni* is intended to "look at the problem
of political freedom against the background of the present turmoil

---

[3]The first performance of *Tègònni* in Nigeria was at the Arts Theatre of the
University of Ibadan in November 1998, directed by Òsófisan himself. Since
then, the play has been performed in Nigeria a number of times (Òsófisan, May
2006, from personal correspondence).

in Nigeria – my country – where various military governments have continued for decades now to thwart the people's desire for democracy, happiness, and good government" (11).

The final form of the play and the idea to draw on *Antigone* shaped itself in Òsófisan's mind when he approached Lagos airport to fly to Atlanta, driving past "burning houses, mounted placards, and screaming police and military vehicles." He writes:

> I remembered the story of the British colonisation of Nigeria and the defeat of my ancestors. And I remembered the valiant story of Antigone. The two events–one from history, the other from myth–would help me add my voice to the millions of other small voices in Africa, all shouting unheard and pleading to be set free–voices that are waiting desperately for help from friends in the free world. (10)

As this passage demonstrates, Òsófisan directs *Tègònni* at a Western audience, but not only to appeal for their help, for he also explicitly holds Britain, France and Germany responsible for selling their conscience and supporting the military dictatorship to safeguard their economic interests (10).

Òsófisan's address to the West does not mean that he absolves Nigerians themselves from responsibility for their country's crisis. At the heart of the Nigerian predicament he diagnoses a distorted consciousness that shows itself in "collective amnesia and inertia, in cowardice, and in inordinate horror of insurrection" (*Revolution* 15-16). It is this distorted consciousness, which is largely a distorted *historical* consciousness whose anaesthetic force disables change, that Òsófisan sets out to heal from within. Accordingly, his theatrical practice is characterised by a critical re-evaluation of the past as a prerequisite for socio-political change in the present. Within a context of oppression, moreover, this calls for a special strategy, which Òsófisan describes as "surreptitious insurrection": a way for the "dissenting artist" to "triumph through the gift of metaphor and magic, parody and parable, masking and mimicry"; a "covert and metaphoric system of manoeuvring" with which the terror of the state can be confronted and demystified (11). Performance, then, becomes such a "surreptitious" strategy by which to circumvent repression but also actively attack it.

In line with his project of re-evaluating the past to change the present, Òsófisan does not set *Tègònni* in contemporary Nigeria but instead, turning to the root of Nigeria's predicament, situates it towards the end of the 19th century, at the height of colonial expansion. By enacting a moment of socio-political change set within this past, performance becomes a way to transform history into an active site where a renewed (historical) consciousness may start to take shape. Performance, to draw on Wendy Brown's words, thus literally "opens the stage for battling with the past over possibilities for the future" (151). Because, as Òsófisan explains in a discussion of his play Morountodun,

> by continuously juxtaposing scenes from myth and history; from the present and the past; and from the play's present, and the real present, ... the audience is made aware all the time of the options available, and those chosen. ... The intention is to turn the stage into a problematic space of ideological conflict, through which the audience can see itself mirrored and, possibly, energized in its struggle with history. (*Theatre* 9)

Another way in which Òsófisan explores different ideological positions and socio-political problems is by borrowing from and challenging antecedent texts. His dramaturgy is characterised by such recourse to existing plays, both from the Western and the Nigerian theatre tradition. Thus, he engages with Samuel Beckett's

Waiting for Godot in his *Oriki the Grasshopper* (1981), with Wole Soyinka's *The Strong Breed* in his *No More the Wasted Breed* (1982), with J. P. Clark-Bekederemo's *The Raft* in his *Another Raft* (1988), with Shakespeare's *Hamlet* in his *Wèsóò Hamlet!* (2003) and with Euripides' *Trojan Women* in his *Women of Owu* (2004). Òsófisan gives his re-workings both local and political relevance. The first is achieved by drawing heavily on myths, rituals, songs, proverbs and parables taken from the Yoruba tradition in which he was brought up; the latter by subjecting these traditional elements to constant re-evaluation, releasing them from their possible repressive weight and granting them contemporary socio-political relevance. An example in *Tègònni* is the inclusion of the Yoruba parable of the Tiger and the Frog, teaching a moral that in the context of contemporary Nigeria acquires great political bearing: "the one who was swallowed gained a throne, while the one who usurped power fell to disgrace" (100). Tradition, then, is not treated as something that is grounded outside of history or that has no political viability but, instead, as something that has a place within the (political) present; a place, however, in need of continuous reconsideration.

The Politics of Representation

The main question Sophocles poses in *Antigone* is whose claim is more "just": that of Antigone, who stays true to the laws of the gods and her private morality, or Creon, who insists on the superiority of the laws of the state and public morality instead. In a chapter on tragedy and politics, Suzanne Said explains that in 5th century B.C. Athens, such on-stage negotiation between conflicting interests and ideologies had an important didactic function, since it represented the dialectic of the political process held high in the young democracy of Athens (Boedeker and Raaflaub 282). Tragedy, then, primarily served to instruct the art of debate to audience members. In Òsófisan's adaptation, written within a context of oppression that forbids such debate, the confrontation between Creon and Antigone acquires a different relevance and comes to represent the opposition between oppressor and oppressed. Within this larger field of injustice, the Sophoclean complexity of the conflict is reduced, and the ethical question of justification is rendered irrelevant. With regard to *Tègònni* it is therefore more constructive to think of Antigone not as the character from Sophocles' tragedy, but rather as a concept, a concept that has travelled widely through philosophy, art and literature and, while travelling, has taken on different forms, shapes and meanings.[4] In Òsófisan she has travelled to Africa where she becomes the representative of the struggle against oppression.

Òsófisan structures his entire play along the lines of *Antigone*, so that the "valiant story of Antigone" (10) is transformed into that of Tègònni, princess of the imaginary Yoruba town of Oke-Osun. Creon, in turn, becomes the British colonial Governor Carter Ross, who rules the town with an iron hand. Similar to Fugard, Òsófisan departs from Sophocles' ambiguous character-presentation. His Governor becomes the undisguised representative of brutal colonial oppression, a man who longs for the time when "you knew you were right, because you believed in the Cross and in the Empire" and "You hammered the Union Jack down their throats, and made them sing 'God Save the Queen'! For if you didn't do that, they would quickly resort to barbarism, to cannibalism, to living apes" (131). Sensing the dawn of a new "enfeebled" age, Òsófisan's Governor obsessively clings to the historicist view that,

---

[4]See Mieke Bal's study on *Travelling Concepts in the Humanities* (2002).

as Dipesh Chakrabarty explains, enabled European colonialism in the first place. Since historicism "posited historical time as a measure of the cultural distance (at least in institutional development) that was assumed to exist between the West and the non-West," it was essential to the construction of colonial otherness, while it also legitimised the idea of civilisation in the colonies (Chakrabarty 7). Òsófisan's Governor personifies this view and loudly proclaims that it is because people like him that civilisation acquires its destiny (131-132), though he also shamelessly states that "we're just here to give the orders, it's the niggers who do the fighting" (60).

Unlike Sophocles' Creon, who only comes to power after Antigone's brothers have died, Òsófisan's Governor is actively engaged in the civil war and eagerly applies the strategy of divide-and-rule by supporting one of Tègònni's brothers with his army and treating the other as his enemy and forbidding his burial. Tègònni, like Antigone before her, disregards his decree and sets out to bury her brother's body. But the Governor represents more than brutal colonial force and also refers to the military dictatorships that have held Nigeria in its grip for so many decades. Showing the ways in which the past still haunts the present, Òsófisan engages with socio-political problems that are painfully familiar to his contemporary Nigerian audience, thereby calling for their active engagement. Accordingly, Tègònni is also more than the unambiguous symbol of resistance against colonial oppression, as she also becomes the agent of social and emancipatory change in a repressive traditional society.

Like Sophocles' heroine, Tègònni is presented as different, as someone who refuses to play according to the rules of the patriarchal society in which she finds herself. She is the founder of the first Guild of Women Casters and practices a trade formerly unknown and not allowed to women. Rather than propagating a return to an idealised pre-colonial past, Òsófisan paints an unromantic picture of a society that not only needs to break free from colonial oppression, but also from the repressive forces of tradition. Tradition, like history, becomes something to be battled with, and Tègònni and her sisters and friends take on this battle. With regard to Òsófisan's larger oeuvre, this is not surprising because, opposed to the tendency in Nigerian theatre to portray women as underdogs, almost all of Òsófisan's plays portray women as agents of social reconstruction. In his view, the empowerment of women is crucial to the prospective programme of liberation and modernisation and, accordingly, many of his female characters are determined to struggle collectively to transform their society (Onwueme 25).

In Sophocles, there is no definite answer to the question whether Antigone's act of defying Creon is motivated by the desire for social change or whether it primarily stems from individual knowledge and interest. Her political reproach of Creon's "one-man rule" causing the citizens of Thebes to "lock up their tongues" would suggest the former (556). However, it is equally significant that Antigone ultimately acts alone, without the support of her fellow citizens, without the support even of her sister Ismene. Òsófisan's play leaves no such ambiguity: his African Antigone, Tègònni, succeeds in unifying a group of women and her private act of defiance acquires collective relevance as it turns into a struggle for freedom from colonial oppression and for societal change.

In a way, the stark contrast between Tègònni and the Governor seems to challenge Òsófisan's intention of eliciting his audience's active and critical engagement. After all, it permits an escape into the simplistic Manichean opposition of coloniser versus colonised which, in turn, reinforces rather than heals the distorted consciousness Òsófisan wishes to correct. However, Òsófisan moderates this opposition by including the romantic relationship between Tègònni and colonial officer Allan Jones (a relationship that is more prominent and more developed than that between Antigone and Haimon in Sophocles). Though the character Jones is set in opposition to the Governor, he does not simply embody all that is good and honourable. On the one hand, he is portrayed as sympathetic, kind-hearted and generous and, importantly, as the one who protected Tègònni when she set up her bronze casting workshop and was taken for a witch by her own people. This means that, to a great extent, Jones (the coloniser) facilitated Tègònni's (the colonised) emancipation in Oke-Osun's male-dominated society, which further complicates the opposition coloniser-colonised. But Jones is also presented as essentially powerless, too weak to stand up to the Governor, too careful to avoid confrontation and too eager to settle for compromise.

Though the love between Tègònni and Jones suggests the possibility of bridging racial, political and cultural boundaries, their marriage seems doomed from the start, and within the colonial context, their idea that it could remain outside of the political sphere seems rather naïve. The Governor, of course, does realise the marriage's political implications. His fatherly affection for Jones, echoing the relationship between Haimon and Creon in Sophocles, soon changes into a loathing for his impotence as an imperial officer: "You thought you were being a fucking hero, didn't you!" he shouts at Jones, "You'll marry a nigger woman, and show us all! Teach us a lesson perhaps about the equality of races! Rebuild the world with your penis!" (120-121).

The union between coloniser and colonised and white and black symbolises a transgressive moment in history that the

Governor, as the representative of Empire, is obviously not comfortable with. But neither are most people of Oke-Osun. Tègònni's sisters do wholeheartedly encourage it, but Òsófisan invites his audience to contemplate for what reasons. It is interesting, after all, that the support of one of Tègònni's most committed sisters, Kunbi, seems to depend largely on the political usefulness of the marriage. She says: "Just think of what the town as a whole will gain by having a whiteman as our in-law, rather than our antagonist! We will be feared and respected by all our neighbours" (22). Through this remark Òsófisan forces his audience to recognise that the opposition between oppressor and oppressed can never be neatly drawn and that resistance, no matter how committed it may be, is always to some extent informed by complicity.[5]

Although, as stated earlier, Òsófisan reduces the complexity of Sophocles' original in making the conflict between Creon and Antigone representative of that between oppressor and oppressed, the previous analysis shows that this does not make his play simplistic. Rather, the different political context requires that different questions are posed and that complexity is to be found elsewhere. In Òsófisan, this is achieved by complicating the opposition oppressor-oppressed and extending it to represent more than the binary coloniser-colonised, but also have it refer to contemporary political power structures. Additionally, rather than posing answers, Òsófisan invites his audience to critically re-evaluate the past and become actively involved in changing their

---

[5] The complicity of resistance with the workings of power is discussed by Gayatri Chakravorty Spivak in her "More on Power/Knowledge" (1993). Reviewing Michel Foucault's analysis of "pouvoir/savoir", Spivak proposes a reading of power and resistance as not merely repressive and liberating, but as mutually dependent mechanisms in a shared complex field of forces.

future.

Performing *Antigone*

Òsófisan not only structures his entire play along the lines of Antigone, telling the story of, as the title suggest, an African Antigone, but he also metatheatrically brings Antigone on stage to interact with her African twin-sister. The word "metatheatre" encompasses all forms of theatrical self-reference, all ways in which plays call attention to their own theatricality, such as story-telling, the play-within-the-play and role-play. Gilbert and Tompkins explain that for post-colonial playwrights metatheatre holds great political potential, because it is a constructive method to engage with the politics of (self-)representation, while also offering ways to reconstruct past and present (23). Many critics analyse such metatheatrical practice in Brechtian terms, but it is important to realise that, despite Brecht's significant influence on Òsófisan's dramaturgy, metatheatrical techniques are equally characteristic of indigenous African performance practices (Richards 72).

In her study on the metatheatrical device of role-play in South African theatre Haike Frank points out that the effectiveness of role-play on stage has to do with its power to confront audiences with their (different) knowledges and experiences of role-play off stage, knowledges and experiences which make them especially susceptible to recognise the performative potential of role-play to bring about change. Frank's study can be extended to any society negatively based on role definition, where groups of people are oppressed because of class, religion, sex or race, where people are forced to perform and conform to certain imposed roles. It also applies well to the Nigerian context of Òsófisan. The scene from

Tègònni that best illustrates this is one in which the character Antigone orders her retinue to change roles and play members of the Hausa constabulary, the army that the British raised to colonise West Africa.

Experiencing that playing soldiers is "no fun at all," because all they do is carry corpses, build execution platforms, terrorise people and collect bribes, the actors soon ask Antigone for different parts, after which she promises them a scene in which they can change roles again (28-30). Antigone, then, takes on the role of theatre director and imposes roles on her attendants, roles that they do not want to perform – roles, moreover, that not only refer to the military forces in colonial times, but that will also be familiar to Nigerian viewers still experiencing military control in their daily lives. Still, this scene does more than showing the audience how different ideological positions are projected by individuals; it also presents them with the possibility of changing reality and of changing their own roles within this reality (Dunton 69-74).

Antigone's presence, then, does not remain hidden behind the mask of Tègònni, as Òsófisan metatheatrically brings her on stage as a character as well. Antigone's introduction of herself is telling:

> ANTIGONE: I heard you were acting my story. And I was so excited I decided to come and participate.
> YEMISI: Your story! Sorry, you're mistaken. This is the story of Tègònni, our sister. Funny, the names sound almost the same, but–
> ANTIGONE: Tègònni! Where's she?
> YEMISI: Back in the compound there. Preparing for her wedding.
> ANTIGONE: And for her death?
> FADERERA: What kind of thought is that, stranger?

169

ANTIGONE: Antigone

YEMISI: Yes, Antigone, whatever your name is! Have you come to curse our sister?

ANTIGONE: No, oh ho. Please don't misunderstand me. I know what I'm saying. I've travelled the same route before.

(...)

ANTIGONE: Antigone belongs to several incarnations.

KUNBI: But you...you're black!

ANTIGONE: (laughs). And so? What colour is mythology?

ANTIGONE'S CREW: We're metaphors. We always come in the colour and shape of your imagination. (25-27)

This passage demonstrates that it is not Antigone the heroine from Greek tragedy who comes on stage, but Antigone the metaphor, unbound by time, place or race and willing to travel to any society in need of revolutionary change. For, as Antigone proclaims:

> Many tyrants will still arise, furious to inscribe their nightmares and their horrors on the patient face of history. But again and again, as many times as such abortions creep up, as many times will others come up who will challenge them and chase them away into oblivion. Ozymandias will rise again! But so will Antigone! Wherever the call for freedom is heard! (127-128)

Ozymandias is the name the Greeks gave to Ramses II, the Egyptian pharaoh from whom Moses and the Israelites fled during the Exodus. It is also the title of a poem on dictatorship and the fall of empires by the English romantic poet Percy Bysssche Shelley (Raji 148). In the scene that follows, Antigone and Tègònni together recite this poem, while linking hands like true revolutionary twin-sisters. This image demonstrates that mythological relevance transgresses temporal and spatial barriers and emphasises that Tègònni does not exist by virtue of Antigone. In this way, the historicist view of "first in the West, and then elsewhere" is emphatically rejected (Chakrabarty 6), but does this also imply that Òsófisan's engagement with Antigone should be considered as a way of writing back to the Western canon?

Beyond *Antigone*?

The question remains whether, in addition to an intertextual work, Òsófisan's reworking of *Antigone* is also an example of "canonical counter-discourse", where writers develop a counter text that, by "preserve[ing] many of the identifying signifiers of the original while altering, often allegorically, its structures of power" seeks to "destabilise the power structures of the originary text rather than simply to acknowledge its influence" (Gilbert and Tompkins 16).[6] It seems strange that Gilbert and Tompkins, after first making this important distinction between works that are solely intertextual and works that are also counter-discursive, later state the following:

> Sophocles' *Antigone* has (…) received considerable counter-discursive attention because it disputes the state's definition of justice and champions a figure who is imprisoned for maintaining her sense of moral and legal principle. The differences between two systems of justice and the triumph of the stronger power of the weaker can easily be articulated in a colonial context. (41)

They seem to suggest, then, that articulating the power

---

[6]The term "canonical counter-discourse" was coined by Helen Tiffin (1987: 22).

relations of Sophocles' original into a colonial context *equals* giving this text counter-discursive attention, whereas, according to their own definition, a counter-discursive text not only *articulates*, but also purposefully *destabilises* such power structures. Though Òsófisan, like other African playwrights who draw on *Antigone*, reduces the ambiguity of *Antigone*'s power structures and changes their representative value, he does not set out to counter them. And perhaps this is not so surprising, because even if we interpret Sophocles' original to stand for colonial hegemony, *within* this text the character Antigone, in her defiance of authority, is herself the personification of counter-hegemonic action *against* Creon's rule. It is precisely for this reason that Antigone has become so popular on the post-colonial stage. And it is precisely for this reason, also, that Òsófisan presents Antigone as a metaphor that belongs to several incarnations, a source of inspiration for the struggle against oppression which can be conjured up "whenever the call for freedom is heard" (128). Òsófisan, then, does not seem particularly interested in Antigone's cultural origin or her status as a Western canonical figure. His main concern is with her political potential in the present. It is ultimately not Antigone's foreignness but her *at-homeness* that is stressed.

Rather than labelling *Tègònni* as "counter-discursive" it seems more constructive to refer to Wetmore's "Black Dionysus" model, in which "familiarity is celebrated, but not used to erase difference" and "Greek material is seen as the original tragedians saw myth – a convenient and familiar vehicle by which one might critique society" (44-45). "Black Dionysus" is a

> Post-Afrocentric formulation of drama that is counter-hegemonic, self-aware, refuses to enforce dominant notions of ethnicity and culture, and uses ancient Greek material to inscribe a new discourse that empowers and critiques all cultures, even as

it identifies the colonizer's power and the colonized's powerlessness. (44) [7]

Still, within the context of this paper two additional remarks seem important. The first has to do with the juxtaposition of the words "power" and "powerlessness," which implies an uncomplicated binary opposition between those who do and those who do not have power, an opposition that Gayatri Spivak has demonstrated to be erroneous.[8] Secondly, with regard to Wetmore's use of the term "counter-hegemonic," it is important to specify to which hegemony (or, more accurately, to which hegemonies) this term is intended to refer. After all, in the words of Òsófisan, "it is nonsense to think that the hegemony in question is always the colonial/imperialist one, when the political structures of our countries are so deficient and murderous kleptocracies are in place."[9]

A final question remains to be answered. Because if Tègònni indeed does not exist by virtue of Antigone, how then to understand the fact that Antigone metatheatrically insists on the necessity for her story to play out exactly as it did before, for instance by hinting at Tègònni's approaching death in the first of the two passages quoted above? Though Antigone's question if Tègònni is preparing for her death does end with a question mark, it is clearly rhetorical and leaves little room to answer in the negative. And what are we to make of the fact that, as described

---

[7]Wetmore poses his "Black Dionysus" model as an addition to the Eurocentric "Black Orpheus" model, which sees classic material as a way to understand the African, and the Afrocentric "Black Athena" model, which sees Greek material as African material that needs to be reclaimed.

[8]Spivak 1993, see also note 5 above.

[9]From personal correspondence, 27 June 2006.

earlier, Antigone not only comes on stage uninvited, but also takes on the role of theatre director, getting involved with the execution of Tègònni's story? A story, moreover, which in the first passage quoted above, she possessively refers to as *hers*: "I heard you were acting *my story*" (25, emphasis added).

In a sense, and this counts for Òsófisan as well as for other playwrights who draw on *Antigone* within post-colonial contexts, the very emphasis on Antigone as *theirs*, as representing *their* struggle, as being relevant to *their* political present, inevitably embeds the dominance of Antigone's conventional representational status: as a white Western woman. In *Tègònni* this is illustrated by Kunbi's exclamation of surprise at seeing a black Antigone. In *The Island* by Fugard, Ntshona and Kani it is evident in the white wig on the head of the black prisoner Winston as he performs his role of Antigone. No matter how democratically available Antigone might be, her origin seems unavoidable and it is in this relation between adaptation and original that a certain inevitable ambiguity resides. By bringing Antigone on stage, Òsófisan presents the illusion that Antigone is "really" there, while simultaneously stressing the distance between Sophocles' original and his African reworking. It is as if Antigone could not migrate without doubling herself.

Concluding, however, it is important to emphasise that it is not Antigone's cultural and historical origin with which Òsófisan is primarily concerned. It is not *her* past he is mainly interested in, but the political potential she has to offer for *his* country's future.

10

Uways

O Ayinde

Conflict in the Sudanese novel might not satisfy Edward Said's thesis to the effect that "every novel is a form of discovery" (82). This is because conflict, with respect to al-Sūdān, is the *Zeitgeist*[1] – the spirit of the age. As a historical construct, the Sudan, since the medieval to the modern period, has been a locale for contests and conflicts between and among disparate ethnic communities and, in the words of Ali Mazrui, "the multiple marginalities" (240-255) that inhabit its rigid terrain. As a post-modern/colonial site, the geographies of the Sudanese landscape is presently being shaped, no more by "multiple marginalities" but "multiple complexities" (Ahmed 71) of the Sudanese subjectivities. As a cultural problematic, the category of conflict in the Sudan continues to defy the simplistic binary between good and evil and between Northern and Southern Sudan. Rather the country has the enviable (?) record, at least with reference to Africa, of being one in which conflict exists, on the one

---

[1]This is taken from: *al-Adīb al-Sūdānī: Ahmad al-Mubārak 'Isā* (ed) A. M. Ahmad ((Khartūm: Dār Izza, 2007) p. 47

hand, between the 'black' and the 'white', and, on the other, among the 'white,' the 'black' and the neither 'white' nor 'black.' As if by compulsion, the Sudan celebrates the uncanny union of the real, the farcical and the absurd; it is a site where conflict is the *nodus* of being; it is a space where conflict is the driving force of existence.

Now, if the subject matter of conflict has become so intertwined, quite paradoxically, with the very essence of the Sudanese nation, then its appropriation by imagination must necessarily be for purposes other than mere re-presentation of its dynamics. In other words, in order for the novel to be relevant in postcolonial Sudan, it should most likely set for itself the task of, in the words of Chinua Achebe, "re-educating" the complex Sudanese subjectivities and "regenerating" (103) the Sudanese cultural values. Put differently, the Sudanese novel that would titillate the Sudanese literary appetite and, therefore, merit our attention should be such as would satisfy, in line with Edward Said, the urge in humanity "to modify reality" (82a). Ahmad Muhammad al-Mahjūb graphically pictures this when, writing in the 1930s in Sudan, he says: "what's the essence of literature if it does not assist people on revolution and change in life...and in propelling...(the people) on to the current of progress and development?" (13).

Thus in Uways' *al-Ruqs taht al-Matar* (*Dance under the Rain* – hereafter, *Dance*), we shall examine how the novel attempts "to modify reality" in Sudan through its representation of the *topoi* of conflict in the country. In order to achieve the foregoing, however, it is important for us to examine intra-Sudanese existential/ historical/ cultural valences that accentuate conflict in Sudan before its appropriation by Sudanese writers. In other words, the starting point of an inquiry into the category of conflict in the Sudanese novel, and one in which the motifs of race, gender and nationalism are embedded, should be an investigation, albeit briefly, of the extremely

176

charged field which spawned racial, gender and national consciousness in Sudan before its appropriation by Sudanese writers. Thus, the following question becomes extremely urgent: what could be the fountain(s) for the conflictual identities of the Sudanese in the contemporary period and how might it be useful in our attempt to understand the problematics of race, gender and nationalism in the Sudanese novel? In answering these questions the probing statements of the renowned Sudanese writer, al-Tayyib Ṣālih, compels our contemplation. Writing in *al-Majallah* close two decades ago, al-Tayyib Ṣālih says:

> One of the reasons why this country is always in turmoil could be attributed to the fact that its name means nothing to its people. What is Sudan? Egypt is Egypt, Yemen Yemen, Iraq Iraq and Lebanon Lebanon. But what is the Sudan? We have continued to trundle on with this hollow colonial legacy. (137)

These statements from al-Tayyib Ṣālih are of high importance to any analysis of the problematic of conflict in Sudanese culture. The statements essay a reasoned gulf between the Sudanese and his/her nation. They portray the former in a state of angst, utterly disoriented with him/herself and completely disenchanted with the very first element that defines his/her identity: *al-Sūdān*. Specifically the question, 'what is Sudan?' mirrors the Arab-Sudanese's rejection of *al-Sūdān*. The name is rejected probably because it effaces, in line with Ibn Khaldun's thesis, "the historicity" of the Arab-Sudanese "as an historical group" (qtd. in Al-Azmeh 38). *al-Sūdān* 'inflicts' 'blackness' on the latter; with it, the most important critical factor for national cohesion and identity formation in Sudan becomes circumscribed by colour: blackness[2]

---

[2]The Arab-Sudanese "considered the word "Sudani" as a synonym for "Black Slave" and felt insulted when they were so called. Many of them refused, after

The rejection, by the Arab-Sudanese, of *al-Sūdān* does not, however, mean the celebration of the name by the black-Sudanese. This is because the circumscription of nation by colour and the inscription of Sudan with the black identity have not, since the early modern period, led to any improvement in the socio-political and economic realities of the black-subjects in Sudan. Throughout the period of the British hegemony over the Nile Valley and years after Sudanese political independence extreme and, perhaps, deliberate under-development of the Southern and Western parts of the Sudan, both of which represent the bastion of black identities in the country, has continued[3.] For example during the British rule "only four government primary schools" (Prunier 26) could be found in the whole of Dar Fur. Schools and other educational facilities were and have not been provided in these areas probably based on the fact that, in line with George Antonius, "without school or book" (Antonius 40) the yearning for a nation by the black-Sudanese would be inconceivable. Thus while the Arab-Sudanese is in conflict with *al-Sūdān* because of 'race'/colour, the black-Sudanese, on the other hand, rejects it because of its empty promises as a 'nation'.

But the foregoing only represents a perspective. In other words,

independence, to apply for passports because they had to register themselves as Sudanese nationals before they could get a passport." For more on this see: Muhammad Khalafalla Abdulla "Mustafa's Migration from the Said: An Odyssey in search of identity" in *Middle Eastern Literature* vol. 10. 43-61 (1998).

[3]For criticism of the British hegemony in Sudan and the origins of contemporary conflicts in Sudan see: A. Muhammad: *Nafathāt al-Yarā'fil Adab wa tārīkh wa' Ijtimā'* (Khartūm; 1958); For North-South dialectics in modern Sudanese history see: Ahmed: "Multiple Complexity and Prospects for Reconciliation and Unity"; F. M. Deng: *Africans of Two Worlds: The Dinka in the Afro-Arab Sudan* (Yale: Yale University Press, 1978); --- "Scramble for Souls: Religious Intervention among the Dinka in Sudan" in *Proselytization and Communal Self Determination in Africa* (ed) A. Na'im (New York: MaryKnoll 1999).

it is not only colour/race and nation that have informed the epistemology of conflict in postcolonial Sudan, lack of consensus over gender role(s) has also served as an important fountain for conflict, frictions and fissures among Sudanese citizens. From the farthest regions of southern Sudan to its northern peripheries, arguments abound not only over the essence of the male or female in nature but also what socio-cultural and political space(s) could be yielded to each in the Sudanese construction of its identity. Within this gender spectrum, however, the Sudanese woman is usually at the receiving end. She has no independent identity. She usually watches as her body is, in the words of Muhsin al-Musawi, "confiscated, sold out, drawn upon, mapped and deprived of its own identity" (al-Musawi 223). During the pre-independence era[4] her body was a contested site between the colonist and the colonized. In the post-independence period, her identity has again been appropriated and invaded by the conflictual subjectivities in Sudan in their inter-racial and intra-national and cultural transactions; on her body the North and the South violently intersect. She is the "necessary allegorical ground for the transaction in national history" (Radhakrishnan 77).

Contrasting the figure of the woman with the man in Sudanese culture yields interesting images for us to behold. Without attempting to explore in-depth how he has been "produced" culturally,[5] the male in Sudan may be categorized into to three: al-rajul (the male), *nisfu al-rajul* (half male, read the effeminate), and *al-rajul al-kāmil* (complete

---

[4]On the dialectics which attend the woman's body and image in the pre-independence period see: A. A. Oladosu: "Authority Versus Sexuality: Dialectics in Woman's Image in Modern Sudanese Narrative Discourse" *Hawwa* 2.1 (2004) p. 113-139.

[5]On the male in Sudanese culture see: R.M. Osman: "The "Gender" of Accounting with Reference to different Concepts of Masculinity and Feminism" *The Ahfad Journal: Women and Change* (ed) G. Badri Vol. 15 No. 1 1998 (Umdurmān) 25-47.

male). The complete male in Sudanese Arab-Islamic culture, for example, is not only the opposite of the female but is the quintessential "spermatic animal per excellence" (Foucault 112). It is with reference to him that the patriarchates have divided authorities in nature into two: the one in heaven and the other on earth; "to God belongs the powers in the heaven; to the ... (complete male) belongs the power on earth" (Wadi 271). At the inter-gender level the complete male is a warrior: the conqueror of the female. At the intra-gender level, men in Sudanese cultural hierarchy acquiesce, either by choice or compulsion, to his authority. Thus the gender problematic, in addition to that of race and nation, could, therefore, be seen as the *doxa* – the dominant issues in contemporary Sudanese life. They constitute, in a contrapuntal manner, "the ideas, the concepts and the experience" (Edward Said(b) 73) from which the Sudanese novel draws support. It is to its portrayal and the representation of its trajectories in Sudanese culture that 'Uways novel, *Dance*, is dedicated.

Narrated by the author, *Dance* tells the story of Stephen Michael Donato, the hero, J'afar, 'Umar, Nafīsah, Robert John Kolant and Tony. Even though the hero and Robert are from Southern Sudan, they are friends to J'afar, Umar, Abdul Gani, Nafīsah, all of whom are Arab-Sudanese. Both J'afar and Nafīsah are children of a medical doctor by name Muhammad Ahmad while Tony, the Southerner, is their house-servant. Apparently born after the attainment of independence by Sudan, all the characters, excepting Robert and Nafīsah – both of whom are students in the law of school – became friends when they met in the Sudanese Military College. Their parents wanted them to pursue such fields of human endeavour as medicine and law but they chose to go for military training probably to mirror the condition of the postcolonial Sudanese nation: a nation at war itself; a nation constantly on the brink of an implosion. Aside

180

from these characters there is Muhammad Ṣālih, the Arab-Sudanese elderly house-assistant to the hero, Stephen Michael Donato.

Dance has two beginnings: one in the South and the other in the North of Sudan. The first conduces to the metaphysical patrimonies and cosmogonic sensibilities of the hero, the second images post-independence Sudanese socio-political landscape; the first attend to the hero's Southern origin, identity and reminiscences, the second patronizes his trials and travails in northern Sudan; the first patronizes symbols and traditional cues in Southern Sudan, the second is *sui generis* in its portrayal of the rigid realities of modern Sudanese life in the North; the first mirrors how the hero, as a young village-boy, goes out into the bush very early in the morning only for him to "return as a grown-up child in his twenties" (8), the second is picaresque of how he departs Northern Sudan as a nationalist in search of his "nation." We shall delay the engagement with the symbolic in our reading of Uways' novel for the pragmatic, in line with the Arab axiom that every ending naturally returns to its beginning.

The pragmatic and the mimetic in *Dance* begin when the hero, Stephen Michael Donato, the Southerner, decides to go for a wedding feast organized by his friend in Umdurmān. Walking steadily as if on a mission, his hands in his pocket, he is seen by a group of young boys who had been playing on the street under the shining moonlight. His appearance immediately catches the attention of the boys. One of them exclaims, "Look at this black slave!!" (8). When a Southerner is seen in the northern parts of Sudan, his/her presence occasions an inner conflict in the xenophobic Northerner; the racialist alarm in the psyche of the latter automatically rings. His emotion is full of contempt and hatred for the black subject. The boys, three in all, thereafter walk up to the hero. One of them confronts him thus: "We are in need of a servant who will take care of our house!!". The second says: "Would you accept to work with us...The work is not difficult...cleaning of the house and utensils and laundry...we shall give you money that suits your service" (9). These statements are reminiscent of a perspective in the dialectic image of the black-African as constructed both by the Arab-African writers and their counterparts in sub-Sahara Africa[6] which essays the black subject as an entity whose essence inheres in slavery and servitude. The statements made by the boys also call attention to the possibility of the continued incidence of slavery in the post-independence Sudan; the possibility, in line with John Eibner, that the "Sudan is the only place (in the contemporary period) where chattel slavery is not just surviving but experiencing a great survival" (Eibner 6). Instead of responding to these inflammatory comments, the hero decides to keep his calm. But his silence and sturdy posture only infuriates the boys the more. The hero, therefore, calmly says: "I have a job already, can I go please?" But the boys appear unprepared to let him have things his way. One of them then says: "Bring your mother instead!" (10).

By saying "Bring your mother instead" the boys, who, in the words of Bakhtin, could be referred to as "centripetal forces" operating in the midst of Sudanese "heteroglosia" (272) want to infuriate the hero; they desire to transform the texture of the conflict from the verbal to the violent. This is because in typical African societies, mothers are sacred entities – they are revered as the source of life and living[7]. Thus in instances when mothers are ridiculed, it is expected that their children should rise up and defend their honour.

---

[6]On the figure of the black subject in African fiction see: A. A Oladosu: "*al-Sud*" in African Fiction: Rethinking Ayi Kwei Armah and Ihsan Abdul Quddus" in *Journal of Oriental and African Studies* Vol. 40 (2005) p. 211-230.

[7]On the sacred mother see: L. C. Birnbaum: *dark mother: African Origins and godmothers* (San Jose: Universe, 2002).

But rather than trying to redeem his mother's honour, the hero pleads with the boys once again to let him go saying: "I'm on my way to a wedding party, please let me go" (Uways 10). But the boys would not let him have things his way probably because the North-South interface thrives only when it becomes violent. Thus the hero seeks recourse to his professional training: he engages the three in physical combat. Violence occurs in the text as an effect, the cause being the refusal of the black subject to remain where he is put by the Other; the refusal of the Southerner to carry the can of guilt; the sturdy refusal of the black subject to profess and confess his inferiority. A police officer soon emerges unto the scene. He asks the boys what went wrong. In unison they chorus: "It is this hopeless Southerner...he is trying to rob us" (10). The policeman does not think twice before saying: "O! these Southerners would cause nothing but trouble...follow me to the station" (10). Here reference to the hero, neither as a black man nor a slave, but a Southerner means the word is the third variable in the polyglot; the third in the panoply of adjectives usually employed by the Northerners in reference to their compatriots from the South. The employment of the word "Southerner" enjoys plausibility not only because it is a racial concept but also because it affirms the political binary in Sudan: the North/South, Muslim/Christian and Arab/non-Arab divide. In the reckoning of the Northerner, the Southerner is "primarily a non-Northerner" (al-Effendi 372) the same way the Northerner is primarily a non-Southerner. This political game denies the possibility and in fact the reality that not all Southerners are Christians nor are all Northerners Muslims. It also refuses to instantiate the fact that not all Northerners are Arab (white) and that not all Southerners are black. When it becomes clear to the hero that he is being seen as the perpetrator, not the victim of racialism by the agent of government – the police, he reaches for the inner chest of his pocket and brings out his identity card. This achieves the desired result. The police officer discovers that the hero is an officer in the military and begins to plead out of fear and humiliation saying, "Sorry sir! You can go" (Uways 10). The hero eventually arrives J'afar's house. There he meets his friends and associates all of whom seek to know the reason for his late arrival to the party. The hero's response is brisk and terse: "a small problem on the way" (11).

A couple of days thereafter the hero pays Robert a visit on campus. He enters a canteen, requests for a hot cup of tea and awaits the arrival of Robert who joins him. A short while thereafter, the hero catches sight of Nafīsah, the younger sister of his friend, J'afar, who is also engaged in a conversation with her colleague by name Rashid. A short while after the exchange of pleasantries between the two, the hero goes back to his friend, Robert. He has hardly taken his leave when he hears Rashid whisper to Nafīsah: "Who could this slave be?" Nafīsah replies: "He is one of the friends of J'afar!!" Rashid then says coldly: "Is it that your brother can't find the free born he could pick as friend?" (21)

Although Rashid says this silently he fails to reckon with the possibility that in the conflictual terrain which Sudan has become, in the racialist spaces of Khartūm and Umdurmān and one in which the black subject is, in the words of Frantz Fanon, "over-determined from without…dissected under the white eyes" (*Wretched* 116), the hero's "antennae" would "pick up the catch phrases"(116) of racialism as soon as they are let loose by the racialist. In other words, apart from the guilt complex, conflict ensues in and outside the text in Sudan for "psycho-affective" (40) factor – a factor which operates in the temporal spaces occupied by the racialist and the racialized subject in the country. In other words, the affectivity of the racialist and racialized subjects in Sudan is constantly on "edge like a running sore flinching from a caustic agent" (50). The hero would not let such derision and demeaning comments from Rashid pass without seeking redress. He goes back to the spot where Nafīsah and her friend are sitting but only finds Nafīsah who is completely engrossed in a book. He then goes on to confront her thus: "I regret the fact that you are reading law!" ('Uways 23). Nafīsah opens her eyes wide in utter confusion and humiliation especially when she realizes that the statement is directed to no other person other than herself. The two characters, thereafter, engage each other in a confrontation:

> "Nafīsah! Have you learnt in law that human beings are in categories based on their colour and skin? What kind of law would that be?
> Nafīsah looks the hero straight in the face and retorts saying:
> "Listen Sergeant Michael, you have your world and we have ours!
> "I'm not a slave to anybody, Nafīsah! I was created black by God, but he has not left in me any seed of stupidity and insignificance…my ears caught the conversation between you and your friend a while ago and I felt blood rush to my veins. I nearly returned to slap his ugly face…" (23)

Days after the confrontation between the two, Nafīsah's mind remains fixed on the encounter. In the night she stays awake. Images of the hero and their hot exchange occupy her heart. She is particularly disturbed by the challenges the hero posed to her and his interrogation of her identity and world-view. Being an Arab-Sudanese and daughter of the rich she shares the anti-South/black sentiments of the North. She sees the black-Sudanese as an evil. She says to herself: "…nothing is worse than these (black) people!!" (25). She begins to contemplate the ideals that the hero stands for: "Stephen desires to change the order of nature! Never! Perhaps he thinks…he could (in reality) be counted as one of us…" (27). Here "the order of nature" references the privilege which the 'white' enjoys in ruling and running over the 'black'. By saying "…he thinks…he could be counted as one of us…" Nafīsah also invites reminiscences of Frantz Fanon's sharp analyses of life in the colony: "…what divides this world is first and foremost what species, what race one belongs to" (xx). Thus post-independence Sudan becomes a replica of the British-Sudan. In the former the Sudanese authorities become postmodern colonialists; the black subjects become postmodern colonized subjects. But the encounter between the hero and Nafīsah dramatically functions in establishing a relationship between the two. Both characters eventually move from conflictual /adversarial postures to that of consensus and mutual respect; from mutual respect to affection. Nafīsah begins to adore the hero's masculinity, intellectuality and uncanny perspectives to life; the latter, in return, starts to appreciate her preparedness to rediscover herself; her preparedness to discover the solemn and profound knowledge of the world wherever it may be found. Thus gender-racial conflict, in *Dance*, is conceived.

In Aristotle's thesis conflicts sometimes ensue in human societies based on, among others, disproportionate growth of one part of a city in comparison to the other, the adversarial interface between the poor and the rich and the contest between justice and injustice (Bickford 398-421)[8]. Tony, the house servant, the hero and other Southern Sudanese would probably have remained in Southern Sudan had it been the case that basic necessities of life have been more equitably distributed by the authorities. Thus when the Southerner comes to the north, s/he does that not as a tourist but in search of living; in search of, in Aristotelian parlance, 'profit'. Once s/he arrives the North, the latter ceases to belong only to the

---

[8]For a study of Aristotle's theory on conflict see: S. Bickford: "Beyond Friendship: Aristotle on Conflict, Deliberation and Attention" *Journal of Politics* Vol. 28 No. 2. (1996) 398-421.

Northerners. Rather the North becomes, de facto, a no-man's land.

Thus the hero derives confidence in protecting the young Tony. In doing that, however, he achieves two things in the text: the establishment of black consciousness in the face of white affirmation, not the creation, of an uncanny solidarity between the working class as a counterpoise for the oppression of the ruling class. The solidarity that exists among the working class, the oppressed and the poor in Sudan is instantaneous; it precedes the oppression of the oppressors; it is innate and immanent, not acquired and contingent like that among the rich. By saying "You aren't god by virtue of your being white", the hero is affirming the truth of black consciousness which gains strength in the same way that "the truth of the ruling-class consciousness", in line with Fredric Jameson's thesis, "is to be found in working-class consciousness" (290). Yet the statement "You aren't god by virtue of being white" still raises a number of questions. What makes an Arab-Sudanese "white" in relation to the Black-Sudanese but "black" in relation to the British? Is reference to the Arab-Sudanese as "white" either by the Arab- or the black-Sudanese valid? Is the "white" subject truly white like snow or common salt? These questions are pertinent not only for their relevance to any discourse which concerns itself with the categories of race and nation, but also for our attempt to make sense of postcolonial intra-African relations. Thus by saying "you aren't god by virtue of being white", the hero appears to be desirous of separating colour from status; he seeks to deconstruct the age-long notion which equates blackness with evil and whiteness with goodness and virtue. The hero seeks to establish the humanity of all Sudanese in order to dismantle the "modern day colonialism" (Uways 28) in his country; in order to place the Sudanese on a socio-political and social spectrum where equality and justice would be the touchstone of intra-social and inter-communal relations.

But the hero would soon discover the reality and the elasticity of racialism in Sudan. He is accused of being responsible for Nafīsah's refusal to marry Rida, the choice of her family. He is visited by his friend J'afar who asks him: "Sergeant Michael, tell me what's between you and Nafīsah." The hero contemplates his friend and says: "Nafīsah is my friend and sister O! J'afar. I have great feelings of respect and honor for her...I haven't entered your house with the intention to dishonor it"(59). But J'afar has ceased being a friend to the hero. He retorts: "Dog...you dishonorable negro, if you go near her, I would shatter your head with bullets, listen ...She is going to marry Rida in a weeks time...do you hear me? (59). By calling the hero a dog, J'afar employs what is known in Arabic rhetoric as *Kināya*. *Kināya* is a rhetorical trope which, according to the medieval Arab critic, Abdul Qāhir al-Jurjāni, references "a meaning which you comprehend not by way of the word(s) used, but by way of the meaning expressed" (*Dalāil al-'Ijāz* 330). Thus the description of the hero as a dog is with a purpose: J'afar desires to attribute to him the notions of bestiality and inhumanity that are ordinarily inherent in a dog. Dogs, in Arab-Islamic culture, are not fit as human companions; at best they are employed in games and hunting. His reference to the hero as a 'dog" also travels the familiar track in modern Sudanese narrative discourse in which the black subject is given series of names and adjectives all of which portray him as depraved and an irrational being. Thus when reference is made to the black subjects such as *Kilāb al-Mas'ūrah* (Mad Dogs), *Adawāt mawt al-Sawdāh* (Black Instruments of Death), *Thīran Āijah* (Violent Bulls) and *Dhamāu li al-Dimā* (Blood Thirsty)[9] we are awakened to racial politics in the text; we are reminded of the politics and poetics of colour in Sudanese culture; we feel impelled to engage the problematic of race as it

---

[9]On this trend in Modern Sudanese narrative discourse. See: 'Ajūba. Mukhtar: *al-Qissah al-Qasīrah fī al-Sūdān* (Khartūm: Dār al-Tālif wa Tarjamah, 1972)

appertained to Sudan in earnest. Thus we begin our return journey to the beginning in *Dance*.

Racial Conflict

In reading specifically for "race" we begin with the symbolic: the role of blood in the construction of the epistemology of race in Sudan. The hero remembers having asked his father once: "My father do you hate the Arabs?" But the old man refrains from offering an immediate answer to the hero's question. Rather he picks up a broken bottle and makes an incision on his arm. Then the following dialogue ensues between the two:

> "What's this Stephen?"
> "Blood"
> "What's its colour?"
> "Red"
> Then the old man says as follows: "Every child of Adam is created by God with a red blood, this is the origin, then he created for them different colours." (20)

Here blood becomes a signifier: the signified being the primordial equal status of the human race. Here, again, colour becomes secondary and arbitrary: its employment as a standard in measuring human quality and in bestowing honour and privileges becomes arcane, invalid and an infringement on divine wisdom. In Southern parts of Sudan, the human blood is held to be sacred. To share the same blood group is to share the same racial identity; to share the same cultural traits; to carry the same genetic codes from which proceed evil and good. There in Southern Sudan, the Arab-Sudanese are seen to be as bad as the blood that runs in their veins. Thus the ordinary Southerner has the notion that the possibility of a union between the North and the South of the country is as remote as the union of the heaven and earth. Deng quotes one of them as follows: "The Northerner is a person you cannot say will one day mix with the Southerner to the point where the blood of the Southerner and the blood of the Northerner will become one" (191- 227). But *Dance* imagines this very possibility.

When the hero is accidentally shot in a military parade in the barrack and consequently hospitalized, he is told he would need blood transfusion for him to survive. Muhammad Ṣālih, his Arab servant could not, because of his old age, be of help. The latter, therefore, goes from the east to the west of Umdurmān in search of blood donors all to no avail. Nobody is willing to come forward and save the life of the hero who is already in a state of coma. Eventually Nafīsah steps forward. She offers to provide the blood that would save the hero in return probably for the latter's effort in assisting her in her "search for self-validation" (*Black* 213). When the hero regains his consciousness, the first person he sees by his side is Nafīsah. She gets hold of his hand, places it in her palm and with a voice laden with love and compassion says: "I nearly died of fear over you!" The hero looks her straight in the face and exclaims thus: "Your blood is running in my veins!" (Uways 63).

Thus Nafīsah, the Arab-Sudanese and, the hero, from the South of Sudan, achieve that which is deemed ordinarily impossible by the Sudanese. Both characters overcome the cultural, not primordial, barriers between 'white' and 'black' in order to open new vistas in inter-racial space in Sudan. Both characters migrate from their 'whiteness' and 'blackness' in order to chart new directions for Sudan's fortune and destiny. The character of Muhammad Ṣālih further accentuates this perspective. Muhammad Ṣālih, the elderly servant to the hero is a Muslim and from the farthest parts of northern Sudan. He had previously served the Egyptian Pashas before coming to Sudan to work in the houses of the Sudanese notables. He even worked briefly for Nafīsah's family before he is asked to leave sequel to his old age. At the beginning, he refused to work for the hero. The latter once asked him "Why did you refuse to work for me initially?" Muhammad Ṣālih responds thus:

> "When my people ask me for whom are you working…I would say: a Southerner..!"
> They would then burst into laughter and say: he has become a slave to a slave. (13)

But Ṣālih, the figure of the North – the image of the oppressor and the postcolonial racialist tendencies in Sudan, eventually agrees to work as a servant to the hero, the Southerner – the figure of the racialized and oppressed subjects in Sudan. This reversal of roles appears to partake of the contrarieties and paradoxes in the Sudanese cultural landscape. Sudan is the place where "the moon appears in the afternoon and the sun rises in the night; it is the place where the heavens send showers of fish and the fish in the ocean develop wings with which they fly in the skies" ('Uways 29).

Perhaps more importantly, the characters of Muhammad Ṣālih, the hero and Nafīsah throw up the third category of race in Sudan for our contemplation: the Afrabians. The Afrabians, according to Ali Mazrui, represent that category in African culture which emphasizes the "interaction between Africanity and Arab identity and the possibility of a fusion between the two". (8). The Afrabians among the Sudanese, in line with Tayyeb Ṣālih, prefer to see things "with three eyes, talk with three tongues" (*Season* 151) and relate to things as neither 'white', 'black' nor negroid. The characters of Muhammad Ṣālih, the hero and Nafīsah, therefore, function in awakening the Sudanese imagination to the possibilities of the emergence of a consensus on the country's identities. They also serve in preventing our reading of race in Sudan from, in the manner of the postmodern, "being conclusive or teleological" (Hutcheon 8).

Conflict of Gender

What knowledge about gender does *Dance* furnish and how does it accentuate the conflictual spaces of the narration? How does the female see herself and the Other? The female in this novel is represented by Nafīsah and the prostitute. Both provide two conflicting perspectives of gender for our contemplation. Nafīsah sees herself as a traditional woman who, even though she belongs to the upper class of the Sudanese society, believes her essence ontologically lies in her procreative ability. One night, before her relationship with the hero begins, she contemplates her own image and destiny. Nafīsah's notion of herself conforms to tradition: that women's place is in the home; not necessarily in the school nor in the offices[10]. The female in Nafīsah also considers herself incomplete in the absence of the male. This gives credence to Wadi's thesis to the effect that "everything is easy in the life of a woman except the man: he is the source of her conflicts and tribulations; he is the fountain of her happiness and sadness…" (Wadi 50)

But how do women see men in Sudan? The quintessential male, according to Nafīsah, is he with dreams and "means." The male of her choice is he with "good looks, lots of money and a beautiful car such that the hearts of the ladies should skip each time they see him"

---

[10]Recent studies on the image of and challenges confronting the Sudanese women include: T. U. al-Hajj: *Tatawur al-Mar-ah al-Sūdāniyyah wa Khusūsiyatiah* (Khartūm, 2007); M. M. al-Amīn: "Is-ām al-Mar-ah al-Sūdāniyah fī majālat al-Ilmī wal 'Amal" in *al-Mar'ah wa al-Ibdā' fī al-Sūdān* (Khatrum: Markaz al-Dirāsāt al-Sūdāniyah al-Dawliyah, 2001). In English see: *Women and Law in Sudan: Women's seclusion in Private and Public life* (Sudan, Women and Law Project, 1999).

(Uways 26). In other words, the male of her dream should be materially comfortable. He should be such whose presence, as we have it in early Sudanese short stories, should lead to conflicts among the ladies over who should be his lover. This is, however, not the only perspective to heterosexual politics in Sudanese culture that we read of in the novel. The prostitute in one of the brothels in Umdurmān provides another perspective.

> One night the hero pays a visit to the brothel. He meets the prostitute who welcomes him with excessive joy and happiness. She walks coquettishly in front him and, within a twinkle of an eye, begins to remove her night gown. As she does this she whispers lustfully thus:
> "O! I'm lucky tonight!! The female teacher, Safiyyah, used to say that Negroes are the most capable of all men on earth, I detest men who are soft!" (34)

This statement reminds us of men's identity as constructed by Bint Majdhub in Tayyeb Şālih's *Season of Migration to the North*. According to her, a man's worth lies not in his ability to provide material comforts for his woman but in his ability to satisfy her in bed. In the presence of her son-in-law, Bint Majdhub confronts her daughter thus:

> "O! Amīnah this man has not denied you of any of your rights...your house is beautiful, your cloth is beautiful. He has also stuffed your hands and neck with gold. But it appears from his face that he is incapable of satisfying you on bed. Should you desire real sexual satisfaction I can introduce a man to you, if he comes to you he would not leave you until your soul breaks." (al-Tayyib(b) 80)

Women who share this notion of men see themselves as men's sexual plaything; as objects in the hands of men; as "the impalpable gate that opens into the realm of orgies, of bacchanals, of delirious sexual sensations" (*Black* 177). They are also active bearers of the "look"; they look at men as sexual objects in the *leitmotif* of erotic spectacle. But the foregoing does not necessarily lead to conflict in *Dance*. Gender conflict ensues in the text when Nafïsah begins to assert her agency through her refusal to marry the man her family has picked as her husband. She is immediately confronted by J'afar, her brother. The latter is the figure of the traditional Sudanese Afro-Arabic culture which sees the woman as an estate that belongs to the male. When he hears about her refusal to marry Rida, the choice of her family, blood rushes to his face. He considers her a threat: a threat against his masculinity. He also considers her refusal an affront against the patriarchal authorities as represented by his father. He therefore insists her sister would marry nobody else except Rida. Thus Nafïsah finds herself in conflict with her family when she decides to migrate, in the manner of Hassanah bint Mahmud in *Season of Migration to the North*, from the locale of the "*female*" to that of the "*feminist*"; when she ceases being, in the words of Trinh Minha, the "made woman" (264) in order to become a woman in the making.

Nafïsah refuses the marital contract her family enters into with the family of Rida sequel to her discovery of the "new Nafïsah" (63); she rejects Rida after having discarded the old Nafïsah: the Nafïsah "who has a veil on her heart and a covering on her intellect" (63). Her refusal to accept Rida implies an elaboration of oppositional discourse by the female; her rejection of the society's tradition which defines her as a thing to be possessed, a spoil of war. Thus the marriage is dissolved as soon as it is solemnized.

Conflict of Nation

Still in the pursuit of the geographies of conflict in *Dance*, we come to the third in the categories we have identified, namely nation. What elements are constitutive of a nation? Using the theory of *nation* as evidence, Homi Bhabha proposes "the condition of belonging" (45) as fundamental to the emergence of the political entity known as a nation. But close to a century ago, the Arab congress, in 1913, made the following proposition:

> "In the view of political theorists, groups are entitled to the rights of a nation if they possess unity of language and of race according to the German school; unity of history and of tradition according to the Italian school; and unity of political aspiration according to the French. If we are to consider the case of the Arabs in the light of these three schools, we will find that they have unity of language, unity of history and of traditions, and unity of political aspirations. The right of the Arabs to nationhood, therefore, finds endorsement in all schools of political theory." (qtd. in Nuseibah 49)

What the Arab Congress probably failed to take into consideration is the problematic known as *al-Sūdān-* a state which simultaneously and paradoxically enjoys that which it lacks: unity of history and tradition, unity of race, and unity of political aspiration. *Al-Sūdān* is like a magical pot. It constantly boils with Africanity, Arabicity and Arabfricanity. None of these Sudanese identities fathoms what the word nation means to the Other. It is with reference to this problematic that the hero, the black-Sudanese, asks Nafīsah, the Arab-Sudanese, thus: "What's the idea of the nation with you?" ('Uways 22). Nafīsah looks the hero in the face without offering a response. She offers no response probably on the assumption that the hero is aware of the fact that as far as the ordinary Arab-Sudanese is concerned, the word "nation" means the Arab-Sudanese at war with the black-Sudanese. But in waging war against the black-Sudanese both the Arab- and black-Sudanese subjects are employed by the

195

'nation' in Sudan. This is represented by characters like 'Uthmān, a black-Sudanese and 'Umar and Mahmūd, the Arab-Sudanese. Despite the years he has put into the 'service' of his 'nation', 'Uthmān is arrested by the authorities on trumped charges of sedition and treason. He is accused of cooperating with insurgents in western parts of Sudan, probably Dar Fur, where new Sudanese subjectivities have emerged to redefine what it does mean to refer to Sudan as a nation and, perhaps more importantly, what it does mean to be a Sudanese. 'Uthmān is consequently "put in solitary confinement, then summarily executed" ('Uways 39). Upon his death, his children become orphans; his family is forced to return "to their village in Western Sudan" (39).

The circumstance of the Arab-Sudanese in the Sudanese army is equally not better. 'Umar, returns from the war front and goes straight to the hero's house. Suddenly, he bursts into hot tears; his body starts to shake as if under a spell. The hero, assisted by Muhammad Şālih, carries him into the inner room. After a while he stutters thus: "O! Stephen…scattered corpses…even flies wouldn't do what we did…my friend it was at the White Nile, we destroyed thousands without mercy…" (42).

The hero and Muhammad Şālih begin to mourn the unfortunate Sudanese who have suffered the fate 'Umar has just painted. But the latter is not done yet. As if he is purging himself of his sins, he goes on to paint more pathetic details of the operation. 'Umar thereafter proceeds to resign from the army. He could not do what Mahmūd did at the battle front. The latter goes mad upon seeing the extent of the bloodshed and savagery the soldiers perpetrated. When he eventually regains his senses, he turns his gun on his forehead and shoots himself dead (44).

'Umar's story reminds the hero of the night in which his father was killed, sequel to the invasion of his village by the government forces. The story also brings images of his lost friends and close relations all of whom have either died in the violent conflict between the North and the South or have been permanently displaced. A couple of days after this incident, he also tenders his resignation from the army. The hero disengages from the army probably out of fear of losing, like 'Umar, his humanity; he disengages from the army as a nationalist in search of the 'nation' (73).

Conclusion

What has been done thus far is to grapple with meaning in *Dance*. Meanings, according to al-Jurjāni, are of two types: intellectual (*aqlī*) and imaginative – takhayilī (*al-Balāgah* 241). Intellectual meanings are "realized by reason and it is true for all people in all generations..." while "Imaginative meanings are those which cannot be said to be either true or false, nor can what it asserts be taken to be true or what it negates be taken as truly negative" (241). Using this proposition as our guide, and having the contours on the Sudanese political and cultural landscape under our focus, it could be argued that the meaning we derive from *Dance* is true, intellectual and objective. If, however, the characters and the conflicts in the novel are seen to be poetic and imaginary, the meanings we discern from the novel would then straddle the shifting *topoi* of truthfulness and falsehood. Whatever perspective we choose, it is axiomatic from this study that the Sudanese novel is, in the words of Jean Paul-Sartre, "in the midst of action fully engaged in ...(its) epoch" (*Les Temps* 1954)[11]. Its vocation includes the deracination of the Sudanese subjectivities, the promotion of more gender friendly society, and the

---

[11]This is quoted by M. T. Amyuni: "The Arab Artist's Role in the Society: The Three Case Studies: Naguib Mahfouz, Tayeb Salih and Elias Khoury" *Arabic and Middle Eastern Studies* Vol. 2 No. 2, 1999. p. 203-222.

construction of a nation where consensus would be the touchstone of intra/inter-national/communal relations.

11

Bessora

J Westmoreland

> "La ca't de séjou', plus fort que la
> minute de silence dont on fit une
> symphonie, que l'Empire State
> Building filmé en continu pendant huit
> heures, que le pot doré de Beaubourg,
> et que les frigidaires superposés."
> (Bessora 29)

A NEW poetic and literary trend among Francophone African diasporic authors, specifically those writing from Paris, is the use of surrealist techniques in a "postcolonial" context. This practice dates back to Negritude's affiliations with such European surrealist writers as André Breton. Whereas traditionally in African diasporic context, Surrealism has been used to articulate a sense of solidarity or belonging (as in the formation of the Negritude and Black Power movements), Bessora employs surrealist imagery in the immigrant context to articulate a sense of unbelonging or anxiety-filled, hybrid state of the female immigrant in Paris.

In her semi-autobiographical novel *53cm,* the Swiss-Gabonese writer, Bessora, satirizes the exaggerated significance of the various "cartes" that will permit her protagonist, Zara, to become part of the French Nation through the acquisition of citizenship. In ironic tones, she fetishizes these seemingly unattainable objects, thus underscoring the absurdity of the immigrant situation as created by the French government.

The contradictions inherent in the immigrant position are clearly manifest in the continual adherence to a false hope: becoming a French citizen despite the impossibility of attaining the requisite "*cartes.*" By fetishizing the *cartes,* Bessora inflates their importance to the point at which they become absurd. In the case of Zara, it is not necessarily the *carte* itself that is ridiculous but the legal processes and rigorous physical rituals one must undergo in order to obtain the desired status of citizen.

In this quest, Zara is forced to negotiate not only complex bureaucratic obstacles, but also physical ones as she forms her body into the "condition" required by the nation. As Zara explains it, acceptance into the French nation is highly conditional, based on the correct "condition" of not only the body but of one's identity itself. Therefore, to become "French" not only the normalization of the body is required, but the normalization of one's identity as well. In this case, the hybrid or impure identity of the immigrant (the ultimate sign of alterity) must be transformed in order to gain access to the nation. According to Zara, the two cartes one must obtain in order to acquire the *carte d'identité* (the signifier of French citizenship) are the *carte de séjour* (resident visa) and the *carte de gym* (gym membership):

> J'ai conlcu un contrat avec le diable, grimé en troglodyte souriant
> à peau de girafe. Je tressaille. Mais…je dois continuer sur la voie de
> la cartographie. J'ai la ca't du Gymnasium; Il me faut subtiliser une
> ca't de séjou', et additionner ces deux ca't pour obtenir une ca't
> d'identité vichyste. (53)

Throughout the narrative, Bessora refers to these *cartes* in what surrealist thinkers would describe as a convulsive manner, constantly repeating and mutating their titles until the objects themselves are stripped of all rational qualities or "official" status. In doing so, she critiques the impossibility of fulfilling the expectation of the French nation. Framing her work in a surrealist understanding of the fetish and convulsive repetition, one can trace the representation of these *cartes* throughout the novel and examine their significance (or lack thereof) in terms of citizenship, belonging, and normalization of both body and identity. Bessora uses these surrealist techniques not only to counter the official French discourse and deflate the importance of the "*carte*," but also to open up the possibility of new narratives and associations coming out of the immigrant experience.

Before beginning an analysis of Bessora's discussion of the *cartes* in *53cm,* let us situate her corpus within a larger surrealist context. Certain texts, namely her short story "The Milka Cow," have been described as "fantastic." In the introduction to an anthology of short Francophone stories entitled *From Africa,* Adele King describes "The Milka Cow" as "(leaving) politics aside for a fantasy voyage." (King 16). The fantasy world she creates in this short text is accomplished using a surrealist mode, juxtaposing two systems of representation until they meld into one illogical, "hybrid" field of signifiers.[1] Though not all fantasy can be categorized as surrealist, the

[1] Bessora also does this in *53 cm* by inserting historically incongruous figures and at times changing their gender or crucial markers.

techniques used in this text to generate Bessora's fantastic setting in "The Milka Cow" are highly influenced by surrealist thought. However, it is important to note that Bessora does not outwardly claim to be part of a particular nouveau-surrealist movement. For this reason, one might not classify her texts as surrealist, rather as being informed by surrealist modes of expression. A reading of *53 cm* through a surrealist lens reveals certain nuances of the "*cartes*" or "ca't" that would not necessarily be exposed in another interpretation (be it realist or Other). In the context of *53cm*, Bessora's use of Surrealism is a mode of resistance against hegemonic culture or dominant modes of representation. Her work falls under the category of counter discourse defined here by Françoise Lionnet:

> Dominant systems are more likely to absorb and make like themselves numerically or culturally "weaker" elements. But even the "inferior" or subaltern elements contribute to the evolution and transformation of the hegemonic system by producing resistances and counter discourses. (9)

Zara resists absorption into the dominant culture by emphasizing and maintaining her hybrid position (and thus her alterity) throughout the novel. Her surrealist counter discourse proposed in *53cm* serves to expand the reader's understanding of the immigrant position regarding French citizenship. Different from Bessora's use of surrealist modes in "The Milka Cow," *53 cm* does engage with overtly political themes. Bessora is not alone in her practice of using Surrealism to elucidate certain socio-political paradoxes. Since the Césaires and the *Tropiques* journal,[2] Surrealism has been used to subvert dominant paradigms in the postcolonial francophone setting.

---

[2] See: Aimé Césaire, Suzanne Césaire et René Ménil. *Tropiques 1941-1945.* (Paris: Jean Michel Place, 1978).

As T. Denean Sharpley-Whiting notes:

> On an artistic level, Surrealism rejected aesthetics, moral
> concerns, and literary and artistic values as elitist, repressive, and
> requiring conformity. Such values and ideas clashed with the
> Surrealist credo of calling into question "reality" – which was seen
> as essentially rooted in exploitation and inequality – with the hope
> of creating a "superior reality," a sur-réalité…The mind was to be
> freed of rationalism, logic, reason, and Cartesian philosophy, the
> supposed cornerstones of Western bourgeois culture and ideology,
> which occasioned auto censorship and repression of basic drives.
> (84)

In the case of Bessora, this use of Surrealism is contrasted with
the exclusive and limiting role of the French State, a system that seeks
to impose a homogenized identity. Whereas the State accepts only
one sort of "pure" identity, Surrealism relies on the merging of
systems and hybrid constructions to achieve a "sur-réalité," or
alternative understanding of the situations at hand. The purity desired
by the French nation is made clear at the beginning of the *53cm* at the
moment Zara finds herself in "le règne gymnasial." She observes a
young Arab man on a treadmill in the process of purchasing a
purebred feline: " – Merde… j'ai brûlé que 42 calories. Quoi? Mais
non ma chérie! Le singapora est une race félinidée découverte par les
Américains dans les égouts de Singapour; un pur-sang de race
hyperpure, oui." (Besora 11). Here, the feline is only accorded value
after it is "discovered" by the Americans (another colonizing power)
in the sewers of Singapore. The "pure" creature is rescued and
brought to civilization through an act of economic interest. Her value
is analogous to that of the "pure" African female (not one of mixed
origin like Zara). The "real" African symbolizes (or at least did at one
time) cultural capital and exotic value in the Parisian center. Like the

African woman (rescued by the French from the depths of Africa), the Singapora is desired not only because she is exotic, but also because she is pure. This passage underscores the impossibility of entering into the Nation if one is métisse. Purity is clearly associated with bodily perfection in the context of the "gym," thus emphasizing the stringent requirements for citizenship.

Bessora's choice to counter the notion of purity using surrealist techniques is quite logical if one examines the basic tenants of surrealist thought. Michael Richardson emphasizes not only the hybrid nature, but also the cosmopolitan qualities of Surrealism:

> In Surrealism, the universal is conceived in a multiplicity of forms. Within this relation, specific cultural identities are constantly being formed as part of a complex mosaic that makes up any human being. For it should go without saying that all cultural traditions are hybrid, bringing together disparate elements to form an unstable whole, one that necessarily disintegrates under close analysis. (83)

French citizenship is a very exclusive category that demands purity from its members, even if this purity is falsely constructed out of a fictionalized French history.[3] It is a society based on reason and logic, one that is based on the concept of a monolithic universal identity, whereas Surrealism permits the universal to be constructed in a multiplicity of forms. In her article on *53cm,* Patricia-Pia Célérier

---

[3]Since the 17th century, France has constructed its history based on notions of racial and linguistic purity, excluding all histories of immigration. It is not until very recently (within the last decade) that France has begun to recognize its immigrant past. This "coming to terms" with an alternative history is exemplified in the establishment of a new history of immigration in Paris as well as a re-working of the museum of primitive arts exemplified in the establishment of a new museum of immigrant history in Paris, la Cité nationale de l'histoire de l'immigration <www.histoire-immigration.fr> and a new museum of "arts primitifs," the Musée du quai Branly <www.quaibranly.fr>.

uses a quote from Voltaire's *Candide* to emphasize the importance of Cartesian thought for the French and the ways in which Zara (as a hybrid identity) could never fit into the paradigmatic requirements of French citizenship:

> Le racisme est rationnel et cartésien, la Raison et la race dirigent le monde; ils sont le moteur de l'histoire universelle." (Candide). Les choses fonctionnent comme ci les réalités postcoloniales (immigration, économie globale, métissage, etc.) entraînaient une reconception de la notion de "race" et de ses applications, mais en fait les bases épistémologiques qui informent la conduite des affaires nationales sont restées similaires.   En quête de carte de séjour, Zara représente cet écart. (75)

The use of the term "quête" (not only by Célérier, but also by Bessora herself) when discussing Zara's relationship to the *carte de séjour* is indicative of surrealist practice. At various points throughout the text, Zara refers to herself as an "ethnologue." To support this claim, the very structure of the novel reads like an ethnographic document.[4] This stylistic mode is significant in that it subverts the European ethnographic gaze (on the Other), thereby making "official" French culture the object of analysis or exoticization. As Célérier indicates:

> Pourtant, chevillés sur une lecture critique de l'anthropologie, les romans de Bessora ont un aspect plus subversif car ils rendent exotiques les Français "de souche" et ainsi, éclairent et repoussent plus efficacement les processus "d'exotisation" des "gens de couleur." (75)

This practice of reverse exoticism is significant in the surrealist

---

[4]Here, one is referring to the use of the preposition "de" at the beginning of each chapter. i.e. "De l'altérité dans la règne gymnasale," *53 cm,* 11.

context. The surrealists critiqued exoticism (primarily in the colonial context)[5] as a practice that assumed and emphasized the inferiority of the colonies. However, the surrealists did fetishize certain "primitive" objects in their writing and artistic interpretations. This practice could be read either as a contradiction or as a distinguishing between exoticism and the practice of fetishization.

The fetish is, by definition, an element imbued with a certain level of importance (often spiritual in nature). It is usually foreign, meaning that in an ethnographic mode a culture's fetish is usually identified by an outsider looking in.[6] In Surrealism, the fetish typically appears in the context of the journey (often psychic or imaginary). One of the most recognized surrealist fetishes is the female body, made famous by the photographs of Man Ray. In *53cm* the "pure" or perfect female body is fetishized not because it holds some sort of final value, but because it leads to the acquisition of French citizenship. Lionnet comments on the importance of purity in the following passage: "Difference then becomes – on both sides of this binary system – the reason for exoticizing, 'Othering,' groups that do not share in this mythic cultural purity" (14). Zara is regarded as Other in the eyes of the French because she lacks purity of both body and identity. Adopting an ethnographic analytical position, she reverses the traditional gaze (center toward the periphery) by fetishizing elements of the dominant system (the *cartes*). As these excerpts exemplify, this ethnographic approach serves to further

---

[5]In opposition to the Exposition Coloniale in Paris (1931) the surrealists organized a counter Exposition Coloniale whose aim was to decenter common beliefs regarding colonial practice at the time. Drawing on the personal collections of his friends, Aragon brought together sculptures from Africa, Oceania, and the Americas, so that the people could see the artwork of these countries on their own terms, away from the atmosphere of imperialism that pervaded the "Musée des colonies" at Vincennes.

[6]See: James Clifford. "On Ethnographic Surrealism." *Comparative Studies in Society and History,* Vol. 23, No. 4 (1981): 539-564).

objectify this relationship between the *carte* and identity:

> L'accès à la Gaule, vous le savez, exige un long et pénible détour: l'escalade du mont préfectoral. Un temple de dresse sur son sommet, *centre des étudiants étrangers*. Mon premier dessein sera d'y pénétrer pour dérober un talisman appelé *ca't de séjou'*. (Bessora 29)

> En échange du *papier,* l'officiante donne le talisman, *ca't de séjou'*. Il protège de mille oiseaux volants, *charters*, qui boutent les explorateurs hors de la tribu, dans le plus grand secret. *Cat' de séjou'* protége aussi d'esprits vengeurs et innombrables, nommés *Police,* comme l'Eunuque aux cheveux longs. (33)

In both passages, the italicized *carte* is exoticized through lexical gestures to the foreign element. It is imbued with a sort of spiritual significance through references to the temple, the pilgrimage, and the talisman. In this case, Zara's fetishization of the *cartes* can be read through a satirical lens. She does not fetishize them to exemplify their importance. Rather, by employing this exaggerated discourse, she is satirizing their importance to the French nation. Not only is the *carte* "fetishized" by Zara, but in another obvious clin d'oeil to Surrealism, it is displayed as a found object art piece in the style of Marcel Duchamp.

> Avec la *cat' de séjou'* j'entends révolutionner l'art contemporain, inventer mon genre à moi, toute seule. Chère cat' de séjou, ton compte est bon: je saurai faire de toi une oeuvre d'art, car la valeur de l'art, c'est le dollar. L'expédition terminée, je tirerai un bon prix de ta vente à un musée d'art moderne. À moi Beaubourg, le Guggenheim, le MOMA de New York et le MIKO de Kyoto; si l'art ne veut de moi, un musée- cimitière te conservera, toi l'objet mort, tel un vieil appendice dans un bocal plein de formol. Ou alors, le Muséum d'histoire naturelle t'empaillera. Tu seras très bien, entre

les restes d'une girafe et le cadavre sans sépulture d'une vénus hottentote. (Bessora 29-30)

The placement of the *carte* in a museum as a found object further strips it of its official significance (as recognized by the French government). For the surrealists, the importance of the found object was not the object itself, but the conceptual dialogue that surrounded it. In the same way, Bessora devalues the actual *carte* in favor of the various social issues it allows one to address. By aligning the *carte* with the surrealist notion of found object, she is opening up the possibility for counter discourses, led by immigrant voices themselves, that challenge dominant notions associated with the *carte*, specifically the rhetoric of purity, full assimilation, and the impossibility of hybrid identities that has historically been imposed by the French government. In the second half of the passage, the *carte* is not placed in a space where it could even be accorded the status of "art." It is a forgotten relic in a museum of history. More importantly, it is misclassified, thrown next to another forgotten history, that of the Venus Hottentot. In addition to this excerpt, Bessora problematizes the practice of categorization throughout her discussion of the *cartes*. One of the most basic tools of classification is the label, or the Saussurian signifier. In the case of the *cartes*, Bessora changes the signifier all together (from "*carte*" to "*ca't*"), thus allowing for a completely different set of signifieds or associations.

Throughout the novel, Zara plays with the official language associated with the "*carte*," referring to it as "*ca't*." She repeats this term frequently throughout the text and constantly refers back to the *carte* to demarcate the passage of time. Whether Bessora is consciously referencing (or employing) the surrealist practice of convulsive repetition is not clear. However, reading these passages from this perspective further reinforces the complexity of her relationship to the *cartes* and what they represent to the hybrid or "impure" identity. The surrealists used the term convulsive when referring to aesthetics, often associated with the term beauty. This concept appears in writing for the first time in Breton's *L'amour fou*:

> Le mot "convulsive", que j'ai employé pour qualifier la beauté qui seule, selon moi, doive être servie, perdrait à mes yeux tout sens s'il était conçu dans le mouvement et non à l'expiration exacte de ce mouvement même. Il ne peut, selon moi, y avoir beauté- beauté convulsive- qu'au prix de l'affirmation du rapport réciproque qui lie l'objet considéré dans son mouvement et dans son repos. (32)

This particular passage applies well to the immigrant situation. Here, the "objet" could be read as the *carte* or as the immigrant herself. In the context of the immigrant, "mouvement" and "repos" could be read in terms of advancement. In order to advance, the immigrant must acquire the appropriate *cartes*. However, to eventually arrive at a place of "repos" (having finally acquired the *carte d'identité*), Zara must continually move[7] to form herself into the identity accepted by the nation, even if the impossibility of ever reaching at this resting point is evident. Ironically, the absence of the *cartes* needed for this transformation (here, one may think specifically of the *carte de gym*) forces her into a state of stagnation (a forced "repos") at various points throughout the novel.

As if attempting to combat this stagnation, Zara repeats certain terms and themes. This constant activity (or psychological movement) could be examined under the rubric of convulsive beauty. The surrealists, namely Breton and Aragon, used a strategy of convulsive beauty to "hystericize" aesthetic, social, and ideological norms by calling all such assumptions into question. According to

---

[7] Here, movement is present in two forms. The first is by moving (in the gym) to shape her body into the pure state expected by the nation. The second is the continual movement to and from the official government offices in search of the *cartes*. This is connected to the notion of quest or journey in the surrealist context.

their definition, hysteria is precisely that which escapes definition. For the surrealists, hysteria was not uniquely a pathological phenomenon. Rather, it was in every respect a supreme means of expression. Zara's hysteric repetition of the word "ca't" and the (convulsive) frequency at which she mentions the term call into question the "normalcy" of not only the *carte*, but the systems though which one must pass to obtain it. The concept of convulsive repetition also applies to Bessora's recurrent obsession with the body (and normalization of it) throughout the novel. Though she refuses to conform to the bodily ideal, either of "Frenchness" or of the "Other" (the stéatopyge), she constantly makes references to her own body to the point of obsession ["Mes fesses ne poussent pas."] (Bessora 60).

The repetition of the word "*carte*" and the various word associations to follow ("ca't," etc.)[8] call into question the rational significance of the *carte*. Adding yet another layer, Bessora creates a new terminology for the *cartes* that "creolizes" the official titles. The use of Créole is significant for two reasons. Though Zara is of Swiss-Gabonese origin, it is assumed twice in the novel that she is from the Antilles. The underlying notion here is that all immigrants are the same (that is to say, impure) until their identity is normalized by the state. It also calls into question dominant assumptions about race, skin color, and origin. By creolizing these titles, Zara not only satirizes the official status of the *carte*, but illustrates how the "official" *carte* is paradoxically slippery, elastic, and hybrid, lending itself to multiple readings and meanings depending on the context and the reader.

In the following passage, Zara references the "ca't de c'éolité", a fictional construct: "Tu parles français, mais l'interprète du tribunal traduit quand même: tu as oublié de fournir ta fausse ca't de c'éolité

---

[8] Her word plays with "ca't," " cat' " and " act'" could be discussed in terms of the surrealist practice of automatic writing.

'moi y en a pa'lé beaucoup bon f'ançais mon commandant'" (Bessora 68). According to the State, no foreigner could have sufficient mastery of the French language, thus a translator must be present. Again, Créole is chosen as the default immigrant tongue since, with its multiple influences, it is antithesis of a "pure" language.

Zara's status as "étudiante" and "mère" serves to further negate her purity in the eyes of the Nation. When she visits the immigration office to attempt to acquire papers for her daughter, she is systematically denied. The reason for this is not that her daughter is unfit to enter the Nation, but that workers find it unfathomable that Zara could be both a student and a mother:

> L'OMI n'a rien demandé à votre enfant, parce que les étudiants étrangers n'ont pas d'enfants. Ils viennent en France pour faire des études et rentrer chez eux, pas pour faire des enfants et rester en France. Nous n'avons donc plus besoin du certificat OMI: vous êtes étudiante étrangère, célibataire et sans enfants. (68)

Thus, Zara is ultimately hybrid (in race, role, and identity). Her race is mixed (Swiss and Gabonese), and she occupies a specific hybrid social position for which the French have no "*carte*" (that of "étudiante-mère"). In her refusal to deny her hybridity not just culturally (suisse-gabonaise), but socially (étudiante-mère) she reveals the impossibility of both obtaining the *carte* and retaining one's own identity. Her particular identity is based on an image of transplantation rather than rootedness, as is discussed at her first visit to the OMI: "Vous vous nommez Zara S...Sem...Andock; vous êtes née le 25 décembre 1968 à Bruxelles, d'une mère Suisse nomade et d'un père fang gabonais? Mais qu'est-ce que vous faites en France?" (28). This last line underscores the impossibility of retaining such an identity if one wishes to become part of the Nation.

The *carte d'identité* imposes a pure, French identity and forces one into a state of fixedness. In the eyes of the State, you are French or you are nothing. The possibility of a hyphenated identity does not exist. This stasis implies control over one's identity, both physical and psychic. Each citizen of France (naturalized or "français de souche") must carry the *carte* on his or her person at all times. "Le contrôle" is the official term for the act of being stopped by government officials to verify possession of the *carte*. Thus, to a certain extent the French State is continually perceived as watching the activities of its inhabitants. This "contrôle" is one of the greatest sources of anxiety for the illegal immigrant, who does not possess the proper "identité." In this way, the "contrôle" serves as a Foucaultian panopticon.[9] Even if it never actually happens, the threat of the "contrôle" is always present.

Although Bessora uses surrealist modes to satirize the "ca't," her protagonist remains in a bind. The *carte* is still important to Zara not only for her own survival (or success), but also for that of the person who complicates her identity most profoundly, her daughter. Though she is able, through her surrealist interventions, to distance herself psychologically from the importance given to the *carte* (by the Nation), she is unable to escape her eventual dependence on it. For very real and tangible reasons, the *carte d'identité* is necessary in order to access the means to live (or thrive) in the Metropole.

Bessora's text is not the first to deal overtly with the issues of bureaucracy and the *carte d'identité* in the postcolonial context. Rather, it is a part of an extended thematic trend. Here, one is primarily referring to texts such as Ousmane Sembene's *Le Mandat* and Jean-Michel Adiaffi's *La carte d'identité*, both of which take place in Africa and feature African male protagonists who experience many of the same frustrations, injustices, and problematic dependence on official governmental documents as Bessora's Zara.[10]

---

[9] See: Michel Foucault, *Surveiller et punir* (Paris : Gallimard, 1975).

[10] See : Ousmane Sembene, *Le Mandat* (Paris : Présence africaine, 1966) and Jean-Michel Adiaffi, *La carte d'identité* (Paris: Haiter, 1980).

By resituating the dialogue surrounding the *carte* in a feminine narrative, Bessora engages with the power struggles and feelings of physical or cultural inadequacies from the perspective of the diasporic woman. Relying on humour, satire, and discussions of naming, Sembene and Adiaffi's novels ask the reader to consider what identity is for the postcolonial African. While each of these elements are found in *53cm*, Bessora shifts the discussion to a new geographical and gendered space, preparing a complex web of power dynamics and bureaucratic tensions that are never fully resolved. Reading Bessora's *53 cm* in concert with such realist representations of the *carte* situates this text in a geneology of postcolonial narratives that underscore the anxieties surrounding the acquisition of French identity and acceptance signified by the *"cartes"* whether real, imagined, or ideological.

12

I Marques

Couto

TWO stories from Mia Couto's collection *Contos do Nascer da Terra (Stories of the Birth of the Land)*[1] published in 1997 "The Little Girl Without Words: Second Story For Rita" and "The Little Moonbird: First Story For Rita," demonstrate how the Mozambican contemporary writer recreates the traditional African holistic (choric/animistic) 'self' via the use of innovative language and narrative techniques – a self that has been overshadowed by both the colonial and postcolonial orders. Some similarities that exist between African traditional worldviews (epistemologies) and other worldviews such as Western psychoanalysis and Buddhism, could point to the idea that *we* might all have more in common than we think. We all seem to yearn for the connection with our choric/holistic self, even if often we do not know how to regain that connection due to the general fragmentation and spiritual alienation that tends to pervade our rationally ordered modern societies.

---

[1] All translations pertaining to this collection and other Couto's writings/titles are those of the writer.

Couto's stories are generally characterized by a great emphasis on the traditional pre-colonial African ways of life and epistemologies: myth, orature, different cosmogonies, conceptions of time, the inter-relation between the world of the living and the world of the dead, as well as animistic and holistic perceptions of life, where humans, nature and the universe at large are connected in deep ways and often not perceived as separate entities. The characters of the stories are often people who live in rural areas, which in fact constitute the vast majority of Mozambique's citizens, or people who do not adhere completely to and show resistance towards the assimilation of Western cultural values brought about by both the colonization and post-colonization processes. This suggests that Couto is interested in displaying the rural side of Mozambique, the side less touched by Western cultural values, less touched by the colonization and post-colonization processes: the endogenic/internal (or *choric/coric*) side of Mozambican cultures. As David Rothwell notes,

> Couto has always demonstrated an awareness of Portuguese and, more generally, Western influence on his work. Rather than recusing such influence, he understands and then distorts it. He disrupts the paradigms of Western orthodoxy as he fashions identity by turning European epistemology into a raw, repackageable material. (28)

Rothwell further avers that

> Couto's propensity to dissolve boundaries is apparent, particularly those frontiers that enforce the demarcations of Western tradition. The resultant identity he writes is premised on fluidity, and challenges the rigidity of the systems, both colonial and Marxist, imported from Europe that have dominated Mozambique for most of its history. In the latter phase of his

writing, his disavowal of the postmodern project, through an attack on the International Community's invasion of Mozambican sovereignty, logically completes the postmodern and the nationalist strands in his work. He can justifiably be termed a postmodern nationalist.[2] (28)

Most of the characters in Couto's writings[3] seem to be living in the colonial or postcolonial present since there are many implicit or explicit references to those historical timeframes. Yet we often sense a strong resistance to those historical realities on the part of the characters. That resistance is frequently accompanied by a sense of loss, a feeling of nostalgia or a confusion (an existential nausea of sorts), which suggest that the characters live in a time of deep cultural crisis, in a society that is robbing them of what they value most and what their ancestors have believed for thousands of years. This feeling might be similar to what the anthropologist W. E. H. Stanner calls "a kind of vertigo in living" (qtd. in Chamberlin, *If This* 80) felt by the Aborigines of New Guinea, as a result of land displacement and cultural impositions brought about by the colonization process. Couto places the following message in his introduction to *Stories of the Birth of the Land*:

It is not the light of the sun that we lack. For millions of years the big star has been illuminating the earth and despite that we have not

---

[2] Rothwell further argues that Couto's project of endogeniation is particularly clear in his recent novel *O Último Voo do Flamingo* ('The Last Flight of the Flamingo'). See *A Postmodern Nationalist*, specifically section 7: "Finding the Nation's Phallus: Expelling the UN Specter from Mozambique" 158-169 and "Conclusion" 170-2.

[3] See for example, *A varanda do frangipani* ('Under the Frangipani') *Cada homen é uma raça* ('Every Man is a Race'), *Estórias abensonhadas* ('Blissfully Dreamed Stories') and *Terra sonâmbula* ('Sleepy Land').

really learned how to see. The world needs to be seen under another light: the moonlight, that clarity that falls with respect and tenderness. Only the moonlight reveals the feminine side of beings. Only the moon reveals the intimacy of our terrestrial dwelling-place. It is not the rising of the sun that we need. We lack the birth of the land. (7)

This statement is illustrative of the overall nature of the stories included in the collection and of the didactic (and thus political nature) of Couto's stories: it suggests that Mozambique needs to rebuild its identity by looking at (and rediscovering) the land and its old ways. It further suggests that Mozambican identity must come from within that land and not from the outside, or at least not merely from the outside. What Mozambique needs is not necessarily (or certainly not only) the knowledge and the development traditionally associated with the modern world and the West, which has tended to value reason, technology, objectivity, compartmentalization, intellect and masculinity over unconscious, emotion, nature, imagination, femininity and an epistemology of holism.[4] Couto is asserting Mozambique's need to reawaken its non-masculine, non-rational, non-conscious, sacralized, mystical and mythical side so that the old Mozambican epistemologies can be rescued and reinvented and a truer Mozambique can then emerge – a more 'authentic' nation where all Mozambicans will be able to see, place, cherish and express themselves, and where the old epistemologies are taken into account.

"The Little Girl Without Words" is about a little girl who cannot speak, or better yet, cannot make herself understood. The girl's

---

[4]Couto's introductory quotation seems to associate the sun with the masculine, the rational, the compartmentalized and violent forces, and the moon with the feminine, the earth, the tender and the holistic.

inability to communicate causes great pains for her father and mother as well as the rest of her community:

> The little girl did not speak any words. No vowel would come out of her; her lips were occupied only with sounds that did not add up to three or four. It was a language that belonged only to her, a personal and intransmissible dialect? (87)

In an attempt to make the little girl speak, and in order to communicate and connect with her, the father tries all kinds of methods: he holds her hands tightly, speaks to her tenderly and patiently, implores her to speak, cries out of frustration, takes her to the beach, and finally decides to tell her what seems to be a very unrealistic story. In the end, the story proves to be the very medium that allows for the beginning of communication between father and daughter. This story occupies a place of great importance in Couto's collection and, perhaps, even in Couto's overall writings, including the novels, poetry and short stories. The story, which is a series of *mise-en-abîmes*, a story within a story, within a story, within a story... can also be seen as the *mise-en-abîme* par excellence (the big Russian doll, as it were), for it brings to the forefront many of the cultural identity problems affecting contemporary Mozambique, and it even offers a solution for them. One of the main characteristics of stories which employ the *mise-en-abîme* as a medium, is that they aim at teaching the reader something. In the case of Couto's story, the teaching is in fact multidimensional – and the existence of the *mise-en-abîme* can be detected at many levels: structural, semantic, morphological and symbolical. All these levels work together to give the story an even more unified and coherent character, which in itself is yet another *mise-en-abîme* and serves to further reinforce Couto's cultural agenda: the illustration (display) of the metaphysical holistic conception of the world, as shared by traditional Mozambicans.

Couto's use of language and storytelling techniques shows us how language and narration assume the character of tricksters and how such a quality serves different and very important purposes; it brings wonder to storytelling, it creates suspense, and it keeps our soul alive by connecting us with that which is beyond our reach, that which is beyond language: the uncanny. But the uncanny always remains uncanny: just like Couto's language which by mixing words and inventing new terms, is constantly playing tricks and evading our understanding.

Couto's language becomes similar to "dread talk" as used by the Rastafarians in Jamaica. In the same way that "dread talk" symbolized the forging of a new identity (or better, yet, an identity for the very first time) and the refusal or contesting of the colonial cultural legacy for the Caribbean people, so does Couto's language function as the agent that permits the reinvention or building of a new Mozambican identity – an agent that takes history in its own hands, so to speak, by appropriating the language of the colonizer and changing it to accommodate present cultural Mozambican needs, to affirm its own and unique way of life. Moreover, like "dread talk," Couto's language seems to be an attempt to restore the wonder of language, its power to connect us with the mystical forces, the unknown, the spiritual, giving us a strength that helps us bear the difficulties of life. As J. Edward Chamberlin puts it,

> One of the strategies of the Rastafari has been to rename things. It's an old trick, as colonizers have realized for centuries. I have seen maps of Canada where as many as a dozen different names are layered onto one place, reflecting the different traditions of people who live (or lived) there…. The Rastafarian renaming, too, has involved turning language around so that it reflects their own imaginings and recovers their realities […]. The signature of "dreadlocks" of Rastafari are a way of catching the mysterious

power, or of not losing it [...]. (187-8)[5]

Couto's constant use of the *mise-en-abîme*, in all its different manifestations, ends up creating a special effect. When reading the story/stories, one might have the impression that one is entering a circling or whirling dance, a cascade of sorts, a musical realm even, a place where we might feel detached from ourselves and experience the universe with all its powerful energy – as if we were in a state of trance or spiritual ecstasy. Thus Couto's writing teaches at least two things: that traditional (old) epistemologies have something wonderful to offer, and also that, when used well and 'strangely', language can become the very medium that allows one to experience the beauty and power of what lies beyond our grasp and to reach spiritual fulfillment.

"The Little Girl Without Words" has a subtitle: "Second Story for Rita." Such title occupies a central importance in the story, for it suggests that the 'true' meaning of the story is not what it might at first appear to be. Put differently, the 'true' meaning is not, or at least not only, the first meaning, but rather the second meaning, or even the third or the fourth meaning. The true meaning is to be found in the metaphoric, the poetic, the unobvious, the hidden, or in the untold/unwritten even. Not only does the second (sub) title tell us literally that the story has a "second" story imbedded in itself, but it also appears within brackets, as if reinforcing once again (visually in the text) the idea of the importance of going behind what we see and literally read throughout the story: the idea of looking beyond the material/real possibility, and ultimately, beyond language and its meaning. Thus the subtitle of the story is the very first *mise-en-abîme*

---

[5]For further discussions of the concepts of "dead talk" and "overstanding" see also Velma Pollard's book *Dread Talk: The Language of Rastafarians* and J. Edward Chamberlin's *Come Back to Me My Language*.

of the many others that are displayed throughout the rest of story: it is the first Russian doll, enveloping the many other little ones that are to come out after our careful reading of the Great Mother. This Great Mother functions as the protective womb enveloping all the children inside her: like a goddess who wants us to know/feel the immensity of what exists, and at the same time, does not fully (or rationally) show us *that very immensity* because *that* very knowing/showing would kill the transcendental aspect of the divine, which is untranslatable and unnamable.

But surprises (tricks) never end and so… a more careful (deeper) reading of the (first) title will tell us that in reality it already contains the "second story" of the story, for the title does not say that the little girl is mute, but rather that she possesses no words – which is not the same thing. In fact, being able to speak without words might be a better way of speaking, if we take into account the idea that words are only an arbitrary (and thus incomplete) system, invented by humans to name and comprehend that which is ultimately un-nameable and incomprehensible to us in its true dimension. This reading of the first title makes sense, for in the story we do discover that the little girl speaks through music-like sounds and thus, possesses a language. In that case then, the first title is already a big Russian doll (or the Great Mother) with many little dolls (or children) inside, ready to be played with and also play "the player." Couto has stated the following:

> The secret, in my case, is to transport the childhood. […]. We all have preserved in ourselves that childhood, which people have taught us how to tame, how to forget, how to look at as an unproductive place. Children do not fit well into our present concept of what it means to be productive, responsible. [Yet] that childhood has survived in all of us. (*Jeremias* 2)

As the opening paragraph of "The Little Girl Without Words"

indicates, the little girl does indeed possess a language, but one that no one understands. Why does no one understand it? Little girls (and little boys) often have a language of their own, one that is highly poetic, musical, fluid and which does not obey the rules of adult language. In a fashion similar to Julia Kristeva and others, Couto seems to believe that children speak a pre-symbolic language, a language which is detached from social connotations and where gender roles and other assigned social roles and classifications of the world, things and people in general, do not yet exist or are not yet formed. Children are close to what Kristeva[6], following Plato (67) calls the *chora*, that sacred or sacralized (and whole, in the sense of being un-fragmented, un-dichotomized) side which allows them to listen to all their unconscious/subjective intelligence – imagination, instinct, emotion, body, and so on. That *chora* is broken (or at least suppressed and disrupted) when children enter the symbolic world of the adults which imposes roles, regulations and classification on the world and people based on the so-called higher intelligence – reason, science, objectivity, culture, and so forth. This is why the adults do not quite understand children and the world they live in, and also the reason why one can suggest that the father of this little girl does not understand her. In this story, the father has entered the rational adult world and thus broken (or suppressed) his contact with the world of the little girl (the world of his 'little boy,' so to speak) – a world which obeys different linguistic and cognitive patterns. But his *chora* still exists inside of him: it is preserved/kept somewhere, as Couto suggests above, and it only needs to be brought to the surface. In psychoanalytical terms, this loosely means that the *chora* of the 'little boy'/father has been pushed to the very back of his unconscious; it has

---

[6]See "Freud and Love: Treatment and its Discontents" 240-248 in *The Kristeva Reader* and *Pouvoirs de l'horreur* 9-24.

been repressed because adult life and society do not value/favour it, and consider it immature and inferior to the so-called higher intelligences associated with adult life.

The father loves his little girl (and his 'little boy') dearly and so he wants to 'find' them, to understand them, to reconnect with them. He suffers immensely from the fact that he cannot speak to and reach them. The father knows (senses, feels) that the language spoken by them is beautiful: "so beautiful as to enchant," so beautiful as to "imprison [him] in the intonation," and so "touching" (87) that it has the power to make one cry. It is a language that sounds more like a song, a song of yearning for something beautiful and powerful and good – something that one has lost and wants back madly– but does not really know how to bring/call back to us. The song-language sung by the little girl, awakens in the father a powerful urge, an almost visceral need; it is like a demand, seemingly as strong as the one expressed in Derek Walcott's poem "Sainte Lucie": "come back to me, my language, come back cacao, grigri, solitaire, ciseau the scissor-bird" (309). "Fala comigo filha!" (87) ('Speak to me daughter!'), says the father to the girl. It is the magnitude of the father's urge that makes him search for ways to communicate with his daughter (just like Walcott makes use of all kinds of words [i.e., French, English, Spanish, Creole] in an attempt to create a language that will 'tell him' as accurately as any language can allow):

> Her father would dedicate a lot of attention and affliction to her. One night he held her hands tightly and implored, certain that he was speaking to himself:
>
> - *Speak to me daughter!*
>
> His eyes gave in. The little girl kissed the tear. She tasted that salty water and said:
>
> - *Sea…*
>
> The father was surprised from mouth to hear. Had she spoken?

> He jumped and shook his daughter's elbows. *See, you can speak,*
> *she speaks, she speaks!* He would scream so that people could hear
> him. *She said sea, she said sea,* the father would repeat throughout
> the house. The relatives came running and leaned over her. But no
> other intelligible sound was announced.... (87-8)

The communication between father and daughter is hard to achieve. Yet, the need for that communication to happen is so great that it forces the father to keep searching deeper and deeper inside himself, to see if he can find the magic word that will 'speak' to his daughter. Finally, he does come to a brilliant idea: to tell his daughter a story. This idea works. The idea of the story comes to the father because it had in fact never left him; it was in some part of his unconscious self and just needed to be called back to 'conscious' life: it was there, underneath, like a latent, soft lullaby,[7] just waiting and wanting to be brought to the surface, so that the father could feel the wonder again – the wonder of feeling whole, connected, unbroken, the wonder of entering the choric realm:

> It was then that it came to him: his daughter could only be saved by
> a story! And right there he invented one [...]. When he arrived at
> that point the father lost voice and became quiet. The story had lost
> its string and thread inside his head. Or perhaps it was the cold from
> the water which was already covering his feet, and the legs of his
> daughter? And in a desperate state, he said: - *Now, it will never be.*
> Right away, the little girl got up and walked through the waves.
> The father followed her, scared. He saw his daughter pointing at the
> sea. [...] -*Daughter please, come back. Slow down, daughter,*

---

[7] The reason why the song-language of the little girl is able to reach the subconscious of the father: music (like poetry) functions as the pre-symbolic language or way of communicating, which has the power to liberate us from societal (conscious) constraints and allows us to go deeper inwards.

please... Rather than stepping back, the little girl penetrated further into the sea. Then, she stopped and passed her hand through the water. The liquid scar closed itself, instantaneously. And the sea restored itself, it became one. The little girl walked back, took her father's hand and guided him back home. Above, the moon recomposed itself. - *See father? I finished your story.* And both of them, illuminated, vanished from the room, which they had never left. (88-9)

The story told to the little girl is a story where doubt is suspended: it is a story that makes (and gives sense) to the world, without concerning itself with truth boundaries. It is a story (seemingly) very unrealistic which merges the real and the imaginary, reason and unreason, possible and impossible; it is a story full of trickery, as if we were in fact dealing with a real trickster who is constantly tricking us into believing things that are unreal or seemingly opposite.[8] The bridge between such opposites can, of course, be questioned, if we argue that the stories or histories or theories that explain the world and ourselves to ourselves are in fact all human makings – made out of an arbitrary language system – and so we end up with all kinds of 'fabulous' stories about who we are, what we must do, feel, eat, dress and how it is that the world or universe 'really' functions. As well argued by Edward Chamberlin in *If This Is Your Land, Where Are Your Stories? Finding Common Ground,* many (if not all) of the stories (and thus histories) informing and giving sense to our lives, are make-up/made-up fables, which serve to ease our existential nausea, hide our ignorance, fragility and fears of the unknown – and yet, also fables that make us feel at home and give sense and purpose to our lives.

------

[8] As Lewis Hyde puts it, "The trickster is a boundary-crosser," the one who blurs distinctions and connections between "right and wrong, sacred and profane, clean and dirty, male and female, young and old, living and dead (7)."

Couto's first lesson then seems to be that we must all try to reconnect with the world of our childhood, the world of wonder, the world of the *chora* – it is a lesson for all the adults of the world. But the story aims at much more than that. The story can (and should) be read directly in the socio-cultural context of Mozambique. The use of the little girl and father metaphor in this story can be taken as another trick used by Couto to point to the multiple meanings of his stories. Before further exploring the relationship of this story with the Mozambican socio-cultural environment, a look at the other story included in the collection, "The Little Moon-bird: First Story for Rita," is necessary. This story precedes "The Little Girl Without Words." This means of course that "The Little Girl without Words" can be taken as a continuation of the first story – a reasoning reinforced by the fact that it has the subtitle of "Second Story for Rita." This does not invalidate the previous argument pertaining to the subtitle of the second story and its function as the first *mise-en-abîme* of the second story. It actually reinforces it by suggesting that each single story in Couto's collection always contains multiple messages or stories in it, and that what each story says is always incomplete: its meaning always surpasses what it openly says, what the eye can directly catch. Moreover, the first story ends with the question "And then what happens father?" – indicating that the story has not been completed, at least not according to the little girl who was receiving it from the father. In fact, in the first story the father is frustrated with the little girl, for every night she demands a story from him and when he tells her one, she never seems satisfied with its ending and always asks the same (stubborn) question: "And then father what happens?" At the structural level, the first story also contains two stories: the one about the girl and the one about the bird.

After telling the little girl several stories, and not being able to satisfy her constant thirst for knowledge or wonder, the father decides to tell her the story of a bird whose dream was to fly to the moon:

> My daughter has a painful time falling asleep. No one knows the fears that sleep brings to her. Every night I am called to my duty as a father and I invent her a lullaby. I always perform that duty poorly. When I am trying to end the story she asks me for more: - *And then what happens?* What Rita wants is for the entire world to fall asleep. And she always argues a dream that might happen in her sleep: she wants to become the moon. The little girl wants to travel to the moon, and, she tells the two of us, so that I become the land, and she the moon. The Mozambican traditions are still inflating her lunar courtship. [...]. Once upon a time a little bird was dreaming in its little roost. It would look at the moonlight and it would make fantasies go up in the sky. Its dream would become more immense: - *I will land there, in the moon...* (67)

The story about the bird is of course also a story about the little girl and her constant craving for stories of wonder: like the bird, the little girl seems to have dreams, needs and wishes that are far too big for her human capacity. The father's story seems to suggest that only people (and to a certain extent animals) have life: the other bodies, such as the moon are petrified, lifeless entities. It is the "moony" ('enluarado') (67) character of the bird (and little girl) that makes it lose its quality as a bird and become petrified and lifeless. The adjective "enluarado," used to describe the bird here has a second meaning; it is yet another Russian doll, for it implies that the bird suffered from mad ideas, reason why it wanted to fly to the moon.[9]

Thus, the first story has many messages (*mise-en-abîmes*). At

-----

[9] In Portuguese, when someone is angry or acts/reacts in an unpredictable way, we often say that the person "está de lua" (literally meaning 'is with moon') or "está enluarado" ('is moony') or "está com a lua" ('is with the moon'). All of these expressions imply that that the person is mad and has lost the ability to reason properly (he/she is a lunatic).

first glance, it would seem to re-enforce the idea that when one has a dream, a need or a wish, one should try to fulfill it, and if one can not realistically fulfill it, one must resort to the power of the imagination in order to get it, for the imagination can have the power to fulfill our most grand desires. If it happens in the realm of the imagination, it becomes as real and fulfilling as if it were to happen in actual reality. As the Caribbean poet Derek Walcott would say: "I [have] no nation now but the imagination" (350). However, a more careful reading of Couto's story will tell us that too much dreaming and unreasonable desires will lead us to madness and the loss of humanness. An analysis of the morphology of the first title of the story, will also show us that the story has at least two meanings (two more little Russian dolls ready to play), again reinforcing the idea that stories and words possess secondary hidden meanings – meanings which we must aim at understanding so that we can have access to the wonder of the infinite, the mystical, the wonder of "overstanding," as the Rastafarians might put it. First, "The little moon-bird" ('A luavezinha') can be read as "moon-neighbour" ('luavizinha'), a reading that will point to the cosmic holistic conception of the universe shared by many Mozambican groups: it implies that all the planets are deeply connected and close to each other, that the earth is in fact near the moon, like a sister of sorts. By extension, this also implies that birds and humans are part of the greater order and that is why they feel the urge to go beyond their human and animal limits and connect with the rest of the universe. On the other hand, given the closeness between the words "luavezinha" ('little moon-bird') and "levezinha" ('very light'), we can suggest that the story wants to point to the fact that the human mind (our spirit and imagination) is very light – so light in fact, that it can fly away, travel and enter other world orders, other realities, and thus experience the wonder of what lies beyond our physical reach. The story did not satisfy the little girl precisely because the imagination of the father was not light (flexible) enough to travel beyond the moon and liberate the bird, not light enough to be able to allow the bird to be both bird and moon, that is.

It is precisely because of the 'heaviness' of the father's imagination that the little girl remains unsatisfied with the story and demands more with the question "and then father?" Ultimately, the little girl is the metaphor for the Mozambican land, its people and their holistic or sacralized conception of the universe. The little girl is the nation of Mozambique and the father represents the governing elite of colonial and post-colonial states. The constantly repeated question of the little girl "and then father?" has multiple meanings and functions. On one hand, it alludes to the dissatisfaction (and loss of wonder) experienced by Mozambicans who have had their culture and way of thinking dismissed and shattered by the new, modern, secularized and compartmentalized Western order. One the other hand, and because of its constant use, this question actually re-establishes that same Mozambican world order: the repetition causes us to feel that whirling effect that we mentioned previously – the effect of something that has no end, like a cascade where all parts are interrelated and work to produce a holistic and sacralized conception of life and the universe. Again, Couto is killing at least two birds with one stone (or two rabbits with a single stroke, as we say in Portuguese).

But the father feels the dissatisfaction of the little girl. It is precisely because of the dissatisfaction of both father and daughter that the father comes back with another story, a second story, which as it turns out, proves to be much more effective. The little girl's muteness is related to the fact that the new order governing the country does not value or really understand the old Mozambican epistemologies. In other words, it is not purely a matter of the semantics of the language – that is, the fact that the majority of Mozambicans speak Bantu languages and the small elite running the country speak Portuguese, which is the official language of Mozambique – although that of course plays an intrinsically role.[10] In the story, Couto *actually resolves the issue* of separation between the world of the father and that of the little girl, the world of the Mozambican colonial and/or post-colonial state and its citizens and thus the culturally and linguistically alienated situation of most Mozambicans. The Kristevan *choric self* now becomes symbol of the Mozambican land: its people and its traditions, a self that must be reawakened to feed/teach the new order – a *choric self* that had been relegated to the periphery of the state's interests in the name of modernization and civilization. The *choric self* then, becomes the universe at large, where all the elements are joined and where the human self becomes de-centered, only to experience what can be termed as the force of the universe, or God. This *choric self* is what in astronomy would correspond to the time before the big-bang and what is Buddhist Zen terms would equate to the "all in one" or the "Great I"[11], which is also the state that allows for nirvana (emptiness of thought) to occur, a state that 'resides' beyond language and thus is indescribable through it – a state of bliss and mystical apprehension.

---

[10]Couto is a language relativist like Ngũgĩ (see *Decolonizing the Mind*) or Whorf (see *Language, Thought, and Reality*) and others. Language relativists believe language molds the way humans see reality and themselves. Different languages emerge out of different socio-cultural, physical, ontological and epistemological environments and thus no language will 'say' the same thing. By creating new words, Couto is writing in a 'new' Portuguese –just like many other postcolonial writers who write in 'new' Englishes in order to try and recapture a more 'authentic' post-colonial subject, a subject that is more faithful to the pre-colonial ways of being an 'seeing'.

[11] See "Chief Characteristics of Satori" in *The Essentials of Zen Buddhism* 163-168 and *The Quest for Self* 119.

In its original platonic sense, the *chora* refers to that place that merges all the elements: air, water, earth, fire, a place of high power and energy that will give origin to everything – this is why Plato calls it the "nurse of all becoming and change" (67). In Christian terms, these would loosely equate to the "De Profundis" (Psalm 129). All these senses of the choric self are similar to each other, which only serves to show that different traditions (Western and otherwise) do in fact share many of the same underlying beliefs.

Thus, from the child's choric self, Couto moves us to the adult (repressed) choric self, to the Mozambican (repressed) choric self, and then he shows us (discloses) all the *choras* and the wonder that lies there awaiting to be embraced: he is the teacher, teaching us how to dance in the whirls of the greater or larger life. The language sung by the little girl made people cry because it reminded them of the Mozambican choric self, the self that they had forgotten how to connect with and buried deep inside them. Their cry symbolizes their loss and profound yearning and desire to reconnect with the grand order of the universe their ancestors once had. That is why the father goes to great extents to (re)learn the language of the little girl.

It is important to note that it is the emotion (and not the 'reason') of the father that first speaks to the little girl. He had tried all kinds of words and ways to achieve communication with his daughter and yet she had remained mute (and deaf). When the father cries out of desperation, she mumbles what seems to be her very first intelligible word: "sea." On a larger symbolical level, the tear shed by the father has many other meanings. Being a fluid substance, the tear can symbolize the letting go of the individual self and the entering in the choric/cosmic self. This is further supported by the fact that it is by the sea that the girl will finally find a way to speak and be understood by the father. The house (the father) represents the individualized human self, which tends to dichotomize and separate things, whereas the sea represents the decentered or choric self. The sea is the place that can 'liquidize' both the father and the girl so that they can finally enter the larger cosmic realm.[12] It is in the sea that we witness the disintegration of the entire world. It is in the sea that all becomes shattered and the order of the universe is lost but also re-established: it is there that we witness the 'all becoming one', or the 'one becoming all' and thus the holistic African conception of the universe is restored. The moon breaks down, the sea opens up and the earth bleeds. Blood becomes indistinguishable from water and the water indistinguishable from blood. Sand becomes silver and silver becomes sand. It is the end of the world. Or so the father thought. But then the little girl takes charge of the story and literally jumps inside it to help the father reconstruct the cosmic order, to literally give birth to the land.

As in the first story, the father's imagination has not been flexible enough to continue the story he is telling. His rational and compartmentalized self, not used to intricate exercises of the mind, becomes numb: it loses the story's "string" and "thread" (89). He is flexible enough to disrupt the order of the world, but not ingenious enough to re-establish it again. He becomes afraid of the unknown, of that which cannot be measured in rational terms: he becomes afraid of his unconscious, of the dark places of the world, of the universe at large which he cannot measure in human (and Western) quantities, for it escapes his smallness. The little girl is the one who saves both of them and the world from finally disappearing:

> Right away, the little girl got up and walked through the waves. The father followed her, scared. He saw his daughter pointing the

---

[12]In *A Postcolonial Nationalist* Rothwell also discusses the importance and constant presence of water in Couto's writings and its frequent association with the unconscious realm, the realm that allows one to have access to dream and imagination and thus 'encounter' all possibilities (see "Seaing into the Unconscious: The Role of Water in Mia Couto" 91-132).

233

sea. Then he could see a glimpse of it: in the entire extension of the ocean, a deep crack. The father was surprised with that unexpected fracture, fantastic mirror of the story he had just invented. A deep strange fear invaded his entrails. Would it be in that abyss that they would both disappear? - *Daughter please, come back. Delay yourself, daughter, please...* (89)

At the structural level, this story (like the first one) contains more than one story. It has at least three: the one being told to Rita about the little girl who did not speak, the one about Rita (or is it the little girl of the story being told?) literally taking over and finishing the father's story, and the one told in the last line, indicating that father and daughter had never left the room, even though we might have thought they did. Thus, this story (like the first one) further reinforces the idea that imagination is indeed very powerful, and that words give meaning and sense to that which is meaningless and disorganized: words weave the world, literally reinventing it for us, giving sense to the senseless, and ultimately having the power to make us feel safe at home. This serves to show the central importance of orally transmitted knowledge in traditional African cultures; it shows that the mere act of telling a story makes the events being told real; in other words, it demonstrates the magical power of storytelling and language. This magical power can also apply to written stories since language in general (written or oral) is capable of creating an entire world system, of giving meaning to that which has no *a priori* meaning. As Hampâté Bâ puts it,

> One peculiarity of the African memory is its restoring the recorded event *in its entirety*, like a film that unreels from beginning to end, and restoring it *in the present*. It is a matter not of remembering, but of *bringing up into the present* a past event in which everyone participates – the person who is reciting and his audience. The whole art of the storyteller lies in that. No one is a storyteller unless

he can report a thing as it happened 'live' in such a way that his hearers, like himself, become new living, active witnesses of it. (qtd. in *Unesco* 109)

It is precisely this "entirety," the restoring of the past event "in the present" and the "bringing up into the present a past event" pointed out by Bâ that Couto's story tries to reconstruct in the story of the little girl, thus showing his engagement in recreating the reality of African oral traditions. In this story the father does indeed re-learn the old ways; he gets in touch with his little girl, and consequently, with his nation. Let us hope that, like the father, the post-colonial state will also be open enough to allow non-Western epistemologies to be nurtured in Mozambique so that *all* can sing the song that truly speaks, the song of the little girl, who in reality might be the most mature of all. And she sings beautifully indeed.

13

GMT Emezue

Achebe, Ce

COMPLEMENTARY realism in African literature seeks to identify how notions of multi-dimensional existence mingle with cherished communal values to project alternate positive visions to violence, strife, and other realities of modern postcolonial African societies. The arguments of Asouzu, Ejizu and Sofola capture some of the paradigms of complementary or spiritual realism underscored in this investigation of modern storytelling and fictionalising in Africa as embedded in Chinua Achebe's *Anthills of the Savannah* and Chin Ce's *The Visitor*. The African universe, as Zulu Sofola rightly observes, is multi-dimensional, with all things endowed with the same Supreme Energy (4). Asouzu, on contemporary socio-historical experience of the black world, comments that "the fragmentation of (Africa's) historical existence is an essential part of our search for meaning and happiness in this world" (44). This belies the popular but increasingly nauseous argument of "Africa as mere victim of Western Imperialism" which many African philosophers, historians and critics have held. A more valid conceptualization of African reality from a complementarist paradigm is that which presents "a picture of a dynamic unity of interacting forces and beings" (Ejizu 60). It is a world where all life interacts – the unborn, the living, the dead, the ancestors, the past, the present, the good, the bad – in a seeming endless cycle of existence powered by choices.

Twenty-first century science has been able to create and simulate virtual realities that are identical, though smaller, to their original versions – a feat which has prompted new enquiries into the nature of reality. Now the question frequently recurs: What actually *is* reality? Or what factors now and before have shaped our perception of reality? The German scholar and researcher, Erich Von Daniken,[1] argues that extra-terrestrial and inter planetary visitations did occur in the past leaving a more than fleeting impact on ancestral belief and religious patterns. The theories of Immanuel Velikovsky,[2] while suggesting that we are all intricately and electrically connected,

---

[1] Erich Von Daniken's books which include *Chariots of the Gods?, Return to the Stars, Gold of the Gods, In Search of ancient Gods, Miracles of the Gods, According to the Evidence,* bear out his research efforts in proving interplanetary connections as possible sources of world civilisations and religions.

[2] Immanuel Velikovsky's ideas about the nature of the universe, published in his numerous books were vehemently fought by the academia of the 50's and 60's, probably because of the implications of his conclusions concerning the nature of the universe. In *World's in Collision* for instance, he writes "The solar system is actually built like an atom: only in keeping with the smallness of the atom, the jumping of electrons from one orbit to another, when hit by the energy of a photon, takes place many times a second, whereas in accord with the vastness of the solar system, a similar phenomenon occurs there once in hundreds or thousands of years. In the middle of the second millennium before the present era, the terrestrial globe experienced two displacements: and in the eight or seventh century before the present era, it experienced three or four more. In the period between, Mars and Venus and the moon also shifted." He concludes: "if the activity in an atom constitutes a rule for the macrocosm, then the events described in this book were not merely accidents of celestial traffic, but normal phenomena like birth and death. The discharges between the planets or the great photons emitted in these contacts,

question fundamental assumptions about the universe as we have been taught. This revaluation of man and nature finds a wider purport in current debates on ozone layer depletion and its connexion with planetary movements within the solar system.

It is possible that in near future modern man may successfully create or simulate an identical universe comparable in size and sophistication to earth. And the theory of multi dimensional realities will lead to further questions such as: Is it possible that we ourselves are simulated beings in a simulated reality? If we are actually simulated beings, and not the apex of creation in God's entire universe as religions have assumed over the centuries, who then were our ancestor-simulators? And how might this knowledge subsequently affect our entire moral and spiritual worldview? Is existence therefore a mere game, and are we mere 'pawns' in the hands of our 'gods'? What is the *reality* of concepts such as "choice," "free will," "good," "evil," etc? What if we know we shall be "born again" as the condemned robber in *Anthills of the Savannah* who confidently proclaims so before his execution, or as Mensa, in *The Visitor*, who becomes Deego in a subsequent lifetime? How would this knowledge affect our basic notions of existence and non-existence, of life and death? New Age thinker, Nick Bostrom, has articulated three powerful propositions[3] on human civilisation which, strange as they might sound, hint at similar African, Hindu, Buddhist and Lamaist

---

caused metamorphoses in inorganic and organic nature" (388) (*Worlds in Collision*. New York: Doubleday and Company, Inc, 1950).

[3]In his controversial essay "Are you Living in a Computer Simulation?" Bostrom argues that "at least one of the following propositions is true: (1) the human species is very likely to go extinct before reaching a "posthuman" stage; (2) any posthuman civilization is extremely unlikely to run a significant number of simulations of their evolutionary history (or variations thereof); (3) we are almost certainly living in a computer simulation." Then he goes on to state: "it follows that the belief that there is a significant chance that we will one day become posthumans who run ancestor-simulations is false, unless we are currently living in a

philosophical constructs from the East. These go to affirm that complementary-realist perspectives can positively reshape values and value systems in our societies as both Chinua Achebe and Chin Ce seem to present in their work. But before we delve into the selected novels, it will be worthwhile to explore a theoretical premise for "complementary realism."

Complementary Realism and the African novel

I. I. Asouzu in his book *Method and Principles of Complementary Reflection in and Beyond African Philosophy* avers that complementary thought involves the recognition and application of many positive traditional African concepts vis-à-vis trends in western globalization outlook and that practicing the principles of complementary reflection involves "the conscious awareness we bring to world immanent realities and our recognition of their fragmentation". It also includes "the fact that they merely serve as a missing link within the framework of higher values, helps us to recognize their worth" (393). Asouzu goes further to claim that "we can never regard world immanent values as merely disposable objects but values that have hidden meanings that we must find within a context of complementarity" (394).

A corollary of this concept in literature and literary investigations is evoked in a condition where actions and narratives are interpreted from their complementary structural arrangements. Thus our notion of complementary realism in African literature starts off with basic assumptions in African philosophy the focal point being that we have other realities existing simultaneously with our physical universe and that human activities are actually influenced by these realities. This knowledge has shaped some of Africa's value

---

simulation. A number of other consequences of this result are also discussed."

systems and thought and still wields some influence on the African psyche. Although the absorption of Western materialist thought has corrupted this dominant worldview, nevertheless there subsist efforts by some "conscious" African writers as Chinua Achebe and Chin Ce to recover the indigenous vision as a way of resuscitating a fragmented African universe. The Afrocentric writer and critic, Zulu Sofola, for instance, agrees that the African cosmic universe understands the interconnectedness of all creatures who all emanate from one creative force,

> because all things, including man, were endowed with the same Supreme Energy all creatures are essentially one and the same. And since all things emerged from the same supreme essence, it follows that the differences between creatures and variety of cosmic beings lie in qualitative alterations of the same supreme Energy that manifested in various forms of material existence. (4)

From such an understanding of oneness and sameness of being (including gods and humans) and of experience (objective and subjective), life is perceived as springing from the one creative force. Thus within African animism is embedded the ultimate monotheism of ancient Egyptian and Greek mystery teachings. Man is seen only as the apex of the created beings in the physical world alone. As Sofola further argues,

> he is not only capable of evolving a new universe in the form of a society, he is also able to objectify, engage on cosmic level of cognition and thought, and probe the Supreme Mind of the universe. It is also man, through the degree of the divine quality in him that is able to probe and articulate the Universal Moral Order which he, in turn, uses to order and govern himself and his society. And since the African world view, *ab initio*, is positive, he does not perceive himself in essence as a negative force. (5)

The conscious perception of the dynamics of an African universe dictates to a great extent man's relationship with his fellow beings, the environment and other creatures that make up his multi-dimensional universe. This "multiverse" is seen as operating on three levels, although Wole Soyinka draws attention to a fourth level of reality. The first level of reality "is the divine reality of the Supreme Essence from which all that is, emerged, but itself not created and therefore would not die nor undergo change". This supreme essence is followed by "the reality of the created cosmos with all its worlds held together to the Supreme Essence through its spiritual or divine quality, its Eternal mind or intellect, its Eternal Moral Order, and the material manifestations of its divinity". The third level of reality is "man in the universe of his society created from his divine quality ...... And as the apex of created beings, he serves as a link between the created universe and the Supreme Creator and in the African cosmic perception of life as a cyclical continuum" (12). And then the fourth reality which Soyinka draws from Yoruba mythology is "a chasm, an abyss, which exists between the Supreme Creator and the created universe where man seems to bridge that chasm and attune man and the created universe to the Supreme Creator" (12). We must therefore grow agitated when this harmonious relationship is disrupted. It also becomes our duty to ensure that harmony is restored as soon as possible. This restoration is usually achieved through intervening priests and/or creative artists. From this multi-dimensional perception, man orders his environment and infuses it with positive values like unity, brotherhood, fraternal relationships and spiritual contentment.

As rightly observed by Uzodimma Nwala, traditional Igbo philosophy has an ontology that "emphasized their belief in the spiritual nature of things and a type of cosmic harmony in which man and his actions are central, with supernatural powers and forces superintending" (8). Clearly then the whole of Africa's cosmological system is "spirit-regarding," in the sense that "not only is the world conceived as swarming with spirits but everything including man and things are conceived as basically spiritual. Yet everything was integrated in the whole economic activity of the people" (81).

In complementary realism lies the recognition of a multi-dimensional spiritual universe and its diverse levels of interactions. It lays emphasis on "complementary attitudinal" change which is a process through which "individuals and human societies at large, seek to reposition minds in a way that makes it possible for them to anchor always their interests on the dictates of the common good within a universal complementary harmonious framework " (Asouzu 252). It implies stepping "back from the imaginary thresholds that supposedly separate people from each other into supposedly clashing civilisations" and re-examining "the labels" (Said "Collective") and perceptions of our world. Thus a complementary-realist approach to fiction implies that while reading a work by Raja Rao, for instance, we attempt to understand some of the basic Indian thought and outlook that inform such a work. The assumption that every human being, even the atheist, believes in something, and that even the idea of non-existence of being is also a form of belief on its own, can yield a supremely beneficent method of investigation where literary actions, plots, characterization and other features are approached from their underlying moral and spiritual significance.

In many works by African writers, especially from Nigeria, the dominance of this worldview is apparent. From the elder Chinua Achebe, Wole Soyinka, Elechi Amadi, Cyprian Ekwensi and John Munonye through the younger Ben Okri, Sola Olumhense, Bandele-Thomas, Chin Ce and Akachi Ezeigbo to mention but a few, this burden of reinterpreting their reality from an indigenous basis has taken a truly metaphysical importance. This, as correctly observed by

Basil Davidson in *Black Man's Burden: Africa and the Curse of the Nation-State*, is the "apprehension of reality across the whole field of life" and one from which "emerged a science of social control" and of which it is "the task of religious leaders or priests...to safeguard community welfare and survival" (75). Incidentally, this sacred burden of restoring and maintaining societal equilibrium has fallen not on today's priests but squarely upon the literary artists.

Chinua Achebe is one African writer whose works have aimed so much to re-educate the colonised African mind and, in his own words, "show the people where the rain began to beat them" (*Morning* 45). His novels, *Things Fall Apart* and *Arrow of God,* chart the other levels of existence and reality as part of vital religious and sacred institutions of community and the reader's attention is consequently drawn to the powers and influences of these institutions on the environment and life of the people. In his last novel, *Anthills of the Savannah*, these influences of the spiritual domain come through in the subtle actions, thoughts and choices of the characters.

Chin Ce, a relatively younger writer, is obviously a disciple of Achebe[4] although perceived as "most individualistic in blazing a style of his own" (Grants "Background"). His work include two prose fictions, *Children of Koloko* and *Gamji College*. His latest novel, *The Visitor*, set in contemporary Nigeria like Achebe's *Anthills of the*

---

[4]The idea of Ce as a disciple of Achebe may be inferred from reading Ce's first work of fiction, *Children of Koloko*, where the young hero, Yoyo, is reading Achebe's *A Man of the People* on his birthday. This must signify Ce's admiration for Achebe's craft and vision, which grows apparent from further reading of his devastating critique of the Nigerian nation-state in the essay "Bards and Tyrants: Literature, Leadership and Citizenship issues of Modern Nigeria." There Ce is in wholesale agreement with his older compatriot in *The Trouble with Nigeria* where Achebe sums it all up as "simply and squarely a failure of leadership", i.e., failure of the captains of the Nigerian ship of state equally dismissed by Ce as "a confraternity of pirates."

Savannah, is resonant with African images that govern his vision and reflection upon issues that are poignant in contemporary Nigerian society. *Anthills of the Savannah* and *The Visitor* thus provide valid explorations of complementary realism in African writing thereby lending a new interpretation of African works from this point of view. Of course, this does not detract the universal quest for truth from the efforts of many other African writers. On the contrary, the whole novel concept of complementary realism will achieve a wider significance with further scientific validation of the verity of our multi-dimensional existence in a possibly simulated reality.

Anthills of the Savannah

Many of Achebe's fictional works have consistently reflected ideas based on multiple perceptions of reality. In *Things Fall Apart* and *Arrow of God*, this second realm of existence is governed by religious institutions and priestcraft represented by "Agbala," and "Ani" on one hand and "Ezeulu" and "Ulu" on the other. As Florence Stratton observes "The central divinity in Achebe's Umuofia is … a female deity, the Earth Goddess, Ani" (28). But other representatives of the spiritual essence also include Chielo, the Priestess of Agbala and the Egwugwu.

Anthills of the Savannah perceives the spiritual dimensions through an overriding philosophical platform of interaction between the spiritual and mundane worlds peopled by humans and deities. It is on this platform that the events and actions in the novel are played out by the three central characters in the novel – Chris, Ikem, and Beatrice. The diligent messengers of the Almighty God are representative gods like *Sun God, Idemili* and *Agwu*. All these beings have noticeable roles that they play mainly through their human representatives in the novel. From the beginning, the scourging sun, described as the "eye of the Almighty God", ravages the village of Abazon and forces the people out of their lethargy into some kind of decisive action. They decide to visit the Head of State and complain about the scourge. The act is grossly misinterpreted by the power-drunk leadership, especially when Ikem, a 'subversive' in the eyes of the powers that be, is later seen among the delegates. His subsequent arrest, torture and murder spark series of revolts that topple the government. By the end of the novel, through series of connected events, Ikem, Chris and the Head of State are all killed, leaving Beatrice and Elewa as survivors of the debacle.

The significance of the sun as a primal cause in this book is recognized by Ikem the poet and journalist, in his "Hymn to the sun" which he begins thus:

"Great Carrier of sacrifice to the Almighty; single eye of God! Why have you brought this on us? What hideous abomination forbidden and forbidden and forbidden again seven times have we committed or else condoned?" (31)

This address reveals the awareness of an interplay of the spiritual and mundane realities. But then the questions achieve an ironical turn coming at the end of the seeker's (Ikem) demise since, by then, the reader is aware of Ikem's dual role as man and 'possessed' artist through whose 'voice' *Agwu* had chosen to relay his narratives to mortal man. Perhaps, as mortal, Ikem is to blame for his insistence on his dedication to duty even when warned by Beatrice that his persistence could only cost him his life. But as the acolyte of *Agwu*, his fate has already been sealed by this divine 'possession' and his recognition of the sanctity of his role. From the narrative, Ikem appears to be born to play his role as the spirit-possessed artist that must speak, record and point the way for his people. Thus possessed, Ikem seems left with little choice on his fate. He is the hero who moves admirably and quite aware of all it would take to get the job done. But in the course of action, he throws the door open to all forces, seen and unseen. And being finite and limited as a human being, his erstwhile clarity of purpose and vision is blurred as he "staggers to his destruction and death, leaving behind him the nobility of soul that fought with sincerity of purpose" (15). It is the recognition of this noble soul who fights with sincerity of purpose that prompts the respect, homage and tribute paid Ikem by fellow nationals in the novel. Above all, it is in the recognition of a "conscious artist" (Achebe *Morning* 61), the soul and conscience of society, that Ikem's portraiture achieves his messianic status.

Of his mystical "calling" and his response to it, the story goes that Ikem "in a vague but insistent way, had always felt a yearning without very clear definition, to connect his essence with earth and earth's people" but the problem "for him had never been whether it should be done but how to do it with integrity" (141). This is also evident in his chosen profession as a journalist. His choice of a semi-literate girl for friendship also betrays this inner calling to get close to the downtrodden. Ikem's actions in the novel tend to substantiate his role as the artist who "occupies a vital place in the life of his community as a mediator between his people and their divine reality, and as a motivator for the well-being of his people" (Sofola 7). His artistic mediation comes across in his diverse compositions as both poet and journalist. In his "Hymn to the Sun" there is no attempt to moralise on why the sun is so intense: it is not for mortal man to question the acts of the gods. Instead, one learns from past lessons how people had survived an apparently conflicting universe and the options left for further exploration. As he notes: "No one could say why the Great Carrier of Sacrifice to the Almighty was doing this to the world, except that it had happened before, long, long ago in legend (33)".

Ikem, aware of his idealism, says, "Chris keeps lecturing me on the futility of my crusading editorials. They achieve nothing. They antagonize everybody. They are counter-productive" (38); "Chris said I was romantic; that I had no solid contact with the ordinary people of Kangan; that the ordinary people of Kangan (who) ... from all accounts they enjoyed the spectacle that so turned my stomach"(39). It is this major difference between his sturdy idealism and Chris' own practical nature that brings about conflict in the relationship of the two friends.

From the beginning of the novel, Chris perceives his role as a 'detached' observer in the drama of resistance which he helps to create. He says "why then do I go with it now... I don't know. Simple inertia, maybe. Or perhaps sheer curiosity: to see where it will all ... well, end" (2). This assumption leads him to adopt a "detached clinical interest" in all that goes on around him. He is a player in a 'game', but one who has an understanding and awareness (which others lack) that it is all a game, and so needs not be carried away in it. With this awareness comes a commitment to aid as best as he could without forfeiting his own comfort. From this perspective Chris imagines himself the chronicler of events in which he is a participant. In his own summation: "I couldn't be writing this if I didn't hang around to observe it all. And no one else would" (2). His impudence in assuming he could be the chronicler, in other words the story teller, without the recognition and assistance of *Agwu* is like the anecdote of "a foolish forester" who mistakes a mighty boa for a tree trunk and "settles upon it to take his snuff" (125). Since he is not possessed by *Agwu*, then the deity knocks away the story from his mouth. He cannot be the story-teller, no matter how he tries or pretends to be. He learns later through his interaction with the poor that life is for living and one must always give his best no matter the circumstance. The importance of recording or being a story teller achieves a higher dimension in *Anthills of the Savannah* as a result of this spirito-materialistic view of the world. It is significant that this awareness (of value-oriented literary practice) has come across to late twentieth century Europe through the insights of scholars like Wendell Berry[5], Stephen Greenblatt[6], Edward Said[7], and Cheryl Glofelty[8] amongst others.

In most events in the story, Chris' stance as a "conscious" being is clearly stated, yet he misses the greatest of lessons until seconds before his death when the truth hits him that "this world belongs to the people... not to any little caucus, no matter how talented" (232). He dies with a smile of knowingness and recognition that he, in spite of himself, has been led to do the right thing by struggling to protect an unknown defenceless girl from a drunken assailant. Such a selfless act for another underscores the meaning of human existence and tends to elevate a world steeped in segregation, greed, avarice and

---

[5] Wendell Berry observes that "to assume that the context of literature is 'the literary world' is I believe, simply wrong. That its real habitat is the household and the community that it can and does affect, even in practical ways, the life of a place may not be recognized by most theorists and critics for a while yet. But they will finally come to it, because finally they will have to. And when they do, they will renew the study of literature and restore it to importance". ("Writer and Region" *What Are People For?* San Francisco: North Point Press, 1990).

[6] Stephen Greenblatt's *Renaissance Self-Fashioning* championed the case for New Historicism which perceives art alongside symbiotic relationship that exists between literature, historical and social forces and factors.

[7] Edward Said's *Orientalism* and other writings have formed the major background for Post colonial discourse which interrogates power plays, politics, literary and socio-economic factors (for colonial discourse studies.

[8]Cheryll Glofelty, Lawrence Buell, Thomas Dean, Don Scheese, Michael Cohen, Scott Slovic (just to mention but a few) are among the loud voices that advocate Ecocriticism as Value-oriented critical practice that situates the relevance of literature to present world situations by its recognition of the intricate relationship between man and environment, nature and life.

many vices of human society. As the old man explains the importance and significance of everybody as members of a divine community:

> to some of us the owner of the world has apportioned the gift to tell their fellows that the time to get up has finally come. To others He gives the eagerness to rise when they hear the call; to rise with racing blood and put on their garbs of war and go to the boundary of their town to engage the invading enemy boldly in battle. And then there are those others whose part is to wait and when the struggle is ended to take over and recount its story. (123)

The implication of this message is perceived by Beatrice, the last remaining member of the little caucus. This awareness decides her later interaction with the likes of Elewa, Abdul, the student leader, Elewa's mother and other people she ordinarily would not welcome into her world. Achebe's ideal heroine, Beatrice, is depicted as an avatar of *Idemili* who "did not know (the) traditions and legends of her people because they played but little part in her upbringing" (105). Irrespective of this gap in upbringing, Beatrice lives up to her role as the goddess. Many a time she experiences dual consciousness. Ikem and Chris sometimes refer to her as a "goddess", while she calls herself the "goddess of the unknown god" (105). She possesses deep insights and makes prophetic utterances about the lives of Ikem and Chris. Thus while other major characters die by the end of the novel, the goddess remains to interpret Chris' dying message to her acolytes. In many instances in the novel, the author draws parallels between Beatrice's aloof bearing and comportment to that of Idemili who would not brook to be crossed by any mortal. Ifi Amadiume notes that Idemili is the central religious deity of the Igbo living in the Nnobi area of Eastern Nigeria where both she and Achebe were born. Associated with female industry, assertiveness, prosperity and other qualities, Idemili embodies the matriarchal principle, a principle which in its ideological opposition to the patriarchal principle embodies the cult of ancestral spirits (53).

Beatrice's relationship with the two men underscores the process of growth and maturation in the novel. At the end, it is an understanding Beatrice that takes care of Elewa, arranges the naming ceremony of her baby, gives the baby a highly philosophical boy name and coordinates affairs of the other friends around her. Of all the characters in the novel she understands at the end the importance of living a purposeful life, which is that life whose "voice", like that of the cock, "is the property of the neighbourhood" (122). The significance of her survival at the end of the novel becomes poignant when perceived from the viewpoint of her role as an avatar and the only one who recognizes the real meaning of human existence.

There is the African belief in reincarnation which is implied in several ways in the novel. Death loses its mystery and pain with the awareness that one will always incarnate again. The dying robber proclaims in a literal sense: "I shall be born again!"(42). Beatrice, during the naming ceremony of Ikem's daughter is heard "teasing" the dead Ikem once more, affirming his natural survival after death. Thus the characters strive to define their life and existence in complementary terms knowing the illusion of death as a final ending. While people like Chris learn from the experience of their own death, Beatrice learns from the death of Ikem and Chris such values that will maintain equilibrium in her life. Thus Achebe utilizes the artistic tool of characterization to comment on positive values inherent in his African universe. From this broad perspective, therefore, characters in Achebe's novel, though fully developed, are representative of African values. Characters such as Ikem, the old man of the village, Elewa and Beatrice draw from the power of an all-sustaining spirit; they understand that a selfless life devoted to care for others is more satisfying and rewarding than a selfish existence exemplified by the lives of early Chris, His Excellency the Head of state, and all the politicians and military toughies that lead the country to the doldrums. Achebe reminds us of the sanctity of life, but even more important is the life that is outward-driven, selfless and dedicated to serving life in recognition of its multidimensional realities.

The Visitor

While Achebe tries to show yardsticks for measuring successes and failures in human life through character delineation and events in *Anthills of the Savannah*, Ce fully embraces this onerous responsibility of taking us directly into realms of multidimensional existence and exposing the required qualities that place us in our respective circumstances or situations in life. Amanda Grants observes of *The Visitor* as "a story in which three dimensions of existence affecting three principal players Erie, Mensa and Deego interrelate continually to create an unbreakable thread "(24). The plot arrangement foregrounds the dimensions of existence by structurally depicting three different phases interrelating simultaneously through a principal character whose identity changes and interweaves with other characters as the story unfolds. The action of the novel therefore moves at a fast pace with sudden shifts in perspective and story line. From a chronological perspective, Deego falls asleep while watching a movie. Through a trancelike dream he goes to another level of reality (the world of the ancestors) where he (as Erie) tries to come to terms with his true identity. But he can never understand why he is there until he has met himself once again. This necessitates his taking a trip back to earth in another past period of existence as Mensa. Commenting on the plot technique of *The Visitor*, Okuyade Ogaga notes that "at first glance we immediately notice the fragmenting nature of narration" (141) which he explains as a feature of modernist fiction with its lack of emphasis on "logical arrangement, since the world it seeks to reflect lacks any logical or stable meaning" (141). From a complementary-realist approach, this cinematic plotting, which is significantly cyclical, artistically reflects the spontaneity and simultaneity of multiple existence which interweave symmetrically in spite of the seeming confusion. It reflects orderliness behind an apparently chaotic universe governed and controlled by a single intelligent force from which religions have drawn their monotheistic faith. At the end of the story, it is not surprising that a whole new meaning or insight into the several conflicts will be gained.

Events in *The Visitor* are set in three places (realms) – Erin, the spiritual city, Aja, the physical city and a future Deego-Sarah time frame. Ce adopts attitudinal and descriptive contrasts as a way of showing and displaying the distinction and differences between the realms. Aja is one dense, decrepit, morbid "murky ball of blue surf," with "coarse dirty dusts" which "stank with grime and dirt" (135). Erin on the other hand is the "city of his fathers" and a "motherland" with "broad clearly swept roads and walkways" (22). Unlike many science fiction narratives that thrive on the bizarre, the artistic attempt here to draw similarities from ordinariness is not lost on a keen reader. The reason probably is to create that level of association which comes with the familiar and may be justified by the knowledge that "since all things emerged from the same supreme essence, it follows that the differences between creatures and variety of cosmic beings lie in qualitative alterations of the same supreme Energy" (Sofola 4). Hence Ce projects a vision that seems to explain the non-existence of superficial differences on different realms of existence as if confiding that such differences lie only in our attitudes, values, and awareness of spiritual interlinks which inevitably shape our styles of living.

With an enunciation of the positive values of Erinland, a place where "the people of the dark skin like blended bronze had become the carrier of the values that sustained the greatest civilizations in time and space" (25), the author sets a series of considerable events in motion. These noble values, above all, are what make Erin a highly spiritual land. It is the "homeland" where "human productivity (is) in its noblest intentions" and "the sanctity of creation (is) preserved in the micro-consciousness of individual creativeness and mutual receiving", where both "creativity and receptivity" operate from a point of "common equilibrium" (24). A heightened awareness of their great responsibility towards life marks out the citizens of Erin, like Grandad and Uzi, from "visitors" such as Erie, Zeta and the Minister. Further, the enigmatic title *"The Visitor"* drawn from an African traditional song that "we are visitors upon the earth" (6), underscores the temporariness of existence on the physical. But curiously Erie is not "at home" in Erin, the ancestral land. The reason is not far fetched. While Erin offers comfort and home for Zeta who, as we realise, was Sena, Mensa's girlfriend in Aja city, such comfort is denied Erie as a result of his basic ignorance about the true mission/purpose of life. But as Deego in future replay of his life, he could live out a loving existence with Sarah and try to win back the dream he lost in the past. It supports the great symbolism of the earth as a market place where humans visit to do necessary shopping (gathering terrestrial experience) after which they must depart home. This idea is also ingrained in Achebe's *Anthills of the Savannah* through the authorial comment about "the divinity that controls remotely but diligently the transactions of the market place that is their (our) world" (102).

In *The Visitor*, the future, past and present are re-examined closely to show the intermingling of worlds. The central character suffers much pain in both physical and spiritual worlds. While his pains in the physical world are physical and emotional – pains from wounds and betrayed trusts, his spiritual pain arises as a result of amnesia, and non-recognition of his higher self. This non-recognition of his true self is indirectly linked to the violence of his past life. This selfish existence disrupts his spiritual equilibrium. Thus to make some smooth transition into his present world, he has to relive some aspects of this violence, perhaps, to learn the lesson of non-violence. The underlying idea of the story is that time is arranged symmetrically in order to align the human perception, through terrestrial incarnations, to the great need for a selfless and responsible existence. And a visitor who violates the ecosphere must undergo a process of rehabilitation in a suitable realm from where he must start another level of existence in the physical world. Ali Mazrui hints at a similar idea in *The Trial of Christopher Okigbo* but this vision is demeaned by his dogged argument for purity of art and separation of literature from politics – in a word, the 'art for art's sake' dictum.

Within the African universe such an act of desecration as murder, whether by mistake as that of the police officer in *Anthills of the Savannah* and Mensa's killing of Sena in *The Visitor*, or as a deliberate reprisal such as carried out by Mensa, Sena and Omo in *The Visitor*, is ultimately accounted for in the hallowed ground of true existence where Lord Tuma and his council of spiritual guardians preside. In *Things Fall Apart*, the crime of accidental killing by Okonkwo is physically pacified by his exile for a number of years. In *The Visitor*, Erie experiences periods of void, lack of knowledge of self – a 'spiritual' exile and pain consequent upon this lack of connection with the spiritual reality.

A significant part of Erie's healing programme requires his getting back into his former body as Mensa. The narrative achieves this effect with such fluidity that Erie, while being the observer, simultaneously becomes the observed. It becomes as Ejizu observes that "the world and reality as a whole appears to present a picture of a dynamic unity of interacting forces and beings"(60). Like *Anthills of the Savannah*, Chin Ce's novel explores the complementary reality of reincarnation by focussing on the inner and outer realities of three important characters who achieve their parallels in three different dimensions of existence. Erie, the spiritual self, has Deego and Mensa as extensions of his terrestrial existence, just as Sena and Sarah are those of eternal Zeta. In the simultaneous actions in the novel within three dimensions of existence all the characters appear not completely aware of their immortal, spiritual selves and, to an extent, believe that their terrestrial earthly existence in past and future are the ultimate consciousness of life.

Living in the city and earning a humdrum livelihood as tax collector in 2040 AD, Deego is presented here as a movie addict who loves films based, significantly, on violence. This is shown by his attraction to the movie entitled "The Gun" which becomes a symbol of past reality. While watching the action he sleeps off and finds himself transported into two dimensions of existence, one in the physical world city of Aja and the other in the ancestral Erin. In this future-present Deego is married to Sarah, rightly the love of his life, but he is able, via the movie, to connect to the spiritual essence of Sarah: Zeta. Sarah, unaware of this metamorphosis after Deego's dream exclaims: "Nonsense Deego, I am the girl of your dream" (203). Sarah has a mark on her cheek exactly similar to that of her spiritual double Zeta. Deego's role in the postscript of the novel is that of a being that might achieve a partial – never complete – self-recognition at the end. But as Erie, in Erin land, this complete self knowledge and self awareness is Everyman's destiny.

The complementarist paradigm suggests that we are more or less naive visitors to life's experience, like Mensa who has come with all the juvenile notions of survival. He believes in his cunning and might symbolised in the gun. But then a universal idiom goes that one who wields a weapon rather too fondly might end up the same way. Hence Mensa comes to a violent demise through the gun. The tragedy of Mensa's human experience in this life is a universal tragedy of all of humanity who live a 'wasted' existence in ignorance:

> ...he was more than one man in a part of a planet leaving a trail of treachery and violence in the tracks of time. ... He realized it was his blind, unthinking pawnage in an equally blind unthinking existence that had brought him here for serious reappraisal something he must never forget again. (181)

But dwelling on the importance of Erie's new awareness and understanding, Granddad teaches the complementary vision that all experiences are necessary and important in the long journey of awareness.

Analysing the story by the contrasts that abound in it, we find that within the three levels of experience in three different places (Lagos, Erin and Aja) only two (Lagos and Aja) are located on earth and share the same quality of restiveness, pollution and strain. In contrast, the spiritual city of Erin has all the aura of peace and beauty with its three suns that reflect a priceless golden hue. In terms of value, while many on the earth are depicted as vile, greedy and lustful, Erin is the home of enlightened beings like Adaku, Uzi and Granddad who labour for the sheer joy of helpfulness: the complementary vision of reality. This brings out the striking difference between the two cities. Furthermore, the people in Erin move effortlessly and can easily read one another's thoughts while the earthlings have a limited form of communication which is speech. Also, Erin has different shades of colour, while the earth dwellers have a single dominant dull colour and move with much haste and stress. Thus it is that *Anthills of the Savannah* and *The Visitor*, though written by different writers in different years, share an awareness of multi-dimensional realities and project positive values for Africa and the world. Both authors emphasize the temporality of physical existence as that which the planet earth offers all nature and life. This implies possibilities of other universes which Ce actually represents as Erin. Humans are constructed as visitors who must live in service of their fellows, becoming, as Achebe summarizes this fellowship, the "cock that crows for all."

In *Anthills* while the actions focus on three dominant characters, with only Beatrice, the one who gains awareness surviving, *The Visitor* revolves around many multi-personal characters, whose lifetimes at different settings, are deeply interwoven. The characters in Achebe's novel – Ikem and Beatrice – have but vague connections with their spiritual deity with Chris gaining a spiritual insight only on his last breath. In contrast Deego has no idea about his spiritual self until he experiences a past life as Mensa and, as Erie, discovers his true self. His spiritual rehabilitation in Erin ancestral homeland is supposed to help him live a more meaningful future-present life. As to the setting of both stories, Kangan and Aja are similar in their moral and intellectual degeneracy. They are post-colonial settings where the citizenry suffer from consequences of the moral and spiritual downgrading of their higher ethical selves. But Erin, the spiritual complement in *The Visitor*, is a land that is beautiful and holds the truest of ideal visions.

In *Anthills of the Savannah*, Achebe's presentation of the direct interplay of the spiritual denoted by the gods *Idemili* and Agwu with the physical is shown in his argument about the representatives or avatar of these gods: Ikem and Beatrice. Achebe acknowledges that these are 'poor' representatives just like the "ofo" carved sticks. However Ce plunges into the abode of the ancestors to reveal the positive attributes of complementary beingness. While it appears that Ikem and Beatrice do not have much choice over their fate and destinies because of the influence of the deities, in *The Visitor* Mensa is to live a brief span on earth by his own misdirected choice. The intervention of the gods in his life comes in between his dual existence, the hazy transition moments from terrestrial to spiritual consciousness.

Sociologically, Achebe's and Ce's novels pass serious commentaries on the modern nation-state where politics and leadership are negotiated from undue advantages in election rigging, corruption and abuse of authority. Incessant coup plots, greedy leaders and their hungry but docile people litter the landscape of both novels. However, as opined through Achebe's authorial comment, the problem is not necessarily politics but "a basic human failing" (139). Ultimately both works seem to conform to Shatto's opinion that mainstream African novels are "informed by a high-minded social awareness …which, in a serious manner, seek to increase and influence our awareness of the major issues of our time" (130). These issues have been shown here to transcend mundane preoccupations with material problems to a more serious awareness on the part of African writers of the breakdown of spiritual equilibrium in the fragmentation of the African universe through "basic human failings" acutely intensified by colonialism and westernisation.

To conclude, complementary realism reveals underlying value systems that govern the human community. It does this by a consistent recognition of the simultaneous existence and interlinks of our physical and other realities. While the complementary-realist writer accepts the superiority of finer levels of existence, he debunks the idea that we are mere pawns in the hands of some gods, hence life is infused with meaning on all levels of existence. Complementary realism argues that a life well lived, like that of Chris and Ikem in *Anthills of the Savannah*, keeps the people and community in preservation but a selfish existence such as His Excellency the

Kanganian president's, or Mensa's and Jaguda's in *The Visitor*,
fruitlessly throws everyone in spiritual doldrums. The constant
interplay between the spiritual and mundane is given great
prominence. As Achebe celebrates this interplay as incarnations (as
in Beatrice) or spiritual "possession" (as in Ikem), so does Ce attempt
comparative scenic expositions of lives and lifestyles in
multidimensional worlds. It is the recognition of multiple realities
that informs the philosophy of values – value-oriented art and life for
African society. Therefore the *re*-vision of reality by older and
younger African writers like Achebe and Ce is not a fruitless
adventure in bizarre or magical craft, but rather an insistence for us to
reassess our values and spiritual ideals corrupted and disoriented, as
Ce himself comments, by our materialist wandering "through the
wilderness of colonialism and its frills" ("Griot" 13).

 **Section B1**

14

C Ce

Chinweizu

AMONG the few but true griots of their times, in the likeness of their nationalist counterparts who led their generation through the wilderness of colonialism and its frills, Chinweizu, Nigerian scholar, poet and cultural critic raising Pan-Africanist consciousness through his books, and public lectures around the world (*STLAWU*), holds a pioneer's post – the guardian of the Word. Literary history bequeaths this position to the Afrocentric scholar not just for his advocacy of true and original African aesthetics[1] but also for his art 'lured', not by 'cleansing rites' as said of his kinsman (Soyinka 42), but faith in a continent tousled and bereft of direction and whose consequent amnesia could only have found cure by all the doggedness that

---

[1]In their seminal critical volume *Toward the Decolonisation of African Literature* Chinweizu, Jemie and Madubuike outline three major tendencies discernible in African poetry in English one of which is the euromodernist tendency to 'ape' the practices of 20th century European modernist poetry. They repeatedly name Soyinka's, Clark's, and the early Okigbo's poetry as notorious examples.

Afrocentrism demanded of his days.

Energy Crisis (1978), his first volume of poetry introduced the stirring of cultural and artistic sensitivity in an artiste whose roots were beset with problematic responses toward a hollow but endemic frippery of twentieth century western modernism. It left the artiste with the choice of either furthering the prevalent vision of self promotion or joining the bards of ancestral days in elucidating a community aesthetic. One can see this tenuous struggle in *Energy Crisis* which seemed torn between the poet's obsession with self and for his people–his folks–with all their mannerisms and idiosyncrasies as reflected in their social conditions and responses to society. Those poems had come to reflect an artistic awareness and adaptation of his African –contrasted with a powerful but close-minded Western– world to his chosen responses to social experience. It saw the articulation of vision which initially had started jaggedly as of a raconteur, who eager of merit, initially betrays a floundering that nevertheless recedes with one bold proclamation after another. This is the background by which one may assess the importance of Chinweizu (*Energy Crisis* and *Invocations and Admonitions*) in contemporary African poetry.

A rundown world of Crisis

Energy Crisis comprises three sections; 'Wild Oats Farm', 'Commentaries', and 'War and Other Savageries'. In his preface 'Why Publish a book of Poems?' Chinweizu likens the book to an epitaph, 'to show them (his contemporaries) something they had overlooked …or open them to some new feelings or sensations or made them rethink some positions' (iv). For him art devolved in a functional and aesthetic amity between the writer and his audience and not merely from self indulgent experimentations with a 'magnus opus'.

The tag of 'a seamy massage parlour of adolescent wet-dreams,' (Irobi 9) applies very well to the section, 'Wild Oats Farm' – the title itself an erotica for the rundown imagination which presents the poet as a jeering chronicler of various escapades in love marriage and sex. In 'Spring Memories', the persona, in a reverie of the past moments of joy and pleasure, evokes the pain and disappointment of severed love in images of sexuality: '...warm tunnels of fantasy/...bosom heaving with raptures... in orgasmic reverie' (4). Other poems like 'I'll tell you why', 'Weekend Sex', 'Strolling Aphrodisiac', 'Phantom' and 'Desperate woman' are replete with innuendoes of sexual thrills and ultimate doom. They express the poet's cynicism and ridicule of women; more generally, of love and, invariably, every intimate men-women relationships. The treatment of sex as a 'morsel' which a lone dishevelled boy pines for ('Weekend Sex') continues in 'Strolling Aphrodisiac' with the lady walking down the square, a living aphrodisiac provoking unquenchable lusts. His portraiture of women as brief, ephemeral and unreal specimens of nature emerges in the 'Phantom'; in 'Desperate Woman' some love advance is turned down with extreme contempt. Such downright cynicism casts the poet persona in the image of 'Kingfisher' – indifferent and cold to feminine advances. For Chinweizu, marriage is a trap in which couples are 'auctioned' to loss of freedom and happiness ('Chronicle in Matrimony') – a purview of his masculinist theories published later as *Anatomy of Female Power*:

> And thus it is that a wedding is a grand and heartless conspiracy against the bridegroom...You can almost read the thoughts in her mind as she hugs and kisses him in front of the wedding guests: Poor fool, I caught you at last! (63)

In the section 'Commentaries', the jeering note persists rather humourlessly to embrace issues of the African colonial encounter.

'On Welcoming Predators' is said to 'encapsulate the metaphor of white colonial adventures in Africa and the world over with the use of human and animal characters' (Onwudinjo 315). More of such experiments run through other poems as 'Backsliding' and will later stretch into downright satire of wrong-headed white-superiority cults built on Biblical theories and myths in 'The Saviour'. Other times the bouts extend to the nation's Ivory Towers as in 'Faculty Party'. In 'War and other Savageries', the contradictions of statehood enlarge as the poet x-rays the savageries of political repression and hypocrisy at national and international levels ('The Return of the Flies', 'Elegy on the Middle Way'). 'Praise Song for the New Notables' takes a glance at the oppressive culture that permeates the politics of Africa's republics for which his country Nigeria is notorious. 'Clarion Call', the shortest of the poems, combines poetic lyricism in ridicule of a warmongering world – a whore losing her honour somewhere could really be the cause of many wars and plunders that have engulfed nations since Troy.

'Epitaphs of a War' is a threnody of social devastation filled with memories of the Nigerian war, a significant movement in history that helped to shape the new poetry in an equally significant manner. Events unfolding to the war are chronicled in the first stanza. The poem is rendered with bitterness, and recalls the massacre of Biafra's unarmed populace under Nigeria's 'No Victor, No Vanquished' post-war sloganeering. 'The renowned humaneness of the voters was caused by sheer exhaustion of their massacre mission', declares the poet. A sense of loss dominates the poetry and the tragedy of this national defeat is blamed on our leaders for their festering greed/by ethics and statecraft mislearned from alien land (Aiyejina 9).

In his award-winning[2] *Invocations and Admonitions* published

---

[2]Chinweizu's *Invocations and Admonitions* won ANA (Association of Nigerian Authors) Poetry prize for the year.

1986, the nationalist, or, Africanist vision begins to loom large in the poet's consciousness. Significantly, this volume is dedicated,

> to the memory of Cheikh Anta Diop, Egyptologist, scientist, historian great pioneer of Afrocentric history who reconnected the modern African consciousness to black Egypt.

But like the *Crisis*, *Invocations and Admonitions* also dwells on the community, the bard's own folks, and their mannerisms. Women, love and sex in 'Desire', 'That Lady', 'A Gift of Maidenhead' and 'Sex in Space' are treated with his usual masculinist rebuttal. 'Desire' for example maintains a subtle rhythm in the public jeer at womanhood: 'Desire had made her coy/ Tigress tomboy of yesterday/ Desire has tied her tongue'. Cynicism is the attitude toward 'That Lady' who has 'wedded some gent and gone off to make brats'; the 'gift of maidenhead' is politely rejected with 'kisses, caresses, warmth and excuses.'

Other poems – 'The Penis of a God', 'Blest Freight for the Slaughter House', and 'Chant of Hired Planters' – recast the redundancy of the ruling class and their exploitation of the underprivileged through all history. There is sympathy for the workers who actually 'clear the bush, plough the soil, harrow the ground' but are cheated in the harvest ('not for us the harvest time'). On the other hand, there is contempt for Capitalism and its lechery ('what do you expect...we who make sure the roads are built'). Chinweizu often adopts this stance of poet-reformer on a mission. He presumes to bulldoze his art with an acute sense of history ('Admonition to the Black World'), to flatten Imperialism's footholds (Islam, Christianity, Marxism, Capitalism) in our consciousness and, by these 'demolitions', retrieve from the distant past an 'icon' for the inspiration and pride of his generation. For this rare and courageous singer, putting on the garb of the griot in modern writing could be onerous, particularly when lamenting the fall of the heroes of our history ('Lament for a dauntless three') and attempting to capture a historical experience in an artistic memento that evokes the chequered Nigerian independence, its betrayal by a tribe of military interlopers and their civilian counterfeits incarnated even in millennial leaders like Obasanjo[3] and his PDP coterie. Art is thus inscribed for posterity in the serial national conflicts which had come to signify, for recent Nigerian poetry, the point of departure from the aesthetics of the league of euro-modernists represented, in Chinweizu's argument, by the poetry of Okigbo, Soyinka, and Clark.

Thus *Invocations and Admonitions*, distinguished by an Africanist alliance, adopts more complex techniques of expression in various traditional literary forms that had helped to enrich and distinguish the poetry of the new Nigerian writers from that of their older counterparts. This distinction lies in the realignment of heritage from a more credible interpretation and organisation of traditional repertoire. Egudu's observation then that

> the Igbo literary tradition . . . has provided patterns for the various forms of written poetry, and (that) Igbo rhetoric and linguistic mode of expression...furnished writers with verbal resources for achieving semantic and ornamental effectiveness (2)

is particularly true of Chinweizu's griot-poetics as can be seen in its faithful representation of the energy and lyricism of Igbo traditional speech. Even for *Energy Crisis*, rightly observed as predominantly set in the West (Aiyejina 9) and consequently replete with sceneries

---

[3] As close as April 16, 2007. Habib Aruna of the Nigerian *Daily Independent* feeling the political pulse of the nation-state laments the 'cancerous ailment in the body politic of the nation' being militaristic autocracy; he states: 'President Olusegun Obasanjo, himself a quintessential product of military commandism, is emblematic of the abnormality that military rule has begotten (for Africa)'.

of pub, snow, winter, etc., one can easily discern its roots in the oral dramatic and longer narrative forms. For example, we can appreciate the poems 'Strolling Aphrodisiac', 'Phantom', 'Desperate Woman', 'I'll tell you Why', etc., as the commencement of a dialogue. There is always the inevitable presence of an local audience achieved partly by the story-telling nature of the poems,

> Hey strolling aphrodisiac
> Why do you wander about the square...(12)
>
> You there by the bolted door...(21)
>
> He arrived and went straight to the
> city fathers and/declared...(35)

'Mary Lou' and 'Energy Crisis' poems seem to reposition the ballad form not in the 'concentration on a single episode' (Finnegan10) but in the surviving heritage of Africa in the Americas. African-American speech is the idiolect of this story of infidelity and racial prejudice where parallelism and repetitions permeate the narrative and accentuate its oral essence:

> Mah good man, mah good hungry man
> Ah only slept with his name
> Ah only slept with his colour
> Ah only slept with his money not
> with him. (26)

This folk dialogue begins with an admix of contemporaneous artefacts ('VWs, Volvos, Cadillacs, Chevys) and oral patterns ('If your vibes pull you in here'). The ballad tradition of stanzaic refrains and repetitions ('Sorry Mama, I'll like to help you woman/but I've got this energy crisis on my hands') is enhanced by the lyricism of the composition:

> And she started to cry
> Lord why are you so mean to me
> Now I want it he's got none
> Lord why are you so mean to me. (30)

More of these features are employed in 'The Saviour', a dramatic narrative which, in sixteen lines, encapsulates the New Testament story of Jesus. We also perceive further echoes of folk traditions; in 'Praise Song to the New Notables', for example, the panegyric comes to the fore. We have a singer and a chorus. The griot acting as 'Odozi-obodo' is at the centre of the dramatic ('It is I OdoziObodo.../I who set the land right"). But it is a rejection of the graft and corruption of post-colonial states led by 'the Odozi Obodo':

> I eater of taxes
> I graft millionaire
> I swindle tycoon
> I lord of Uhuru. (46)

The first-person narrative, frequent in oral dramatics, is used to merge hero and singer and to create in the audience a wry sense of humour: ('I steal the grain/and blame the rats'). The Chorus introduce the audience participation, and a dramatic enactment is in progress, laden with high praises on the surface but ironical fillips at the paradigmatic levels of meaning: 'slayer of turbulent bulls/who strangles 'castrated goats'. The last lines, 'gobble up our treasure hall, new black star' crystallises in our minds the final purport of the lavish praises on our political pseudo greats.

In addition 'Epitaphs of a War' tells the civil war story on a bitter note. Unlike an epitaph, it is rendered in a long-narrative structure; it is indignant but also solemn and contemplative. 'In the aftermath of battle/beaten commanders are herded off/to die at old age at thirty two' is the poet's reference to the systematic destruction of the Igbo nation after their rebellion – a Nigerian factor that entrenched not unity but cynicism and resentment among the various nationalities. The poet persona is sometimes reflective – 'I remember my flint words of consolation/at his daddy's death...' and strives to teach the younger generation:

> Son should they ask you why we died
> Tell them our leaders were paralysed
> by festering greed... (53)

There is a continuing shift to the first person narrative 'I' which gives, in the words of Alternband and Lewis, 'the greatest possible sense of involvement in a story, [making] empathy ... fully possible [and giving] the illusion of undergoing and sharing... the revelations brought by his experience' (Taiwo 85).

The Bard's Invocation

However manner that *Energy Crisis* handles its story-telling craft in a dexterous mixture of traditional voices, this exploration is brought to great accomplishment in the bard's *Admonitions*. It confirms the artistic concerns of the poet as 'both iconoclastic in their demystifying forays and revivalist in their appeal to African history and nationalism (Oyortev 80). It also restates the poet's fundamental concerns with the harrowing reality of African life. Such 'demystifying forays' may be seen in light of proper diction which Chinweizu and company had advocated in their decolonisation treatise, and which the poet exemplifies here to wit in a word: clarity. In the thinking of the triad of Chinweizu, Madubuike and Jemie, 'Orature being auditory places a high value on lucidity, normal syntax and precise and apt imagery (247)'.

In *Invocations* the griot is more at home with his traditional

271

repertoire: the prayer ('Invocations on a day of Exile'), the abuse: ('The Pagan's Reply'), work song: ('Chant of Hired Planters'), dirge song: ('Lament for a Dauntless Three'), and song of admonitions ('…To the Black World'). The prayer in 'Day of Exile' is remarkable in its adoption of *òfò*, to represent the Igbo poet-diviner. This totem of justice urges steadfastness on the holder through any human or divinely instigated adversity. The persona of this poem is therefore not unlike the exile of an unjust society 'where truth is cast out of the gates and falsehood sits majestic'. It draws from the traditional incantation as the supplicant calls upon his ancestors and gods: 'And you forest spirits/and you spirits of the rivers/and you my ancestors' (16). The journey motif parallels traditional rites of passage: 'I have travelled a road without rest/I am hungry for a patch of earth' and the rhetoricism is appropriately adapted to elicit the element of pathos: 'where can I settle my rump/and cool my blistered feet?'

There is here achieved the merger of human will and divine consent (*Chi*) –*Chi* being a man's 'guardian angel, his spirit-being complementing his terrestrial human being' (Achebe 43).

> though my path is hard
> my chi is alert...
> And what is that crouching in ambush...?
> I say my chi will not permit it
> move out of my path
> my chi is alert. (16)

When a man says 'yes' his chi also affirms, we say; so too for the poet-persona: 'I have said yes/ my chi will also say yes' (17). Thus in this time-old precept of ritual self cleansing do we declare him/her clean and free from incrimination – an expression which is achieved by the accompanying device of rhetorical questions:

> Did I get loose another man's tethered goat?

Did I lean unto my bed another man's unwilling daughter?
Did I loot the public granary and harm another man's
crop...? (17)

The truth of retributive justice reflects from traditional
philosophy and, in Chinweizu's poetry, is deployed with extensive
structural repetitions and parallelisms important in African
communication art:

If prosperity should visit me
It shall find me at home
It shall not overwhelm me
It shall not drive laughter from my teeth
It shall not surround me with faces mad with envy
It shall not kill me before my time. (17)

In 'Lament for a Dauntless Three', the artiste's voice takes after
traditional dirge 'praise of heroes who have finally been defeated by
the almighty spirit called death' (Ogunba 45) and for whom there
abides the traditional honour of praises (Egudu15). Indeed, the
lament is patterned after a local lamentation and quite full of praises
for three heroes of the Nigerian 'revolution', Okigbo, Nzeogwu, and
Murtala. In the words of a critic:

Okigbo is decked in local fauna: a strong and courageous panther
who leapt to 'scatter the granary thieves' and Murtala is the 'strong
arm' that rose to clear the 'debris' of political misrule. These
qualities set the stage for the tragedy of their deaths. When Okigbo
is slain in the battlefield and left to 'wander in the forests of final
nights,' and Nzeogwu is 'betrayed, trapped and gored,' and Murtala
is later cut down by 'bullets sent to fetch his head,' a situation of
utter despair and hopelessness is most powerfully projected.
(Emezue 119-120)

273

In this lament, the subject-heroes take on mythic dimensions, quite disproportionate to actual historical positions. Now they are full of goodness, had elevated the material well-being of their people, helped the poor and made the peace. So their death is made to acquire a tragic outlook that should leave the bereaved utterly helpless as aptly projected in this rhetorical parallelism:

> what voice shall comfort us…?
> what arm shall strike for us …?
> what hand shall cleanse this rot …? (11-13)

With the poet we can traverse further to reconstruct traditional funeral occasions where, as assumed, the deceased is not really 'dead' until a 'thorough search' has been conducted around the familiar places the deceased usually stayed during his life time. When at last he is not found, he is then adjudged dead. 'Lament for a Dauntless Three' is informed by such funeral practices in Igboland. The three heroes are sought after in places associated with their physical and spiritual homelands. For Nzeogwu it is 'the smoke of battle'; for Murtala 'the brush of (Northern) savannah /...to the desert edge', and for the poet Okigbo, let us search the 'song halls in heaven' (Emezue 119). The futility of the search finally establishes the sad fact that the hero is dead, not that they 'are not good enough for heaven' (Amah 13). In 'Lament', the news 'chilled the ears' and even 'multitudes on the Niger bank ...raised a great lament'. 'Earth comets, wind and stars have all joined the lament.' Such elements of tragic fallacy, raising the issue to great tragic heights, are resonant of funeral traditions which evoke 'responses and interjections and small outbursts from the other celebrants who serve as the chorus to the whole ritual' (Awoonor 102).

The towncrier motif, begun by Okigbo, is explored extravagantly in 'Admonitions to a Black World'. The future, present and past millennium of history are compressed in a four-part movement of ritual and tradition aimed at restoring pride in the race. Chinweizuan darts are nowhere deployed more effectively than in this part where the griot dismantles orthodox western strongholds in Africa (namely Islam, Christianity and Marxist modernism) and berates his people for their allegiance to foreign values:

> That one claims he is an Arab
> And when he hides his African tongue
> Stuttering in Arabic
> he is giddy with pride (30)

The Muslim may 'bow in obeisance to Mecca/five times like a lizard', and followers of Marxist modernism may well declare, 'The god of the Dialectic, of Historical materialism'

> Is colour and nation blind.
> From the mud of primitivism
> He lifted me to astral planes
> And showed me the Universal Father. (31)

Chinweizu's Afrocentric position on western imperialism is expounded elaborately in his book, *The West and the Rest of Us*, a profound work of great controversy: 'For nearly six centuries now', he asserts,

> western Europe and its Diaspora have been disturbing the peace of the world...armed with the gun...fortified in aggressive spirit by an arrogant messianic Christianity... and motivated by the lure of enriching plunder white hordes have sallied forth from their Western European homelands to explore, assault, loot, occupy, rule, and exploit the rest of the world. (3)

But here poetry and history take the audience to ancient Egypt. Africa is 'the birth place of monotheism', they proudly assert in the manner of

275

many a rapturous Egyptologist.

> Look! look over there
> Into the dawn mists of history
> Pull off the veil of five thousand years
> And behold your progenitors…(43)

Great kings like Uti, Meni, Khafre,etc., begin to file before our vision. 'African astronomers, architects… poets/Embalmers, geometers, potters, sages/ theologians, sculptors, carpenters chemists/ pharmacists...' A modern griot goes to work eloquently testifying for Africa with confidence, authority, and conviction. The great sage Ptahloptpe wrote 'maxims for the ignorant... in the seven excellent discourse'. There was a highly sophisticated architecture 'building with hewn stone' (invented by Imhotep) great Sphinx and pyramids...' There were great physicians like Teti who compiled works on anatomy. Quite profound is the technique of drama in poetry reenacting, with songs dances and rituals, the drama of the resurrection of king-Saint Unas from an adaptation of pyramidal texts:

> Then the king is purified
> With the chant of the cleansing
> In the manner of the Sun-god Re:
> Cleansed is he who is cleansed...
> Cleansed is Unas in the Field of Rushes
> Hand of Unas in hand of Re!
> O Nut, shy-goddess, take his hand
> O Shu, god of air, lift him up!
> O Shu, lift him up!
> Where upon the King
> Asks for admittance to the sky. (43)

The entire poem overwhelms the reader with facts and figures of history all in the bid to reinvent black consciousness with all its sense of dignity and pride ('The pyramid is our icon'). There is a conscious, overarching dominance of expressions, images, and oratorical locution drawn from tradition. The poet persona represents the voice of the ancestors in its wisdom, warning the people:

> O blacks hear and heed!
> When the final war begins
> To drive white predators from your land
> The jackals of the white race
> Will dash forth to exterminate you. (34)

This ancestral voice is also the voice of prophetic admonition ('If you let them, if you let them…'). The detailed exploration of the rhetorical and dramatic, repetitions and parallelisms, recast the deeper essence of the poem, steeping it in the town-crier's most effective rhythms of delivery that far surpassed Christopher Okigbo's own attempts.

> If you let them, if you let them
> They will use your fears against you
> Your lack of daring against you
> Your craving for trinkets against you
> Your hunger for the world against you ...
> If you let them, if you let them... (35)

'Admonitions to a Black World' is easily Chinweizu's crowning metier not only for the energy of it fast-chanting style but also in the exhaustive recapitulation of Africa's pasts in long, winding, rhetoric, song and drama. At the end if there is a feeling of catharsis, it is from our own exhaustion by the epic enactment, or, for the griot, a successful transmission of a highly significant art. One can re-imagine it as the sum of an artistic maturation in the weaving of language, history and tradition, and in the profound combination of artistic and mythological depositions.

Conclusion

This then is our fellowship with the art and craft of our griot of *Crisis* and *Invocations*. We have sought to present an artistic movement that marks Chinweizu's nationalist consciousness by drawing from hybrid cultural settings (*Energy Crisis*), and the poet's comprehension of local cultural dynamics (*Invocations*) where 'themes are highly relevant ... full of imagery of the right kind (with) a very high competence in the manipulation of language for effect (Obiechina 12). Chinweizu's poetry, more than those of his generation, demonstrate effective use of rhetoric and unify the lyrical and ideological purposes of art in a seamless and lasting impression on the reader's mind.

The example of Chinweizu is thus the unacknowledged definer of the literary conscience of younger artists in their clarity, resonance, and deference to local oratorical devices. These are local methods and manners of rendition never quite matched in Pre-war Nigerian poetry. Thus did the new Nigerian poets – Chinweizu, Ohaeto and Osundare, to mention but three – truly endear the genre in the way that Achebe, Aidoo, and Soyinka had done for the prose and dramatic traditions of their various African societies.

15

I Bala

Mapange

In 2004, *The Last of the Sweet Bananas*, a large-scale book of selected poems from four previous collections: *Mau* (1971), *Of Chameleons and Gods* (1981), *The Chattering Wagtails of Mikuyu Prison* (1993) and *Skipping Without Ropes* (1998) by Malawian poet Jack Mapanje was published on Bloodaxe and Wordsworth label at Tarset in the United States. There are also twenty one *New Poems* to complete the book, and, in a way, justify the "newness" of the title.

Mapanje, distinguished Malawian poet, linguist, editor and scholar was head of Department of English at Chancellor College, University of Malawi before he was incarcerated for three and a half years under the dictatorial regime of Kamuzu Banda. A large number of the poems collected in the book are inspired (the right word is, perhaps, "impelled") by the poet's imprisonment in Malawi's notorious Mikuyu prison under the late dictator, Hastings Kamuzu Banda, from 1987 to 1991 without charges. Many more of the poems in both *The Chattering Wagtails of Mikuyu Prison* and *Skipping Without Ropes* are, invariably, prison poems conceived and written in the form of recollections; since the poet, once incarcerated, is naturally deprived of anything to write with. While some of the poems are simply poems composed in Mapanje's head, later when the poet regained his freedom, he wrote them down from memory.

Any exploration of Mapanje's poetic oeuvre is bound to take cognisance of the suffering the poet endured during his imprisonment. The earliest poems subtly but boldly indicate that Mapanje has always been a radical poet, what his four years long privation did was to simply strengthen and intensify his range of concerns. Therefore, it is difficult for a poet like Jack Mapanje to wholly escape the debilitating narrow tag of "political poet", despite other concerns that his poetry may imbibe from collection to the next, and despite its amazing apotheosis. And there are many (new) poems in the book, which show that Mapanje has other private concerns other than the larger political fate of his native Malawi; politics may well be his principal theme to readers, even though his oeuvre has never exude any explicit revolutionary agenda, (or even tow a particular party line). An early sequence, "Cycles", for instance, takes its title from the Mangochi region where Mapanje grew up, from Malawi creation myth, as well as from colonial history such as the Chilembwe Uprising, and might appear to be a fusion of both the local and the political for some readers.

The use of creation myth deploys animal figures, especially the chameleon, which keeps reappearing in various guises in the poet's later works that are marked by a harsher tone. And these later poems are truly poems informed by experience (instances of the clichéd "songs of experience"). In such poems formal concerns are less important than content, yet the concerns are indispensable to the meaning making process of the poems. The poems, as it were, betray Mapanje's mastery of syntax as in the brilliant "On His Royal Blindness Paramount Chief Kwangala":

> I admire the quixotic display of your paramountcy
> How you brandish our ancestral shields and spears
> Among your warriors dazzled by your loftiness,
> But I fear the way you spend your golden breath;
> Those impromptu, long-winded tirades of your might
> In the heat, do they suit your brittle constitution? (25)

Mapanje's syntax perhaps explains the penchant, if not the obsession, to write in some form of code, especially in his early poems, like the seemingly uncontroversial "Song of Chicken" in the sequence referred to earlier, "Cycles":

> Master, you talked with bows,
> Arrows and catapults once
> Your hands steaming with hawk blood
> To protect your chicken.
>
> Why do you talk with knives now,
> Your hands teaming with eggshells
> And hot blood from your own chicken?
> Is it to impress our visitors? (21).

It is, indeed, easy to spot a "subversive meaning" for those readers with the vision to peep through the textual gimmick of the poem. Certainly, it is even more appropriate, then, that the taunting, cryptic-totemic chameleon which firmly stood over Mapanje's (early) poems, poetry wholly subsumed in the Malawian history and culture, but also envisioning a better, more democratic

Malawi, which might effectively replace the ossifying society that is the legacy of Hastings Banda.

The harsh prison condition, the inherent cruelty and injustice of his illegal incarceration still haunt Mapanje's poetic sensibility more than a decade after regaining his freedom, and effectively resettling in the United Kingdom. As such, both *The Chattering Wagtails of Mikuyu Prison* and *Skipping Without Ropes*, the two collections he published following imprisonment are dominated, even in a distant way, determined and validated by the experience of Mikuyu prison. Indeed, the two books are best seen as an attempt to "exorcise" the demons of prison. First, in *The Chattering Wagtails of Mikuyu Prison* Mapanje has memorably written about the terrible living condition of prison: the harsh routines, the humiliation and the overall denial of justice. Therefore, the poem "The Streak-Tease At Mikuyu Prison, 25 Sept. 1987" is quintessence here, for it describes the poet's being strip-searched on the night of his arrest, which at first is compared innocently, even naively with "the strip tease at the Bird's Nest, / London Street, Paddington in the seventies" during Mapanje's postgraduate studies days. Here, the strip search is much bleaker, harsher and unrelenting:

> The streak-tease at Mikuyu prison is an affair
> More sportive. First, the ceremony of handcuff
>
> Disposal, with the warder's glib remarks about how
> Modern handcuffs really dug in when you tried to
>
> Fidget; then the instructions: take off your glasses,
> Your sweater, your shirt, shove these with your

Jacket into their shrouded-white bag or your handbag
Until your release, which could be tomorrow... (84).

The poem ends with the realisation of the grim reality of what he was reduced to:

Now the stinking shit-bucket tripped over drowns

The news about the lights being left over night for
You to scare night creepers, as the putrid bwezi

Blanket-rag enters the single cell & staggers on to
The cracked cold cement floor of Mikuyu Prison (86).

The rest of the poems in *The Chattering Wagtails of Mikuyu Prison* are equally couched with the same indignation and outrage while simultaneously bristling with the rare ability to laugh at the absurdity of what transpire in prison, and at the stupidity of Banda's cruelty and self-aggrandising repressiveness.

In *Skipping Without Ropes*, the spirit of resistance subsumed in the taunting laughter is further tackled in greater scope than in the previous book. The eponymous title poem, for example, is a hopeful, nay powerful declaration of the poet's resistance and resilience in the face of suffering. The poem refers to the activity by which Mapanje kept fit while in detention; he was, as expected, denied even a length of rope to exercise, fearing that he might harm himself. The poet foresees how skipping may be the new metaphor for his life, and for that he will "hop about, hop about my cell, my/ Home, the mountains, my globe" and with near-manic mockery in childlike playful tone, he enthuses:

Watch, watch me skip without your
Rope; watch me skip with my hope
A-one, a-two, a-three, a-four, a-five
I will, a-seven, I do, will skip, a-ten,

Eleven, I will skip without, will skip
Within and skip I do without your
Rope but with my hope; and I will,
Will always skip you dull, will skip

Your silly rules, skip your filthy walls,
Your weevil pigeon peas, skip your
Scorpions, skip your Excellency Life
Glory. (129).

Considering the twenty-one *New Poems* Jack Mapanje's poetry appears to have moved from the need to indulge in cryptic encoding to more lucid narration. From *The Chattering Wagtails of Mikuyu Prison* to the *New Poems*, there are only a sparing references to Mapanje's earlier object of identification: the totemic chameleon. It is safer to say, then, that the "transition" from cryptic, obscure metaphor to fabular, storytelling idiom allows the poet to consummate his poetic skills on developing the art of storytelling in his poems. Mapanje's seemingly unrelenting and unending search for points of reference and identification, invariably, avails him the most apt of platforms to conjure a timeless parable of experience that is rooted in hisand our humanity.

The first poem of the *New Poems*, "The Stench of Porridge" aptly underscores the horror for the way in which the smell of prison tenaciously trails those who even regained their freedom:

Why does the stench of prison
Suddenly catch us like lust?
Didn't the spirit govern once for all,
The groans of prisoners dying next cell
The pangs of prisoners gone mad,
The weeping blisters on our elbows,
Knees, balls, bums, buttocks, wherever
And the blizzards blustering
The rusty tin roofs
Where helpless chickens
Drip in the storm?

For how long does this
Stench intend to trail us?
Or is it really true what they say,
'Once prisoner always prisoner'
Why? (191-192).

The *New Poems* too are pervaded by the overriding metaphor of prison; for even supposedly love poems for the poet's wife are centred on Mapanje's incarceration as in the poem, "The Seashells of Bridlington North Beach" which begins:

She hated anything caged, fish particularly,
Fish caged in glass boxes, ponds, whatever;

'Reminds me of prison and slavery', she said (204).

Another poem worthy of mention is "Rested Amongst Fellow Hyenas, Finally" which celebrates, in a mock laudatory tone, the death of Hastings Banda. The poem is reminiscent of Wole Soyinka's "Exit Left, Monster, Victim in Pursuit" and "Where The News Came To Me of the Death of Dictator" (collected in *Samarkand and Other Markets I have Known* [2002]), which, in a similar fashion, celebrates the death of Nigeria's dictator, Sani Abacha in 1998, though not with the same tenor that underlines the anger and a sense of relief which inform Soyinka's. Mapanje's poem, like Soyinka's, points at the inevitable mortality of so ruthless a dictator like Banda, showing that even the most-feared despots are human after all:

> So the undertakers have buried
> Their lion of the nation for life
> Among the hyenas he ridiculed
> At political rallies once?
>
> [...]
> And were those battles he fought
> To become another Almighty God
> Worth spilling his people's blood
> For, eventually? And will the taxis
> Really show us the solitary barbed
> Wire cemetery where his rabid hyenas
> Gather at night stomping about and
> Foaming for his bonesglory be! (198-199)

In the end, the only thing out of place, askew from *The Last of The Sweet Bananas* is the wanton absence of notes offering contextual information (as in *Of Chameleon and Gods*). This absence of contextual notes makes the poems a bit obscure. And it is also difficult to fathom the compulsion to rearrange the poems, which, in the original individual volumes, formed a kind of autobiographical whole in a sequential order.

In the last analysis, like so much African poetry in English expression, *The Last of the Sweet Bananas* is a representative collection arising, evidently, out of a noted level of commitment to the idea of poetry as a form of an intervention; as a kind of social commentary. The book is certainly bristling with satire and irony intended to clearly expose and undermine the hypocrisy and cruelty of the dictatorial regimes not just in Malawi but also in the whole of Africa.

Yet it is difficult to understand how Mapanje's early poems could constitute any real or imagined threat to a dictator like Hastings Banda. But one thing is certain, though: those dictators like Banda who react so repressively to a clutch of supposedly critical poems say a lot about the level of their insecurity when confronted with honest criticism.

16

A Kehinde

Brathwaite

THE POETRY of Edward Brathwaite is the quest for identity and an attempt to come to terms with a past that was overwhelming in itself "and still remains overwhelming in its undesirable intrusion into the present" (Egudu 8). Brathwaite's main artistic preoccupation is to achieve 'wholeness' through poetic reconstruction. For him, therefore, "the eye must be free/seeing – an attempt to retrieve his world through his poetic vision" (Dash 122). In fact, the importance of Africa in West Indian writings cannot be overestimated, either as providing alternative metaphors of cultural difference or as a fully developed Negritude.

The trope of Africa is a recurrent feature of West Indian literature. As Kole Omotoso rightly observes, Africans in the Caribbean suffer two major psychic wounds:

> They have been violently taken away from their ancestral homes through conspiracy of their own people and the white slavers and thus been permanently deprived of the revitalizing effect of their home culture, something which the Europeans of the Caribbean

depended upon to survive their sojourns and the Indians looked
back to in exile ... The second damage stemmed from the denying
of the values and worthiness of African culture and consequent ongoing denigration of continental African culture. (30)

Omotoso echoes Coulthard who believes that for the African
slaves and their descendants in the Caribbean, the impact of these
psychic wounds have been so profound that their consciousness has
over the centuries been afflicted by the crisis of identity (25). Indeed,
it is this very crisis that basically informs the creative imagination of
the average Caribbean artist. All kinds of cleavages along the lines of
race, wealth, class and political affiliation have caused the alienation
felt by the Africans in the Caribbean. This position is the central thesis
of an informing and insightful discourse by Shelby. In the book,
Steele mildly interrogates some themes of African-American
literature that emphasize racial solidarity (122-128). It should be
stressed that the alienation felt by the Africans in the Caribbean has
become the burden of the West Indian writer attempting to capture the
complexity of his society. In doing this, as one would expect, there are
bound to be areas of common interest among the writers, just as there
are dissimilarities among them. But one thing they have in common is
the need felt by the West Indian writer to recreate and redefine the
essence of his/her black colour and West Indian experience - the need
to capture the reality of the people who seem rootless.

Therefore, the trope of Africa is a case study of "tropological
revision" in West Indian literature. According to Henry Louis Gates,
Jr., tropological revision is "the manner in which a specific trope is
repeated with differences, between two or more texts" (xxv). Karen
King-Aribisala in her perceptive article "African Homogeneity: The
Affirmation of a 'United' African and Afro-West Indian Identity"
declares:

One of the consequences of this predicament is the tendency of

West Indian writers to make actual or imaginative pilgrimage to
Africa, in an attempt to rediscover their ancestral roots. (40)

Given this unified African heritage and shared commonality of
the African historical experience, African and West Indian writers
appear to consciously examine their African heritage in the literatures
of both areas. Brathwaite's sense of awareness–most importantly of
his historical position and situation in society–finds utmost
expression in his brooding, slow but progressive attempt to achieve
'wholeness' out of the debris of his past. His Ghanaian experience, no
doubt, had opened his eyes to this possibility. His comment on this
issue is worth quoting below:

> Slowly, slowly, ever so slowly; obscurely, slowly but surely, during
> the eight years that I lived there, I was coming to an awareness and
> understanding of community, of cultural wholeness, of the place of
> the individual within the tribe, in society. Slowly, slowly, ever so
> slowly, I came to a sense of identification of myself with these
> people, my living diviners. I came to connect my history with
> theirs, the bridge of my mind now linking Atlantic and ancestor,
> homeland and heartland. (38)

Brathwaite believes that the 'middle-passage' experience is not
after all totally a traumatic experience; rather, the experience is "a
pathway or channel between (African) tradition and what is being
evolved on new soil in the Caribbean (38). Also, in an essay,
"Timehri", Brathwaite relates how he had gone to England thinking
he was a British citizen but had his illusions shattered. According to
him: "I found and felt myself rootless on arrival in England". He then
went on exile to Ghana. During the eight-year stay, he discovered "a
culture in which there is a profound relationship of individual and of
the spiritual world to the community" (King 130). According to King,
Brathwaite's stints as a historian, a pamphleteer and a poet have been

to transcend the colonial sense of rootlessness and isolation.

Brathwaite's poetry thematically signifies some indices of post colonial literary discourse. He writes about the themes of Africa, slavery and colonialism, alienations, exile and search for identity of literature and society. Actually, the trope of Africa in Brathwaite's poetry is an example of what Paul Gilroy refers to as 'Afrocentricity'. According to Gilroy, 'Afrocentricity' is "African genius and African values created, recreated, reconstructed, and derived from our history and experiences in our best interests" (188).

Sesan Ajayi comments on the trope of 'Africa' in the poetry of Brathwaite:

> His poetry is thus a rewriting of Caribbean history in its socio-economic dimensions for he knows that 'the sea is a divider. It is not a life-giver.' The evocation of Black ritual cults of Legba, Ananse, Ogun, etc is an instance of Brathwaite's substituting principle, for the Black pantheon is assumed to be capable of restoring 'Uncle Tom' to his symbolic position or potency. (205)

For Stewart Brown:

> Much of his work has been a kind of reclamation of that African inheritance, a reclamation that has inevitably involved a process of challenge and confrontation with the elements of the mercantilist/colonial culture which overlaid and often literally oppressed the African survivals. (126-127)

Apparently, the issue of 'Africa' as a co-text in West Indian literature has received much attention among scholars and critics. Omotayo Oloruntoba-Oju in her essay, "Literature of the Black Diaspora", contends that in West Indies, a literature of transplantation is encountered, that is, a literature highlighting the struggles for emancipation and the yearning for a reunion with the roots – "a yearning which again in the arts takes the form of the employment of tropes from African cultural founts" (139). Perhaps Oloruntoba-Oju's claim is a reference to the view of Bill Ashcroft, Gareth Griffiths and Hellen Tiffin that Brathwaite regards a return to African roots as pertinent to contemporary West Indian. They state further:

> The West Indian poet and historian E. K. Brathwaite proposes a model which, while stressing the importance of the need to privilege the African connection over the European, also stresses the multi-cultural, syncretic nature of the West Indian reality. (35)

In his book, *Race and Colour in Caribbean Literature*, G.R. Coulthard highlights the themes of race and colour as well as the grand motif of Africa in Caribbean literature (67). Similarly, Mark Kinkead Weeke's "Africa-in Caribbean Fictions" attempts an analysis of the intertext of 'Africa' in two West Indian novels (85-111).

The search for an African meaning in the Caribbean began earlier with writers like Marcus Garvey and Edward Blyden and later in the twentieth century with one of the foremost negritude poets, Aime Cesaire, who sustains in his work an impassioned dynamic of protest against the assumption that the black man is an inferior being. Therefore, the Caribbean writer's obsession with the theme of Africa is an attempt "at exploding the myth of his inferiority" (Peter 60).

In the search for identity in the Caribbean, Brathwaite has made a remarkable contribution to the theme of Africa in Caribbean literature. In *Masks*, particularly, he makes a wide range of references to such African empires as Ghana, Mali, Songhai, Benin, Congo and Chad; such African towns as Axum, Timbuctu, Ougadougou, Takoradi and Kumasi; such African personalities as Chaka, Osai Tutu; such African gods as Ogun, Damballa, Olodumare, Tano; the tropical Rain Forest; the Fauna and Flora of Africa, its history, legends, myths and mores.

However, Brathwaite does not glorify or fantasize Africa in his poetry. His reference to Africa comes on naturally. This is to put forward the argument earlier raised by Shelby Steele. About *Masks* in which the motif of Africa finds its utmost expression, Michael Dash comments:

> 'Masks' is an innovation of serenity and reverence totally absent in the violated New World. It is tempting to locate Brathwaite's vision of Africa as part of the mythical, nostalgic picture evident in such poets as Senghor, to cast Brathwaite in the role of the prodigal son returning to his roots. However, it is significant to note the section is entitled 'Masks' and not 'Africa' and to see the extent to which we witness something more complex than blind romanticizing of the ancestral past. (219)

When Brathwaite refers to Kumasi as "a city of gold paved with silver, ivory altars, tables of horn, the thorn bush of love burst on the hill bleeds in the West" (*Masks* 138), he is more or less stating the obvious. This readily brings us to the position which Brathwaite occupies within the Negritude tradition. There is a way in which every black writer can be classified as a Negritudist, whether such a writer lives in the continent or in the Diaspora, and such classification can be upheld as long as aspects of Africa abide with the writer's thematic preoccupations. However, core negritudists like David Diop and Leopold Sedar Senghor glorify, celebrate and create fantasies about Africa. Therefore, using this tendency as our yardstick, it becomes obvious that Brathwaite exhibits a moderate negritude outlook.

Brathwaite's physical and literary excursions into Africa are a resemblance of the Israelites' Exodus. This is clearly depicted in the epigraph to "Rights of Passage":

If I forget you, O Jerusalem,
Let my right hand wither;
Let my tongue cleave to the roof
Of my mouth. If I do not remember you;
If I do not set Jerusalem above my
highest joy (ii).

Brathwaite portrays the plight of the black man in three stages "Rights of Passage", "Islands" and "Masks" – the identification of Africa as his roots, the celebration of the realities of African heritage and the reconciliation with the alienation. The identification of the poet with Africa is the focus of the first part of the trilogy. The title "Rights of Passage" indicates the anthropological term "rites de passage" which can be seen as a transition between one condition to another. Therefore, the trilogy signifies a yearning by the poet for identification with his African origin. It also becomes a semiotic of transformation in Brathwaite's consciousness of his own identity. The tone of the third part of the trilogy changes, and this marks the first phase of the transition. Although Brathwaite lived as an alien in Africa (Ghana), he henceforth acknowledges his African blood and desires to be identified with it. This is perhaps a psychological transition, and it is based on this that the meaning of the epigraph is derived from 'Exodus'. This condition is marked by a denunciation of the European mind referred to as 'Babylon'.

In 'Wings of Dove", Brathwaite mirrors his African consciousness in the temper of the Rastafarians:

And I	Down down
Rastafar - I	White
In Babylon's boon	Man
…	…
Cry my people shout:	dem mock

295

dem kill	man Ian'
dem an' go	back back
back back	to Af-
to the black	rica. (42-43)

Thus the return-to-Africa ideal of the poet is not confined to his individual self but to the entire people of African descent. With this new awareness of going-back-to-Africa, Brathwaite's "Rights of Passage" depicts the unfortunate experiences of the past, and he asks the black people to evolve a new, wholesome image:

let me suffer	O dawning
nothing	Let my children
to remind me now	Rise
of my lost children	in the path
but let them	Of the morning
rise	Up and go forth
O man	On the road
O god	Of the morning (13-14).

In "Tom", there is an assumption of the personality of Africa and a concern about the future of African children both in Africa and in the Caribbean:

let me suffer	O dawning
nothing	Let my children
to remind me now	Rise
of my lost children	in the path
but let them	Of the morning
rise	Up and go forth
O man	On the road
O god	Of the morning (13-14).

Furthermore, in his presentation of Tizzic's case, Brathwaite denounces the tyranny of a foreign imposition such as Christianity that robs Tizzic of its power of enrichment. Through "Carnival's stilts of Song", Tizzic comes nearer to attaining the seventh heaven, but he is doomed to failure (Ismond 58).

For Brathwaite, the implication of these denunciations resides in his search for a religion, which is basically African in conception, to replace the Christian religion. Ultimately, the rejection of western values is a sure step towards his affirmation of an African meaning. It may not be an otiose task to comment in passing the factors surrounding the theme of Africa as a dominant trope in Brathwaite's poetry. His source of inspiration for this African exploration can be found in his three-way journey from the West Indies to England where he lived as a student, then to Africa (Ghana) where he worked for upwards of eight years and back to the West Indies. Therefore, he finds in this personal experience of excursions a prototype of the larger ordeal of his ancestors, the memory of which psychologically arouses his consciousness.

Indubitably, Brathwaite sets out to explore the theme of rediscovery of the black race in his poem. To this end, he progresses through a series of dominant themes. The dominant ones however are themes of African Diaspora. For instance:

E-
gypt
In Af-
rica
Mesopo
tamia
Mero
e

the hills of
Ahafo, winds
of the Ni-
ger, Kumasi
and Kiver

the
nile
silica

297

glass	down the
and brittle	coiled Congo
Sa	and down
hara, Tim	that black river
buctu, Gao	("Rights", 35)

The above lines show the migration of Africans from Egypt to West Africa, where they were eventually sold into slavery. The disjointed nature of this poem has a graphological poetic effect; it is meant to show the way the black people are scattered all over the world.

"Rights of Passage" is a poem of protest in which Brathwaite tries to recreate the past and examine it to build a better tomorrow for his people. He is indeed an example of a poet in an emergent literature operating within the European "avant garde" technique attitude, which can be adopted to express the cultural concern of a new notion of the third world.

The theme of Africa finds its utmost expression in "Masks" which explores the culture of the slaves' ancestors in its modern living forms in Africa, especially in the Ashanti region of Ghana. It is the poet's pilgrimage to find his people's cultural origins and psychological genealogy in the history of black empires, in the fashioning of ceremonial drums, in celebrations of the agricultural year, in appeals to the gods for guidance, in commemorations of disasters, in invocation to the Divine Drummer to 'kick' the representative persona awake. "Mask" is indeed a religious poem put to cultural, political and psychotherapeutic purposes on behalf of the whole people. "Masks", therefore, repeatedly 'returns' to "the dance, symbol of transcendence" (Gikandi 113). Brathwaite's coming to terms with Africa in "Masks" manifests itself in a radical and profound sympathy, both psychological and artistic, with the African culture. Nothing signifies this better than the very style of the volume

– the grave measured and meditative tone of the poetry. "Masks" celebrates the life Brathwaite found in Africa, particularly among the Akan. Africa is depicted in this segment of the poem as a land of glorious past history, a land of worthy music, dance, ancestors, customs and, especially, religion.

In "Masks", Brathwaite makes use of the methods of traditional African poetry which account for his shifting personae and consequent modulation of tones and of the voice which is at once private and public. The more formal inheritance from African poetry includes his adaptation of the praise poetry, the lament, the dirge, incantatory verse, the curse and the abuse. Samuel Asein has identified the following lines as traditional (African) incantatory verse and compared them with the overture in Christopher Okigbo's ritual poem, "Heavensgate":

I who have pointed my face   tossed among strangers,
to the ships, the winds'   waves' whitest con
anger,   sonants, have returned
today have returned, eat-   where the stones

ing time like a mud-   give lips to the water:
fish; who was lost,   ("Bosompra" 136-137)

Brathwaite's "Masks" is a celebration of Africa. According to Asein:

> His intimate knowledge of the spiritual basis of African social organization is evident in the graphic representation of religious situations, relying on specific invocations of certain gods and deities, re-enacting rituals and stimulating sacrificial rites without losing the poetic vigour of his lines. (11)

"Libation" opens with a prelude of incantatory verse of prayer and invocation:

Nana frimpong
take the blood of the fowl
drink take the eto, mashed
plantain,
that my women have
cooked
eat

and be happy
drink
may you rest
for the year has come
around
again. (*Masks* 91-92)

This poetry is described by Kwabena Nketia as the kind that may be heard on social and ritual occasions (59). It is both secular and religious. "The Making of the Drum" concerns the sacrifices that sacramentalize ordinary objects in African life. "The Barrel of the Drum" is a celebration of the wood from which the drum is made:

Hard *duru* wood
with the hollow blood
 that makes a womb

...

You dumb adom wood

"The Skin" is an incantation about the goat whose skin will be used for the drum:

First the goat
must be killed
and the skin
stretched

will be bent,
will be solemnly bent, belly
rounded with fire, wound-
ed with tools. (*Mask* 95)

The two curved sticks of the Drummer Gourd and Rattles, The Gong-Gong, are among the various musical objects given a religious significance. "Atumpan" has an awakening motif. In the previous instance, Brathwaite gives evidence of his mastery of the traditional speech, mode of prayer and invocation as he invokes the spirit of the tree:

300

Funtumi Akore	We are addressing
Tweneboa Akore	you
Spirit of the cedar	Ye re kyere wo
Spirit of the cedar	Listen
tree	Let us succeed.
Tweneboa kodia	(*Masks* 99)
…	

Here, Brathwaite addresses himself to the spirit of the wood and not to a physical entity.

The next section of the poems is "The Pathfinders" – those poems that treat African heroes and places of the past. Before he proceeds to celebrate the tribes in sequence that is reminiscent of the epic catalogue, Brathwaite announces the sectional theme:

> summon the emirs, kings of the desert
> horses caparisoned, beaten gold bent,
> Archers and criers, porcupine arrows, bows bent;
>
> recount now the gains and the losses;
> Agades, Sokoto, El Hassan dead in his tent,
> the silks and the brasses, the slow weary tent
> ("Masks" 102)

This reveals that African history has been a betrayal of brother by brother, tribe by tribe, and it is discovered in the poems that Africans are partly responsible for their own enslavement by the Western world. "Pathfinders" treats the exploits of heroes and features of the important places of the past, like Chad and Volta. The poems are in form of praise songs.

"Islands", the final part of Brathwaite's trilogy, attempts a new stocktaking of the Caribbean man. It continues the religious mood and imagery of "Masks" by probing the possible ways in which God,

301

the remote fisherman, may be trying to gather his fish, the common people of the black Diaspora. Old bridges of song (spiritual, blues, work songs) collapse in the mechanized cities, but the primeval rhythm is not totally expunged; the Ananse tales are thin remnants of plenteous African mythology.

"Islands" is a demonstration of the black man's attempt, spiritually, to come to terms with his new world. It is also the rejection of European culture on one hand and the recognition and affirmation of his African roots on the other, all leading to the creation of a new identity within the new world context. As Abiola Irele observes,

> The return to the Caribbean scene in 'Islands' is ...prepared by a new awareness developed from the earlier phases of the poet's adventure. The most significant feature of this volume appears to the poet's insistence on the direct line of culture and spirituality that form the African antecedents of common folk to that overwhelming vigour of life and expression which is their special contribution to the heritage of the islands, to the identity of the Caribbean; it is certainly not too large a claim to state that the experience of "Masks" stands behind this insistence. (30)

"New World" which is the first sequence of poems in "Islands" is an invocation:

> Nairobi's male elephants uncurl
>   their trumpet to heaven
> Toot-Toot takes it up
>   in Havana
>   in Harlem
>   ("Islands" 162).

There is also a reference to music in this poem, which is Brathwaite's symbol for black creative inspiration. According to King, Jazz is used as an analogy for poetic art (7). Various allusions to Jazz musicians,

Jazz dances and Jazz styles offer an impression of the artist in the fallen world, symbolized by "New York, creating blues of the New World.

Section V of the sequence of the poems in *Islands* is called "Beginning". It is a form of new beginning or renewal. In these poems, Brathwaite rejects the imitation of European culture which he thinks should not be imitated dogmatically and goes further to suggest the restoration of African roots in the new world:

> Now waking
> making
> making
> with their
> rhythms some-
> thing torn
> and new ("Islands" 270).

"Islands" thus embodies self-knowledge and the eventual restoration of the black man in the New World.

It has been rightly observed that the motif of 'Africa' in Brathwaite's poetry has left us not only a historical but also literary legacy. This remark proves illuminating enough when we come to consider the poetry of Brathwaite. Although the Caribbean literature remains inevitably distinct in that it also draws heavily on its immediate social and geographical environment, the Caribbean writers often attempt a literary migration to African culture, norms, mores and artifacts. It is for this reason that the entire black literature, both African and Diaspora, are seen as a cohesive project.[1]

---

[1]IRCALC editors in their preface to the *Journal of African Literature and Culture* JALC, No. 3 argue for an "all-expansive African heritage in spite of regional or national groupings…" and aim towards "substantiating the cultural uniformity of Africa in terms of literary and cultural movements."

17

K Eke

Ce

CHIN Ce stands out as a prolific writer among the new generation of African writers. His creativity permeates many genres of literature. He has to his credit works of fiction such as *Children of Koloko* and *Gamji College* in addition to a full length novel *The Visitor*. Chin Ce also has three published volumes of poetry: *An African Eclipse*, *Full Moon* and *Millennial*. His essay "Riddles and Bash: The Creative Wit of Ala's Children" argues for the riddle in Africa as "a literary genre in its own right" (99) while in "Bards and Tyrants: Literature, Leadership and Citizenship Issues of Modern Nigeria" he parallels the "lacunae of imaginative thinking" in most Nigerians with "the vacuity of the leadership" (4).

However, this paper shall focus on the romantic sensitivity that runs through Chin Ce's *Full Moon* (abbreviated FM). One of the remarkable things about romantic poets is their interest in natural objects. Writing on romanticism, David Wright, states:

> Romantics elegize and idealize nature. Nature is seen by romantics

to be consoling or morally uplifting; a kind of spiritual healer... nature is invested with personality; human moods and moral impulses are seen reflected from it. (xv)

Wright's perception of the anthropomorphic nature of romantic poetry is striking. Seen against this background, the common denominator of such poets is their ability to treat natural objects as human beings as C.M. Bowra declares:

In nature all romantic poets found their inspiration. It was not everything to them, but they would have been nothing without it; for through it they found those exalting moments when they passed from sight to vision and pierced, as they thought, to the secrets of the universe. (13)

Bowra corroborates the idea of the romantics' great respect and admiration for nature. This group of poets believes that a moment with nature can generate visionary powers. What matters most is this interpenetration of human mind and nature. Although one of the dominant traits of the romantics is their intermingling of nature and mind, Abrams warns against the danger of perceiving them only in terms of their interest in nature and natural objects:

To a remarkable degree external nature the landscape, together with its flora and fauna became a persistent subject of poetry... (however) it is a mistake, to describe the romantic poets as simply "nature" poets. (116)

One of the most reliable critiques of romanticism is the celebrated William Wordsworth himself:

What does then the poet? He considers man and the objects that surround him as acting and re-acting upon each other, so as to produce an infinite complexity of pain and pleasure.....(258)

Thus Wordsworth, a major romantic, conceives of nature as serving two purposes: nature's dual role as a source of joy and sadness. As Wordsworth reveals, the common fact of romantic poets is to read meanings into landscape.

Chin Ce as a Romantic

One can hardly think of a poem in Chin Ce's *Full Moon* that is not connected with nature. Nature is the strongest element in his poems and it is the connecting thread running through them. Full Moon poetry is not so much a description of natural objects as of the feelings associated with them. In many of Chin Ce's poems there is a natural background, but they deal more with relationship between human mind and nature. One can therefore refer to the sensivity which runs through Chin Ce's poems as romantic.

His passionate desire for oneness with nature finds expression in the poem "In the Radiance" where Chin Ce finds delight in adoring the sun.

> My heart takes a leap
> When the warmth of your presence
> stirs the dying embers. (32)

A close reading of "In The Radiance" (FM 24) reveals the poet's technique of deliberately investing natural objects with human attributes:

> Which sparked and glowed
> in the wind.
> Strength filled with your loving breath
> my fire lights…(32)

307

The pleasure in nature is here depicted in his loving and minute description of the sun. These descriptions never move far from the natural object before him, and are the work of the most thorough observation. In the first place, there is a "leap" in the speaker's mind because of the "radiance" of sunset. The sun lives and works in real sympathy and fellowship with the human soul because of the warm light shining through. Besides, the radiant heat of the sun is said to stir "the dying embers" of the speaker's "heart." To discover the insight that the poem reveals requires careful reading and deep sensitivity. Chin Ce's rhetoric is highly metaphorical as he shows us a picture of dying fire. The purpose of this metaphor at this point is used to paint the depressing mood of the speaker. Through the evocative power of language, the fire that is burning low is likened to the speaker's low spirits. This method of comparing a low burning coal to the depressing mood of the speaker supports the statement that poetic creation "makes the stated fact appear in a special light" (Langer 536). However, the spirit becomes elevated from of the radiance and energy from the sun. The poem tries to show how the mind may be affected by the external world, signified by the sun. The sun, which is giving a warm bright light fills us with the spirit of gaiety, and leaves our mind in great happiness.

The poem "In the Radiance" conceptualizes the effects of a loving observation. As hinted earlier, the sun is alive, and not dead. It has not only life, but also feeling. It is a living being endowed with "loving breath". The sun is endowed not only with life and feeling, but also with the ability to build up "strength" in the speaker. Chin Ce gives to the sun features of humanity. Here we are not so much observers as lovers of nature. The sun does not exist by and for itself alone; it radiates and works on a scheme of interchange and mutuality with us. The radiance of the sunset does spiritually correlate with the moods of the speaker. To the sensitive mind the sun is a symbol of peace, order and joy. What strikes one forcibly in reading Chin Ce's poem is the anthropomorphic imagery that runs through:

> You tended this fire
> To dance in orange glows
> And now here's my light and life
> in the radiance of your eyes. (32)

The radiant sun imposes upon the mind, and we cannot but read spiritual or loving connotations in the sun's face. In the above, the spreading out of warm light is seen as an act of volition. Nature becomes to the speaker an inspirer of a passionate and comprehensive "love", a deep and purifying "joy". The poet conveys this to us through his art of suggestive power. Through the poet's imagination, one visualizes a pot in which a goldsmith is heating metals into gold. Just like a goldsmith is smelting metals into gold in a laboratory, the sun is said to be radiating "joy". In this connection, we cannot but agree with the statement that poetry is the use of "unorthodox or deviant forms of language" (Leech 136).

Further in what seems to be a deviation from the accepted norms, Chin Ce equates the sun to both a lover and a goldsmith.

> Flames
> Fed by the tinder
> of your love
> and smelted in life's blazing crucible
> for joy only pure and golden. (32)

There is "joy" to be found in natural objects, especially in the sun's "orange glow". This interaction between man and nature, or between lovers, is not merely an abstract thing, but something physically experienced. We become conscious of the world outside ourselves as a living, moving phenomenon. In particular, the radiance and dancing presence of the sun or a loved one are very therapeutic. They are means of associating the nature and primarily with peace, tranquility and joy. But, more importantly, is the speaker's sense of the correlative and intercommunicating force of the sun's radiance and the human mind.

"Jos"

The primary concern of another poem entitled "Jos" (FM 56) is the power of nature to move human spirit to joy. This intuitive turning to nature is the fundamental impulse behind this poem. Like many other romantic poets, Chin Ce derives his solace from the spirit of nature:

> I like to be like
> these rocks of the endless age
> crouched and slumbering
> in the Northern heat.(64)

The "rocks" are no longer mere natural objects, but a thing of vital and mysterious power, and an object of love. To produce the kind of pleasure which the poet speaks there has to be closeness, even a familiarity with these "rocks" in Jos, Nigeria. In these lines, there is evidence of an entirely new relationship with nature. To Chin Ce, the "rocks" have a strong organic unity with man, there are no borderlines and man becomes part of the rocks. Chin Ce, again, uses anthropomorphic imagery with startling effects. His imagination recognizes the life of natural objects and hence he decides to enter into a relationship with these rocks not just seen for their beauty, but for their ability to carry out such human activities as sleeping and crouching. By the personification of the rocks, the poet provides a transition to guide the reader from his innocent way of looking at

310

rocks to a manner of transcendentalism which he continuously celebrates. In the sleeping and crouching states of the rocks, the poet draws a source of inward joy, which could be shared by all human beings. Here this lofty feeling of intimate communion with nature is most expressed and much of our enjoyment of this poem comes from the recurrent anthropomorphism that extends to the second stanza:

> How long is your meditation
> You giants bored and
> (all around the greenery)
> barely seeing?(64)

Frequently the triumph of Chin Ce's art depends on the success of his investment of humanity on nature. The poet recasts the external world of the rocks only in order to get beyond it. He attempts to locate visionary power through their several layers. What makes the poem unique is that it expresses not mere outward beauty, but the meditative mood of the landscape. One is struck by the skill with which the poet draws the intellectual from the visual. So the rocks are not just seen for their giant nature, but for their ability to express some of the elusive truths and perceptions of the mind. Chin Ce projects into the landscape his own feelings and sentiments; his joy is transferred to natural objects. One of the pleasures of reading the poem lies in how the poet ascribes meditative abilities to the rocks. This being the case, we feel we can commune silently, privately and spiritually with nature. One may derive additional pleasure from reading the third stanza,

> Through seasons of wind and mist
> nothing can rile your colloquium
> grim monarchs
> with the clouds of guards above.(64)

311

and would very likely relate the poem to a relationship between man and nature. Thus Chin Ce's poem begins and ends with the appreciation of nature. The poet chooses particular words because of their richness of implication and their range of suggestion. It is the poet's firm belief that we can learn from nature wisdom and truth. In his imagery of the "rocks" as one large conference hall, the poet embodies the idea of nature as a teacher. This image serves more than a pictorial purpose. Rather, it indicates an attitude towards nature that includes a belief in nature's power to teach mankind. It is the study of nature, here represented by the rocks, that best brings out the inner life within us, that best suggests to us the worthy and the noble. Hence they are perceived as "monarchs". The rocks will teach us more than we can learn and men become wise as they make nature their teacher. To see nature in this light is the source of exuberant joy. One moment of communion with nature gives us much wisdom because they are rocks of "endless age". In describing the natural objects as beings in a seminar hall, the poet provides an index of his own happiness. This image is employed not only to stimulate our imagination, but also to convey romantic feelings. The poem sharpens our perception of the natural objects around us, showing us the happy interaction between mind and nature.

"Tenderly"

Chin Ce has great and engaging capacity for the adoration of nature. This is one of the most striking and persistent features of "Tenderly" (FM 40-42). The romantic poets have always been celebrated for their love of natural objects. "Tenderly" evokes the tender flight of swans with inexhaustible enthusiasm:

> The wind and tide shall rise

>   to her name, the swans
>   of the skies far as
>   Everest's cold peaks.(48)

The foregoing may seem only superficially about the rising tide of water and the windy atmosphere. The poet takes interest in the ebb and flow of the tide because it is close to the swans' natural habitat. In other words, the swans live in the immediate environs of water. So the poet looks minutely into the world of these birds, starting from their immediate environment. The bond between the "tide" and the "swans" is felt, not just expressed. The rising tide urges each swan to take a flight across the sky. Then as the "wind" starts to blow quite strongly, each swan can fly as high as Mt. Everest. The poet has been elevated into a state where he delights in the beauty of things that exist at the level where the swan lives. This symbiotic relationship between the birds and other natural objects, such as the wind and streams is what excites the speaker. The whole of nature still combine to make the "swans" happy as they perch on the mountaintop to

>   … rally round to beckon she
>   who dwells in a heart dancing
>   and swirling with the chirruping
>   birdling…(48)

These great moments are those in which the beauty of circular flights and melodious songs come alive. What the speaker experiences is a share of the birds' own happiness. For the world of the swan, the world of love, is full of beauty and joy. We attain a state of happiness through appreciating the flights and songs of nature. To the speaker, the swans have no part in misery, as they are seen either "dancing" or "chirruping" with joy. This is because it is common to see them swirling happily. While flying across the sky, they twist and turn in different directions and at varying speeds. This goes to

313

indicate that they are free from the stress of this world. He ascribes a state of perfect happiness to life. The melodious songs of the swan further heighten this state of happiness.

> The wind in her wings shall ride
> till the very end of time
> swinging in hearts
> that reach to heights of love. (49)

Here the swans flying in the winds fill the speaker with the spirit of happiness, and leave in his mind a joyful and permanent memory. The speaker looks at the flying swans as a source everlasting and spiritual refreshment. Thus from those lines we can best know that the birds are living a life of happiness.

If the poet is seen to speak of immediate joy in the presence of nature, the following lines make it as clear as possible:

> Only to light up the fire
> of my heart
> A shining aurora in my dreams. (49)

One cannot ignore the feelings concerning natural things, for they are not uttered casually, but frequently and consciously. One senses a probing curiosity into the workings of the mind that so beautifully compares to the happiness of nature. Anthropomorphic images are the elements or body of his poem. The whole frame of the poem is one, which suggests the happiness of the "brook", "tide" and "swans".

> The brook shall rise to join
> the tide
> when her radiance
> lights up the spheres. (50)

The poet's description of the natural world clearly derives from first-hand experience. At a point the field of reference moves from the physical world of the "swans" and other natural objects to the mental world of the poet.

> And my eyes shall see
> the glory
> of that tenderly soothing shimmering. (50)

There is the blending here of mind and nature. The feelings that nature arouses are one that all can enter into relationship with. This fitting of the individual mind to the world of nature is apparent in the word "aurora". This indicates how natural objects have vitalized the poet's spirit. It also indicates a luminous atmospheric phenomenon, which has helped to brighten up the poet's mood. The word aurora is used to illustrate the joy, which is embodied in the mind's responsiveness to the beauty of natural objects. Here, aurora stands apart in its emphasis on a symbiosis between the happiness of the swans and that of human kind. Chin Ce does idealise nature. To him, nature is one source and nourishment of our feelings and part of our being. Thus there is not a moment of any day of our lives when life (the "swans") is not producing "glory".

"Queen of the Night"

It would be correct to assert that Chin Ce's *Full Moon* is an affirmation that man can get all the happiness he needs from nature as revealed in "Queen of the Night" (FM 53-55). The pleasure that nature inspires is possible only in watching the Queen's "crescent" which is usually "calling forth in joy". This is a point of crucial importance for the appreciation of the poem. It is a vision of the

315

universal order of which the moon and flowers are parts of a landscape of joy. "Queen of the Night" is Chin Ce's attempts to reconcile the blossoming nature with that of man. One looks at the "full-rounding" of the moon and flowers as a kind of happiness one gains from nature. This is because when the flowers are in blossom it always "cast a golden spell" on human kind. In this context the "Queen" is an image of triumphant beauty.

The poem's strength of refreshment comes from its reminder of the "brimming" powers of the moon. This is capable of pouring "richly splendour/in many lives that hunger". These lines achieve their purpose, which is to emphasize that the air is always fragrant with scents from the "Queen". So the speaker's senses are open to the beauty of the moon's fragrance like flowers around him. This appeal to the senses of smell and taste is to show that nature seems to be actively beneficent to man. The "Queen" is definitely operating upon the speaker's sensibility, shaping it, making his mind fit to the external world:

> How I watched you brighten
> when cuddled in my bed
> my night with your luscious gazing
>
> Your light is warmth of my dream
> And the dark may look as day
> when coming out to pee
> To behold your full bright gaze. (62)

Here as elsewhere, one notices a process by which the objects seen in the landscape are invested with fragrance and brightness by the speaker's own mind. Man and nature, mind and the external world of flowers are geared together in unison. The "luscious gazing" of the flowers, illustrates that the speaker's mind is actively imposing a pattern upon the Queen. So there is peace of mind from the "light" and

316

sweet fragrance of the Queen. In this case, one can say that the Queen affects the mind, and the mind reciprocally affects the Queen. Besides, in presenting the Queen as "cuddling" on his bed, the speaker ascribes feelings and passions to her. This shows us how the world of the flowers and the human mind are harmoniously adapted to each other; so the great union of mind and nature is consummated.

"Night"

In "Night" (FM 15), there is genuine pleasure of feeling the freshness of the natural world. For the speaker there is joy to be found in the calmness of the night:

> The night is calm
> And commanding stillness reigns. (23)

Chin Ce continues with the practice of ascribing to natural objects human feelings and emotions. He does not see the external world as a dead matter, devoid of human attributes. In the poetic context, the night has a power, which can inspire love. The nocturnes are said to be peacefully at rest too.

> Even the crickets have slept
> Like tired children after moonlighting. (23)

This is to indicate that nightfall is the norm, a worldly paradise to which living things must return to regain their lost calmness.

> Out of my closet dances my dream
> joyfully
> I feel the radiant light of love
> Halo over my head. (23)

317

Moreover, the "commanding" ability of nightfall is an attempt to enable mankind to live in the material world by entering into harmony with it. Man is integrated and subservient to the powers and processes of nightfall. Man works in partnership with his environment. No poem better illustrates that there is harmony between the inner and outer, between mind and nature:

> And around my cheeks
> sweet swinging songs
> palpitate with the living breath
> And I can feel another life. (23)

There is evidence of an entirely new relationship with nightfall. Here the poet associates night with "love" both physical and spiritual.

> The night is the dawn
> of your never-ending love
> As it comes surrounding me. (23)

Nightfall radiates the type of beauty and pleasure that never changes. Besides, the "night" itself has become a living thing. In the poem delight springs from the fact that nightfall is able to breathe new "life" into the speaker. The night's breath and the breathing within the speaker, are brought together, and then interlinked. There is recognition of man's affinity with nature and the unifying spirit that runs through all things. This unity marks the attainment of inner peace. It therefore symbolizes permanence in the midst of change and decay.

Chin Ce expresses the permanence of natural beauty and its joys. In his poetry nature calmly fulfils herself forever.

18

MZ Malaba

Kahengua

KAVEVANGUA Kahengua is a leading Namibian poet and author of the volume entitled *Dreams*.[1] Kahengu's poetry book of *Dreams* has since been noted for its

> deep-rooted concern about human relationships, the plight of the poor battling to survive on the margins of post-colonial Namibian society and the struggle to maintain cultural values in times of political and economic transition.[2]

Most of the poems in *Dreams* date from 1984 to 2000. The later poems, that form the basis of this study, build on the themes outlined above, but adopt a more critical tone that reflects the author's alarm over the growing gulf between the haves and the have-nots. Namibia has the unenviable distinction of being one of the countries with the

---

[1]Kavevangua Kahengua. *Dreams*. Windhoek: Gamsberg Macmillan, 2002.

[2]See M.Z. Malaba. "Kavevangua Kahengua's Dreams". *Englishes: Contemporary Literatures in English.* No. 29, Anno 10, 2006, pp. 83 - 95.

largest income disparities in the world, a trend that seems set to continue.

Kahengua points to the selfishness that pervades the society in "Subjectivity", where narrow self-interest takes precedence over rising to the challenge of fashioning a mutually beneficial social contract:

> When we engage in discourses
> When we argue
> When we bargain for our views
> To prevail
> Subjectivity pervades
> The employer speaks for maximum profits
> The trade unionist defends the dead wood
> We all know consciously and subconsciously
> Subjectivity is irrational, when each party
> Defends its rationality
> We become pawns of circumstances
> Of survival, survival of the weakest for the strongest thrive
> It depends on whose subjectivity has prevailed
> Whose rhetoric has won by the end of the gruelling hour.

This ironic poem highlights the dogged defence of vested interests which, not only in Namibia but within the sub-region as a whole, masquerades as discussions over wages and conditions of service. The Darwinian notion of "the survival of the fittest" tips the scales in favour of the powerful – the "pawns", as the "weakest", will never "thrive"! The sad reality is that both, in the long run, are losers.

The soulless nature of capitalism is brought out in a poem that bears that title:

> I know capitalism
> It takes more

From us than
It gives
This ain't no mockery
Like a wrestler my sister has
Developed sinewy arms
As a result of carrying dishes
Serving rich customers
Where she *casuals*
Without benefits.

The exploitation of "marginal" people compounds their sense of powerlessness, their perception of leading undignified lives. The poem, however, hints that the day might arise when those who are taken advantage of as casual labourers could flex their muscles.

The city is most often portrayed as soul destroying, in Kahengua's poetry[3] and the satiric poem "Everybody Needs You" catalogues the various pressures the poor are subjected to:

Don't be ill
In the city you live on
Borrowed hopes
Borrowed money
Borrowed time
You prop the city not
Withstanding its massive
Weight of debts

The electronic device for
the privileged?
The TV which supposedly
Communicates knowledge,

---

[3]See, for example, "Old Man Walking" and "Here I want to live" in *Dreams*, op. cit., pp. 31, 12.

> Its document, its licence
> Will usurp your valuables
> As you sink into the
> Quicksand of Black
> Economic Impoverishment
> BEI.

Granted that some of these problems are self-imposed, but the extravagant gestures of the poor often reflect pathetic attempts at self-validation. A striking feature of Windhoek is the number of "micro-lenders", as loan sharks prefer to be known! The precarious existence of the needy is underlined by the oft-repeated line: "Don't be ill", since even "The medical insurance will/ suck you like a tick".

The self-serving nature of Black Economic Empowerment initiatives is caustically exposed in "Two Bees":

> Two bees
> One whose sting
> Has fatal venom
> Especially if you're allergic -
> This you can swat!
>
> The other bee
> Can inject economic power
> Into your blood
> Especially if you're...
> Sorry, I mean excuse me
> I mean to say if you're
> Black like me
> Though I'm not sure I'm black...
> Just soothe the pain
> Of the injection.

The poem focuses on the esoteric manner in which BEE initiatives have been implemented within the region (in South Africa and Zimbabwe, for example) in order to boost the well-connected, rather than as part of transparent affirmative action programmes. Crony capitalism has led to the downfall of many African nations, as avaricious cliques consolidate their grip on "economic power".

Municipal officials are also targets of Kahengua's satiric gaze, as seen in "Chief Inspector,"[4] where a "Private" is promoted to the rank of "Chief Inspector of Cracks," in order to ensure that the city is kept spotlessly clean, so that nothing "might harm our Esteemed/ Tourists". Rather than devote their energies to improving the welfare of the inhabitants of zinc shacks, the officials' priority is looking after "our Tourists of Honor".

The legacy of inequality is explored in the fascinating poem "From Within", which deals with the divisions between the rich and the poor:

> Down Nelson Mandela Avenue
> In Klein /Ae//Gams
> The affluent are privileged
> To live in the privacy of hills,
> Among the rocks
> Like rock rabbits
> Amid the silence of a cemetry.
> "BEWARE OF THE DOG"
> Snarls at me.
> From behind the fortress of walls
> Dogs bark at the sound of feet,
> Of the presumed poor intruder.
> The clack of the electrified fence
> Makes me an outright alien.
>
> Here down Nelson Mandela Avenue

---

[4] "Chief Inspector", *The African*. June/July 2005, p. 20.

In Klein /Ae//Gams
The chosen occupy large spaces
In accordance with the master plan
As laid down to ensure
The postcolonial continuum.

Here down Nelson Mandela Avenue
In Klein /Ae//Gams
The rich discard tidbits
Amounting to full plates
That tantalize the watering mouths
Of the poor.
Here housing is a status symbol
Here streets are wide
As highways,
Yet happiness is concealed in the privacy
Of mansions one wonders
What sins have their owners committed
To possess such riches!
Or whose labour have they exploited?

Down Bethlehem Avenue
In Katatura ke tu Our beloved
Katutura
In the midst of poverty
Adults chat animatedly
Children play cheerfully
Though days and nights are insecure.

Down Bethlehem Avenue
In Katutura ke tu
People like ants are huddled
In small places.
Here shelter is a basic need
Streets are as narrow

As elephants' trails.
People here lick plates filled with
Nothing
Yet their spirits are visibly exuberant,
Against the odds
The young are hopeful.

Kahengua has deftly woven complex emotions into this poem. The stark imagery of the opening stanza highlights the persona's sense of alienation in the "affluent" suburb with the deliberately hybrid name, which blends the German suburban name, Klein Windhoek with the Nama name for Windhoek. The hybrid brings to the fore the "mixed" nature of the Namibian "postcolonial" dispensation. The well heeled enjoy "the privacy of the hills", safely barricaded from the indigent by the "fortress of walls" and the "electrified fence", with dogs as the last line of defence. Ironically "Nelson Mandela Avenue" conjures up symbols of imprisonment, rather than liberation!

Yet the splendid isolation has its charms – the "privacy", the quiet environment, the measure of security which, like magnets, draw the new members of the elite. The segregation of the past, on the basis of race, is superceded by the new dividing line -wealth. The conspicuous consumption of the suburb contrasts sharply with deprivation of the township. The "alien" "intruder" initially discerns the "master plan" designed to shore up the economic divide between rich and poor, rather than lead the "masses" to the promised land, as revealed in the second stanza. Significantly then, he lapses into religious idioms to explain these divisions which suggest that social transformation is not possible. One may, however, argue that the change reflects a pragmatic acceptance of the fundamental principle of biblical economics: "To him who has will more be given." "Mansions", "sins", "wonders", call to mind the divine "master plan" which is deliberately "concealed" from human understanding pending the final revelation. Significantly, Bethlehem is associated with the lowly, "*In Katutura ke tu.*" The concluding verse of the hymn "O little town of Bethlehem" resonates with the images of joy and spiritual regeneration found in the last two stanzas of Kahengua's poem:

> O holy Child of Bethlehem
> Descend to us, we pray;
> Cast out our sin, and enter in;
> Be born in us today.
> We hear the Christmas angels
> The great glad tidings tell;
> O come to us, abide with us,
> Our Lord Immanuel.

The "intruder" feels more at home in "Bethlehem Avenue", which throbs with life, than in the "silence of the cemetery" he experiences "Down Nelson Mandela Avenue"; he identifies more with the "basic" shelters of the poor than with the "mansions" of the "affluent", despite the privations. Ironically the:

> Children play cheerfully
> Though days and nights are insecure.

The prevailing insecurity validates the ostentatious security that is the hallmark of Southern African suburban bliss -possessions are precious and, "From Within", the better-offs try to secure what they have painstakingly acquired through their "labour", as opposed to "sins"! Kahengua's wry humour points to the paradox of the relatively carefree existence of those who have "nothing".

"From Within" composed November 2002 and its hopeful concluding note contrasts markedly with the bleaker vision of "A Happy Poem" written in 2006:

My heart yearns
To write a happy poem
But my mind
Denies me the will

A happy poem
For the street children
Is a misfit.
Holding my gaze
Beyond the horizon
I see a bleak
Bleak future
In their eyes.

Kavevangua Kahengua's poetry reveals the poet's sensitive assessment of the perspectives of various sections of Namibian society. His ironic style seeks to reconcile "the hopes and fears" of different groups, by drawing attention to the structural inequality that lies at the heart of the nation, which urgently needs to be addressed in a bid to counter the "bleak/ Bleak future" he foresees.

19

F Orabueze

Enekwe

OSMOND Ossie Enekwe was born on 12th November, 1942 in Affa, Enugu State of Nigeria. He graduated from the University of Nigeria in 1971 with a Bachelor of Arts degree in English. He earned his masters and doctoral degrees from Columbia University, New York. He is a scholar and a prolific writer whose teaching experience spans several universities in two continents: America and Africa. His international reputation is primarily as a poet, but he is also a theatre scholar, director, musician and novelist.

Like the English Romantic poet, Blake, Enekwe was apprenticed to an artist but his longing for education propelled him to abandon that career for education. His competence in these several professions bears on his works, especially his poems. Today, his works are published in several local and international academic journals and books. Some of his poems, particularly those in his recent collection of poems, *Marching to Kilimanjaro*, are already in Tijan Sallah's *New Poets of West Africa*.

Enekwe's poems generally may be categorized into two. The

poems in *Broken Pots* are lamentations on the pointlessness of human suffering, and the consequences of war. The vision that man is essentially selfish is essentially that of Thomas Hobbes' in the *Leviathan*. Enekwe believes that this latent selfishness in man explodes into a destructive force during the physical and psychological trauma of war. The psycho-neurotic man can do anything: lie, cheat, steal, kill and main as long as he benefits from his actions. His former yardstick for the measurement of achievement and heroism has been eroded and replaced by a new gauge of violence and destruction.

Marching to Kilimanjaro his second collection constitutes Enekwe's second category of poems which, while still lamenting the man of violence and bloodbath, promise some rays of light at the end of the dangerous tunnel of life in which man is wayfarer. In *Marching to Kilimanjaro*, he advocates that the chains of bondage, servitude, humiliation, degradation, suppression and injustice must be broken by a bloodless revolution, where 'rockets' and 'bazookas' are replaced with new weapons: 'knowledge', 'intellection', 'work', 'love for truth and beauty'. The poet seems in agreement with Richard Wright's *Black Boy*, and William Blake's "The Tyger" that it is only through the power of knowledge 'burning bright/in the forests of the night' that broken humanity can overcome the unequal chasm that separates the mighty from the weak. It is only through this violence-free revolution that they can create an egalitarian society where all men will live in peace and love.

In *Marching to Kilimanjaro*, the poet following the footsteps of Ngugi Wa Thiong'o of Kenya, Ayi Kwei Armah of Ghana and a host of fellow visionary African literary artists, aims his satire with a clear view to a reformation of our tyrannical world system. All these men of letters in Africa unanimously agree that at the dawn of independence in every African country, black tin gods replaced white ones to unleash untold economic, social and political stagnation of the continent. One poet presents the situation thus:

> Freedom is strapped in cuffs again,
> Human rights crushed to dust.
> We're back to scratch
> Groping anew for freedom's light.
> (Olusunle "Rights" 51)

The African prose narrative is not left without a voice calling for an internal revolution to be led by Africa's marginal societies:

> Tomorrow it would be the workers and the peasants leading the struggle and seizing power to overturn the system of all its preying bloodthirsty gods and gnomic angels, bringing to an end the reign of the few over the many and the era of drinking blood and feasting on human flesh. Then, only then, would the kingdom of man and woman really begin, they joying and loving in creative labour... (*Petals* 344)

However Enekwe's own use of language is much more remarkable as a poet. His themes of his poetry are not divorced from their manner of portrayal. He brings to bear on his poems his mastery of different art forms: painting, theatre, directing and music. He describes people, things, places, situations and events with the minutest detail and vivid colours. He pays attention to details, whether in his description of the battered and shattered broken humanity in *Broken Pots* or the alienated, traumatized, and damned of the earth in *Marching to Kilimanjaro*. The lyricism of his poems and the use of artistic distancing have been eulogized. Sometimes reading Enekwe's poems *might* feel like reading William Blake in the vision that man can attain self-fulfillment if man-made obstacles are removed. They are both concerned with the underdogs, particularly the plight of children, in every society. They both use simple and descriptive language laced with imagery that stimulate different sense impressions. Enekwe, particularly, personifies objects, events and ideas and employs mythologies from diverse cultures to express his world-view. As H. G. Widdowson suggests, "At the heart of literary creation is the struggle to devise patterns of language which will bestow upon the linguistic items concerned just those values which will convey the individual writer's personal vision" (42).

Ossie Enekwe deviates from his predecessors who eulogized and romanticized Africa as an unadulterated continent until ravaged by slavery and colonialism. He is also not in the league of African poets who vehemently challenged racial discrimination against blacks in Africa and in the Western world, which is not to imply that Enekwe is immune to Western exploitation of his homeland and its brutality to the black race. In "Manhattan" (*Broken Pots*), he presents the face of racial discrimination and shows his disagreement with the city's emotionless treatment of blacks.

> Hate me every moment of your life
> So I can sleep in peace
> in your basements where mice
> and all uncivilized beings
> search for food in the ribs of the night.
> Give me white hate that yields itself day or night.
> Why should I sing for your love?
> me, a nigger-trash barking
> the bark of a black dog
> in a dark deserted alley. (37)

As stated earlier, *Broken Pots* concentrates on the pointlessness, the waste and loss, of war. The poet is not only dealing with the Biafran war, which he participated in as a young undergraduate. Whether the World Wars, Liberian civil war, Rwanda genocide or the war in Iraq, Enekwe's vision about war has a universal application.

The poem "Pot of Unity" is symbolic of the unity and preservative force that was lost in Nigerian nationhood. It was carried by leaders without a sense of direction, and this could only lead to its loss. Its first bearer 'faltered by the cliff' because he is perplexed by the 'groping populace' and his successor, being unsure of himself as he moves through the chaos created by his predecessor, stumbles and falls; the pot breaks and its content is lost. The journey motif that abounds in every literary culture illustrates the difficulty of holding a country together. The similes and personification in the poem do not hide the accusing finger that points to the hesitancy and injudiciousness of Nigerian leaders who lead the country to strife.

> Standing like an Iroko
> terror hit him in the face
> He stumbled and the blood-thirsty snakes
> trailed off to the four corners,
> boiling with venom. (35)

The civil consequence of the pot breaking and its content pouring out is that war engulfs all parts of the country. This must be the poet's apocalyptic admonition to emergent African countries that are basking in the euphoria of independence. The poet foresees that the new leaders have a Herculean task. In the opinion of Fanon, they owe their people a grave responsibility.

> Diplomacy, as inaugurated by the newly independent peoples is

not an affair of nuances, of implications, and of hypnotic passes. For the nations spokesmen are responsible at one and the same time for safeguarding the unity of the nation, the progress of the masses towards a state of well-being and the right of all peoples to bread and liberty. (61)

In the postcolonial state there is political, economic and social tension; there is the blatant exploitation some parts of the entity, and where there is the gross violation of the rights of citizens whose aftermath is uncontrollable violence that ends in war. The pot breaks and blood-thirsty snakes trail to the four corners carrying their venom.

Enekwe's poem "Shadows of Osiris" wonders whether supernatural powers or gods cause violence and wars. It explores this belief using 'Osiris', the Egyptian ruler of the dead and the underworld. In this myth, the god is supposed to die and resurrect in order to renew the fertility of the earth. However, in this poem, the god must demand human sacrifices to renew itself. Instead of the symbiotic relationship that exists in the original myth, the poet creates a parasitic relationship between earth and man. Human beings must be sacrificed for the earth to carry out its primary responsibility of renewing or fertilizing itself.

> Once in every season
> the earth that we feed
> and sit on
> asks for food
> and we hurry
> to do her will. (4)

The irony here is that man does not hesitate to carry out the wish of the gods. He wages ferocious wars with very dangerous weapons in battered and shattered battlefields. In the process of satisfying the demand of the supernatural force, he dies with his foes.

> Forget fear,
> fellow tillers
> of the soil,
> forget fear
> as we cut fangs and lead
> from the lungs, sharpen
> on the crooked stone
> the dull edges of our hearts
> and rush across tattered fields
> to meet our foes. (4)

We cannot but admire the poet's language which lyricism is brought about by the chiming or the alliterative /f/ in 'forget', 'fear' and 'fellows' and the repetition of 'forget fear' in two lines of the stanza. The soldiers are 'fellow tillers' and the devastated battlegrounds 'tattered fields'. These descriptions enunciate the suffering and abandonment associated with war. The fields are tattered because the youths who are supposed to till them are mowing down each other. Therefore, the image of a symbiotic relationship created in the first stanza vanishes in the second. There is a reversal of role as the earth now feeds off man instead of the other way round. As it swallows him up, man dies in the war as he 'cut fangs and lead' on his lungs.

In "Whatever Happened to the Memorial Drum", the poet continues with his idea of futility and waste involved in wars beginning with a roll call of heroes and villains from different climes, times and faith: Achilles, Caesar, Hannibal, Sulliman, Chaka, Churchill, Hitler and Napoleon. Nevertheless, he warns humanity that despite the eulogies and blames of history, war involved so much human wastage and destruction of all hopes.

> Wars came and men died.
> Hope rose, swayed and shat;
> soldiers marched, kissed the dust,
> and we made gods of them out of mud and copper. (10)

In "Broken Pots" where the collection derives its title, tales of his childhood and the rural environment paint the peaceful nature of his home which contrasts sharply with the violent humans that inhabit it.

> The heavy bosomed hill
> Lies close to our hut
> And the winding narrow path
> Stumbles into our farm.
> Up above where squirrels prance
> Or the little naughty birds twitter. (13)

The cold harmattan runs its fingers on their bodies 'like a drunken lover....' It is in this peaceable atmosphere that young virgins are won and their blood flows as a 'little fountain'. As the naïve or innocent narrator describes his childhood experience, the reader understands that the pot is not the earthenware for fetching water in rural communities. It symbolizes the loss of virginity and innocence, in extension, the loss of national aspiration for Nigeria. The 'broken pots' symbolize the agony of broken humanity, especially the youth whose dreams and aspirations are destroyed in war. This sequence continues in "Ripples of Apocalypse" which recollects a time when the people lived in unity.

> There was a time
> before the death of the Moon
> when apes lived in the forest,
> time when all the malignant things
> that crawl through grass and bushes
> passed indifferent to our cause. (19)

However, the harmony is lost when 'love was buried'. The end of love marks the beginning of anarchy. "But now all the demons have returned with hatchets and spades, and lizards sharpen their teeth on our sinews" (19). The consequence of this is the slaughtering of kinsmen and women, which he sarcastically calls 'a pogrom sweeter than orgasm'.

> For on that day, the rivers, even the mighty ones
> will turn to stone, and tress will rush like warriors
> across the wilds, the ivory beads around
> the necks of your maidens will turn to cobras. (19)

Enekwe's "No Way for Heroes to Die" seeks to immortalize Biafran war heroes. He borrows the roll calling sequence in Yeats's "Easter" to lament the ignominious treatment of heroes, Nzeogwu, Achibong and Atuegwu, whose corpses were defiled and not given a proper burial. Their demise 'foretells the apocalypse of a muscle-bound people'. The brutal killing and mutilation of their corpses violate the tradition of civilized societies and the principles enunciated in humanitarian law.

> Nzeogwu died like a lamb ripped apart by
> invisible claws,
> his body drawn in the dust that could not rise enough

337

to tell his people of his whereabouts.
Achibong's head dropped when a coward found heroism
in a hatchet chopping the head of a fallen soldier.
Atuegwu died in a dark cell while he waited for prosecution. (21)

A further point of consternation is neither in the unbefitting killing of heroes nor the defilement of their corpses left to the vagaries of weather, unmourned and uncelebrated, but that 'hungry historians and starving professors' have trivialized their cause by turning 'their resolve into folly'. Thus the lament that it is not the way for heroes to die.

It is doubtless that the poet struggles with language and imagery to communicate emotions that seem to overwhelm him. In the *Broken Pots* collection, he chronicles his personal experiences in that war and those of others he witnessed. As Edith Ihekweazu rather enthuses in her introduction to the volume of *Broken Pots*:

> Ossie Enekwe's poem, simple with few exceptions cannot be labelled as being influenced by any author or school. They are his very personal and own reactions to situations where ordinary language cannot absorb the shock of a shaking experience and where poetry is the rescuing medium. (iv)

The poet foregrounds his personal groping to find the words that adequately portray the degradation and brutalization of unsung heroes of the Biafran struggle for self determination. In the first stanza he laments:

Carcass of heroism stung by rainbows,
Stung till blanched, it was abandoned by flies
Femur and joint juggled by the wind....

These lines create images of abandonment and degradation of the bodies of fallen heroes. It was part of war barbarism that victims are deliberately left in the field for natural elements and insects to deal with them. The second stanza also continues with the issue of deliberate abandonment and humiliation of fellow human beings.

> their scattered bones jeer at the azure sky
> and snared at the masked terrors of rainbow
> Raindrops endow them with the colours
> until they dissolve in the perpetual
> moulding of the earth
> Where the worms that groan endlessly in the mud
> Tumble them through their guts.... (21)

In the third stanza the poet presents the violent and barbaric killing of three Biafran soldiers with terrible pictures of their violent end.

> Nzeogwu died like a lamb ripped by invisible claws his body drawn
> in the dust....
> Achibong's head dropped when a coward found heroism
> in a hatchet chopping the head of a fallen soldier
> 'Atuegwu died in a dark cell while he waited for
> prosecution. (21)

A conglomeration of epithets, 'carcass', 'abandoned by flies', 'scattered bones jeer' and 'sneer', 'worms that groan endlessly', 'disintegrate' 'ripped', 'invisible claws', 'drawn in the dust', 'hatchet chopping the neck' and 'died in a dark cell', create mental pictures of destruction, suffering, sorrow, abandonment, cruelty and barbarism. The poet has intentionally foreground his imagery to send a message to the reader on the barbarism and human wastage involved in the Nigerian Civil War.

In "The Defiant One", which he writes in memory of fellow poet, Christopher Okigbo, he praises the immortality of Okigbo's poetry despite the fact he was one of the unsung soldiers on the Biafran side.

> You lacked the drift
> of the aged smoke
> ubiquitousness in time
> and colour, despite drought
> and wreckage of the shrine. (22)

And in "To a Friend Made and Lost in War", the poet-persona painfully remembers the loss of a friend and fellow soldier. He recaptures the agonizing and traumatic experiences of the physical and spiritual journey to find a friend who had escaped death from enemy weapons in three different locations in the heart of Biafra only to be knocked down and hauled into a ditch by a 'hungry driver' in control of a 'tired truck'. Here again Enekwe succeeds in using clear diction to paint a horrendous picture of human suffering, despair, destruction and death. His knowledge of art brings to bear in his metonym the colour 'purple' for blood, and 'soul' for life. The engine of human life is the blood and soul and their escape from him means his death. The colour 'purple' also symbolizes the death of Mamman Vatsa, a poet and general of Nigerian army implicated in the botched attempt to topple the corrupt military regime of Ibrahim Babangida.

Further in "Mass for the Dead", the poet imprints a lasting impression on the reader's mind about the suffering and degradation of genocidal wars. In the lyrical persona's lamentation of the dead, the dying and living dead, the poet backgrounds the beauty and faithfulness of natural objects in contradistinction with human vagaries and bestiality at war. The persona describes the ill-clad, ill-fed, poorly dressed and tired soldiers marching to and fro with their weapons of mass destruction as nature continues with her eternal cycle, unmindful of the violence that human beings unleash on themselves.

> At sunset…
> bloated edges of humanity,
> abandoned mud forms of their mates,
> drift from the red horizon
> to march back tomorrow behind the Sun. (27)

Thus rather than being filled with serene, pastoral tranquility, the valley is filled with death as images of 'battered bells' that daily announce the demise of the youth, and a long line of malnourished people troop out to pray for soldiers dying in the battlefield and for themselves dying from starvation.

However, Ossie Enekwe cannot be described as a poet that celebrates only the dark side of life: the suffering, horror, barbarism and death seen in wars. He points out that despite human vices there is only one virtue that can heal the wound of wars: love can quench the fire of hatred, bitterness and negative emotions that kindle war. The reader gets a peep into this love in the poem "To a Friend Made and Lost in War." Here a fallen soldier's friends show him a rare act of friendship and love.

> We only wanted to identify your portion
> and stand over you awhile,
> at east to prove to you
> that you had friends. (24)

341

In postcolonial African countries, the ruling powers appropriate the wealth of the nations to themselves and their families to the exclusion of the rest of the country. "Homeless in the City" with its ironical title directs a bitter satire on the privileged class in every society, especially those in the industrialized and civilized countries of Europe and America. Enekwe shows himself as a humanitarian who is disturbed by the welfare of the poor and broken humanity. The poem starts with an apostrophe in the first line of the first stanza: 'See the great wonders of civilization'. The reader naturally expects the wonders of either ancient or modern civilization, but finds:

> Scavengers loose in the streets,
> Picking old clothes, cans and bottles
> Haunting for food
> in the anus of the city. (6)

Enekwe points out that modern man violates the basic or fundamental rights of other human beings. The destitute are the alienated and marginalized phenomena in industrialized, scientifically and technologically advanced, capitalist countries. This idea is advanced again in "Big Fish, Small Fish" where the poet directs his searchlight on the inequality that exists in modern human societies. The title is symbolic of the oppression and injustice that thrives in what ought to be an egalitarian society. Its four stanzaic refrain brings out the idea of a parasitic eco-system.

> Big fish eat small fish
> Big men, small men
> In the belly of the night. ("Sallah" 83)

Ossie Enekwe is undoubtedly a humanistic poet who is

sympathetic to our traumatized, alienated and broken humanity. Wars will end where there is friendship and love. There must be an internal revolution to end an unfair social and economic order. The missiles to be fired in the revolution are education and the appreciation of beauty and truth. In a language that is simple but replete with imagery he brings out his unique vision of life in a new and egalitarian world order where peace and love will prevail.

20

Cabral, Tcheka, Proenca, Ytchyana, Borges and Miller

GMT Emezue

WITH the publication by Heaventree Press in the United Kingdom of an anthology of Guinea-Bissau poetry, *Para Vasco; Poemas da Guiné-Bissau (For Vasco: Poems of Guinea Bissau)*, more light may have been thrown on the new literature of the youngest and poorest nation of West Africa. Ana Raquel Lourenço Fernandes et al, editors of the volume, explain their choice of Guinea-Bissau being 'first in ...series of anthologies of postcolonial poetry from Lusophone Africa' (*Poemas* 6) as the clear necessity for a 'greater awareness by the outside world of this Guinean national culture' (6). According to a record of statistics from the book of twelve poems 'only six extant books of poetry and one novel at the time of writing' (6) are available from that Lusophone African country where the collection *Poemas da Guiné-Bissau* derives. Hence a recent anthology of Guinea Bissau poetry is relevant in the context of African literature as illuminator of cultural, historical experiences of the people. As scholars from the Universities of

Birmingham and Warwick remark, more poetry shall yet be written of its epic 'dramatic national journey' (9) and the ultra nationalistic zeal of Amilcar Cabral in uniting the various ethnicities and eliminating the exploitation and division that characterised them.

Cabral

The poet of 'O último adeus dum combatente' ('The last adeus of a forest fighter') – Vasco Cabral – has been identified as 'the first Guinean intellectual' (7). Having fought in the war of independence to become vice president of the new nation, Vasco's poems are full of high patriotic sentiments. 'The last adeus' resonates with the age-old emotional pangs of parting, and the loyalty of the freedom fighter split between his personal and national interests. This choice, between which lies the distinction of higher and selfish human values, and as a question of commitment, naturally must fall to the triumph of the higher cause.

> That afternoon I left and you remained,
> we felt, us two, the *saudade*'s sorrow.
> I suffered the bloody truth of your tears.
> You're not my only happiness, *amor*,
> I left you there for love of Humankind. (12)

Like the South African resistance against white minority rule the Lusophone African struggle took a similarly organised but more intensive emotive configuration and this was mainly because of the relative smallness of the country and the organised guerrilla warfare which it had to contend with. All through the 1960s Amilcar Cabral conducted a war of liberation against Portugal and effectively controlled every part of Portuguese Guinea not occupied by the

Portuguese army (MERL 2003). The 'last *adeus*' points to this philosophy of the revolution in the temporary satisfaction and subsequent denial of self; the acceptance and separation from the comforts and yearnings of the body for the cause of communal liberty in which self sacrifice is nevertheless embedded in the hope of return.

> Believe I never will forget your love,
> and, if I am the one your love burns for,
> carry the hope that one day I'll return. (12)

Proenca

In the interaction of individual happiness and sadness, discovery and loss, it is thus not uncommon to find the expression of poetic thought and feelings as a missive in which the personal intimacy yields to a condition of inner peace in an otherwise uncertain and chaotic world. This yielding of understanding, intended to evoke the sense of comradeship and revolutionary sympathy, is as stable as the themes of love and sacrifice that run through the poetic universe of struggle, affirmation, invocation and hope. Helder Proenca's 'Uma carta para ti, amor' ('A letter for you, amour') seeks this replication of traditional themes through an intensive device of syntactic parallelisms.

> I want to march with you, *amor*
> ...
> I want, and only this way,
> to march strangely
> holding your waist
> ...
> I want, and only this way,

to listen to the melodies…(16)

Again as in the apartheid years of South Africa when the liberation chant of 'Amandla' recurred frequently in tune with the rejection of conditional freedom from Robben Island prison by Nelson Mandela in that famous speech, 'The struggle is my Life,' so between the Guinean and his love is there is no other way but 'only this way' – the way of struggle which endears the merger of personal and public responsibility. Since universal triumphs are won at the willing sacrifice of individual selves, 'the vigil' in the /stilled silence' equals the voluntary impairment or incarceration of selves while negotiating the difficult hurdles to political self determination. These nuances of sacrifice are equally apparent in the poem 'In memory of Kauh Nan Tungue' where the communality of poetry evidences the marriage of the universal and personal feelings as in the passionate ejaculation,

> I would, oh Mother Africa! feel
> the warmth of blood that gestated us
> in atmosphere of resistance and war. (20)

Hélder Proença's 'glorification of the liberation movement' (8) in not just an intimate 'sexual' sense flourishes in the association of personal intimacy with the wider cause, a corollary which imbues power and commitment to the vision; for the poetry of political liberation is infused in a deeper sense of history, of commitment to a collegiate vision, and of fulfilment that can only find some relevance in its actualisation of the general macrocosmic plan. Yet with a sense of the necessity of sacrifice springs up images of hope that sing of the 'pain time has not healed 'and of 'tomorrow's breeze,' a new smile 'that heralds the new day.' The evocation can only succeed in memories of bloody sacrifices, of the massacres of nationals in their struggle against colonial statutes, against foreign invaders, around which the violence of a whole continent is inscribed.

Tcheka

Tony Tcheka's 'Hino do dia novo' ('Hymn of the new day') can also be seen in the celebration and veneration of the struggle cast in a landscape of 'blossoming flower' and 'red carnations' while yet belonging to the younger generation of voices concerned with national rebuilding after devastating years of war. Significantly, all draw from the memory of the past in symbols of regenerative power and force:

> Let us go to Komo to regain strength
> …
> Let us go to Komo to drink at the same fountain
> where the first nameless freedom fighter
> drank his last drop.

Somehow it is not surprising to find womanhood cast in some of these verses as the ritual source of succour, and positive destiny as it were, in the days before colonial presence upturned local values and imposed its exploitative sexist and racial discriminations on the cultures of the continent. As Julião Soares Sousa's 'Saudade e Esperança' ('Saudade and Hope') testifies, the parallel of 'mother' and 'hope' coming in several repetitions is seen to simulate incantatory cadences that evoke the divining force of the uttered word in order to conjure the idea of survival in the face of continuing disappointments within the postcolonial state:

> I grabbed the sun and *saudade*
> I fought and lived in hope
> so the reluctant land
> would smile in hope
> my hope, Mother... (28)

In 'Cantos do meu País' ('Songs for my country') this postcolonial dialogue has taken the centre stage of the struggle, and the new clamour in that of disappointed sensitivity where the shackles of a native form of colonialism 'still restrain the motion' of national progress and the new victims are still the sacrificed peasantry.

Ytchyana and Borges

An acknowledgement of nativity is markedly resonant in Ytchyana's 'Para ti da tabanca' (For you from the Village') – a dedication to the purity of womanhood and to a peasantry whose 'feet (are) marked by sacrifice', 'hand(s) surrendering to the rhythm of hoes /chanting truth in times of rain' (34). The woman of the modern nation state is the 'suffer-woman, enslaved woman' (36) enslaved that is, by a new political equation that excludes her positive involvement. This is a condition which the poetry of Eunice Borges 'Mulher da minha terra' ('Woman from my Land') would seek to destroy in the cry of what being a woman is not. And the repetition of 'my people' becomes a formula for that constant reappraisal of art and society in agreement..

> To be a woman is not to be weak.
> To be a woman is not
> obeying without understanding
> following without knowing the way

giving without taking.
No! Woman from my land!
Come know what you're worth. (36)

Poetry for Lusophone Africa rightly remains a communal ritual where both the speaker and addressee are linked in a dialogue of forever seeking frontiers of exposition or understanding. Even for its being the first independent Lusophone Africa nation and yet ranking as the sixth poorest nation in the world, the objective of this collection, if nothing more than a new awareness in terms of creative, linguistic and cultural interest in a nearly forgotten part of the world, would have been sufficient honour for the poetic and visionary ideals of the people of Guinea-Bissau.

Miller

In *Kingdom of Empty Bellies*, a poetry collection by a Jamaican scholar, Kei Miller, attempts a poetic chronicle of an exploited humanity who, in the words of Jean Paul Sartre, are witnesses of how 'yellow and black voices still spoke of our humanism…only to reproach us with our inhumanity' (7). Divided in three parts that tend to demarcate its thematic searchlights, the first part tagged 'Church Women' appears mainly concerned with the religious fervour of converts who in membership and activity constitute mostly the world's ignorant and exploited womenfolk. Poems such as 'Caught Up', 'Off-Key', 'Tongues', 'Hallelujahs', and 'Mourning' belong in the first part and together form a passage through the religious or rather superstitious fervour of those 'wretched of the earth' whether at rural nativity or aboard the modern westernised train. The tornado of 'Tennessee' where even 'street lights (are caught up /in a cycle of worship' is cast in the manner of the fox huffing at their motel door

351

(17). In a few lines the poet captures the natural survival instincts (the spiritual fervour) of island experience in the strange milieu and where the poor folks have gone looking for something more than mere shelter.

With insight and wry humour, the chronicle in this first part experience in exile is both physical and spiritual. The values of the western world seem off key to an immigrant world of deeply religious signification for even the mildest of occurrences. Now the fellow convert of 'Off-key I' would not "believe a woman with squinted eyes could see/ Heaven and the Glory, much less reveal/ it to her" (24). There is a mild sense of culture shock arising from ignorance of other different yet common life ways which is apparent in the innocent prejudice of the church member.

> she did not like how
> the tiny woman, baton raised, would lead
> the choir to fold songs, crease them under
> then over, form them into peacocks
> or spiders. (24)

'Off-Key II' is also heavy with images of racial prejudice and discrimination whether on imperial British, French, American or an independent West Indian soil. The 'off-keys' of state persecution, police brutality and racial discrimination would cross distant borders to inflict scars upon our humanity.

> The police never knocked or shouted
> *Open Up!* or flashed their warrants;
> (things don't work like that here)
> just boots and the door collapsing
> a confused woman holding her nightie… (27)

For the 'wretched of the earth,' as Frantz Fanon puts it, religion had long become a means of escape, of reconciliation to one's impotence against state herding:

> That night the woman learned
> how to put Heaven in her voice
> how to prophesy – call down Armageddon,
> flood-water, twenty plagues on Babylon how
> to bawl down Jericho or sing *It Is Well*. (27)

– giving way to further enfeeblement, or re-interpretation of a reality that cannot be faced on its terms.

> even though the ground refuse to shake
> and the jail-walls don't turn to dust and the locks
> don't break – even though
> her son not coming out. (27)

In an eclectic Caribbean society, modern religion has endowed a legacy of public gossips:

> Beware of the church woman; her tongue
> sharp like serpent.
> …
> she will town-cry the soft secret rising
> in Martha's unmarried belly; (25)

of spiritual ignorance:

> gong-mouthed, she will call down
> Heaven-healing

> for the lewd cancer dancing
> inside Billy. (25)

laced copiously with prejudicial mythologies: "Beelzebub salivates on her tongue,/ disguising himself as God" (25).

In the odd alchemy of fervent religiosity, members 'combined /Jesus words with newspaper/ clippings' electrons of emotions 'bounced from filling /to filling, gathered in voltage,/ready to charge' mercilessly at the unrepentant victims of unbelief ('Hallelujahs'). We are thus in agreement with Fanon that 'at whatever level we study it, relationship – between individuals, …at cocktail parties, in the police– is quite simply the replacing of certain species of men by another 'species' (28). We are not left in doubt about the sardonic dimension of the first part of the poem appropriately tagged 'Church Women' for it is through the activities of these believers of ambiguous paradigms that the idea and message of true personal liberty is conveyed. This is made manifest by the magical possibilities of the succeeding part 'Dream Country.' One can note the subtle triumph of culture over artificial and poorly syncretic values of the Caribbean society. In 'Mourning' the church woman will wait 'for two shots /of white rum', she would discard the 'high heels /or the heavy linen dress, not made for movement' and then she will

> lift her elbows
> like scarecrow, knock her knees
> and dance and dance and oh lord
> him gone! (29)

The second section 'In dream Country' x-rays social existence of the downtrodden in the so-called dream country which the modern cities had come to represent for the majority of her immigrants looking for greener pastures. It is a slow tortuous road to a 'nowhere' existence where purpose has been effectively denied in the squalor and neglect under which the people are made to scrounge their daily existence. 'Granna's Eyes' captures this meaningless existence in poetic ballad.

The black community of Granna is a community of hunger and deprivation "where the cries of hungry pelicans/ echo inside our empty bellies" (38). In a way blackness has become synonymous with sadness bigger than the ocean, its wretched homelessness situation integrates with the bare living conditions under which women and children have lived out their lives without memory of anything better. The end of the sorrow in the destruction of the home ends in the usual wry humour of the poet's treatment of religious fervour in part one. The ocean of hunger and privation has its end in the imagination of the faithful *granna* who would walk to meet the rising flood, "her feet planted on two waves/ like Jesus" (42). The dream country is hence a city of atrophy and one filled with self hallucinatory otherness. This might easily pass as a work of magic realism which forecloses the fractured modernity, the vicious cycle of phases and losses without focus or consistency while pitched against the wearied longing for a positive change inured by visionless legacies.

The final section entitled 'Rum Bar Stories' takes us through the sleazy night life, the gossips and daily diversions of pub lovers and hard drinkers typical of western modernity, and after which the Third world cities of Africa and the West Indies are unimaginatively patterned. Part of the props of this society are the usual 'yellow pub' where "…Heineken/ banners sigh/ off the walls…(77)", and of "Tuesday jazz/ singer who dug clean purple notes/ out of cancers" (76). The world of Rum bar stories is a pleasant make-believe in night clubs that offer an escape from the harsh social realities of the outside

355

world as the new Caribbean writer chronicles, through the sharp, concise, and acute detonations of poetry, a contemporary third-world society unabashed in its candour and mockery of modern civilisations.

BIBLIOGRAPHY OF WORKS CITED

Section A1.

Chapter 1

POSTCOLONIAL VOID: ACHEBE, VASSANJI, WA THIONGÓ

Works Cited

Achebe, Chinua. *Things Fall Apart*. London: Heinemann, 2000.

Adejumobi, Saheed Adeyinka. "Neocolonialism." *Encyclopedia of Postcolonial Studies*. Ed. John C. Hawley. Westport: Greenwood, 2001.

Fanon, Fritz. "On National Culture." *The Wretched of the Earth*. New York: Grove, 1963. 206-48.

Feroza Jussawalla and Reed Way Dasenbrock (eds). *Interviews with Writers of the Post-Colonial World*. Jackson: UP of Mississippi, 1992. 25-41.

Ngugi wa Thiong'o. *Weep Not, Child*. London: Heinemann,1987.

Patke, Rajeev S. "Frantz Fanon (1925-1961)." *Encyclopedia of Postcolonial Studies*. Ed. John C. Hawley. Westport: Greenwood, 2001.

Vassanji, M.G. *The In-Between World of Vikram Lall*. New York: Knopf, 2004.

Chapter 2

COUNTER DISCOURSE: COETZEE

Works Cited

Achebe, Chinua. *Things Fall Apart*. London: Heinemann, 1958.

– – – ."The Novelist as Teacher." *New Statesman*, 1965. 160-170.

– – –.*Hopes and Impediments: Selected Essays, 1965-1987*. London Heinemann, 1988.

Ashcroft, B, G Griffiths and H. Tiffin. *The Empire Writes Back: Theory and Practice in Postcolonial Literatures*. New York: Routledge, 1989.

– – –.*The Postcolonial Studies Reader*. London: Routledge and Kegan Paul, 1995.

Attridge, Derek. "Oppressive Silence: J.M Coetzee *Foe* and the Politics of the Canon." *Decolonizing the Tradition: New View of Twentieth-Century "British" Literary Canons*. Ed. Karen Lawrence. Urbana: University of Illinois Press, 1992. 212-238.

Attwell, David. *J.M Coetzee – South Africa and the Politics of Writing*. California: University of California Press, 1993.

Bhabha, Homi. "The Commitment to Theory." *New Formations*. 5.1988. 1-19.

– – –. *The Location of Culture*. London: Routledge, 1994.

Blyden, Edward Wilmot. *Christianity, Islam and the Negro Race*. Chesapeake, New York: ECA, 1990.

Cary, Joyce. *Mister Johnson*. New York: Harper, 1951.

Chinweizu; Onwuchekwa Jemie and Ihechukwu Madubuike. *Toward the Decolonization of African Litearture*. Enugu: Fourth Dimension, 1980.

Coetzee, J.M (1986). *Foe*. London: Secker and Warburg, 1986.

– – –. "Two Interviews by Tony Morphet 1983 and 1987." *Triquarterly*. No 62, 1987. 454-464.

Defoe, Daniel. *Robinson Crusoe*. London: Penguin, 1994.

Emenyonu, Ernest. "Nationalism and the Creative Talent." *Goatskin Bags and Wisdom New Critical Perspectives on African Literature*. Ed. Ernest Emenyonu. Trenton: Africa World Press, 2000. 377-386.

– – –. "Telling Our Story: A Keynote Address at the 15th International Conference on African Literature and the English, Language (ICALEL)." University of Calabar, Nigeria. May 7-11, 2002.

Fanon, Frantz. *Black Skin, White Masks*. New York: Grove Press, 1967.

– – –. *The Wretched of the Earth*. Trans. Farrington Constance, Harmondsworth, Middlesex: Penguin, 1970.

Foucault, Michel. *Power/Knowledge: Selected Interviews and Other Writings, 1972-1977*. Ed. Colin Gordon, Brighton: Harvester, 1980.

Gallagher, Susan. *A Story of South Africa: J.M Coetzee's Fiction in Context*. London: Harvard University Press, 1991.

Jameson, Fredric. "Third-World Literature in the Era of Multinational Capitalism." *Social Text*. 15. 1986. 65-88.

JanMohammed, Abdul R. *Manichean Aesthetics: The Politics of Literature in Colonial Africa*. Amherst: U of Massachusetts P, 1983.

Korang, Kwaku Larbi. "An Allegory of Rereading: Post-Colonialism, Resistance and J.M Coetzee's *Foe*." *Critical Essays on J.M Coetzee*. Ed. Sue Kossew. New York: G.K Hall and Co., 1998.180-197.

Kossew, Sue. "Introduction." *Critical Essays on J.M Coetzee*. Ed. Sue Kossew New York: G.K Hall, 1998.1-17.

– – –. "The Politics of Shame and Redemption in J.M Coetzee's *Disgrace*." *Research in African Literatures*. 34. 2. 2003.155-162.

Lomba, A. *Colonialism/Post-Colonialism*. London: Routledge and Kegan Paul, 1998.

McVeagh, John. "The Blasted Race of Old Cham, Daniel Defoe and the African." *Ibadan Studies in English*, 1. 2, 1969. 85-109.

Milner, Andrew and Jeff Browitt. *Contemporary Cultural Theory- An Introduction*. London: Routledge, 1991.

Nagy-Zekmi, Silvia. "Tradition and Transgression in the Novels of Assia Djebar and Aicha Lemsine." *Research in African Literatures*, 33. 3. 2002.1-13.

Ngugi, wa Thiong'o. *Homecoming.* London: Heinemann, 1972.

– – –. "Europhonism, Universities and the Magic Fountain: The Future of African Literature and Scholarship." *Research in African Literatures.* 31. 1. 2000.1-22.

Osundare, Niyi. *African Literature and the Crisis of Post-Structuralist Theorizing.* Ibadan: Options Books, 1993.

Palmer, Eustace. *Studies on the English Novel.* Ibadan: African University Press, 1986.

Penner, Dick. *Countries of the Mind: The Fiction of J.M Coetzee.* Westport, Connecticut: Greenwood, 1989.

Preckshot, Judith. "An Historical Obsession: Counternarration in Rachid Mimouni's *Tombeza.*" *Research in Africa Literatures,* 34.2. 2003.155-162.

Rodney, Walter. *How Europe Underdeveloped Africa.* London: Boyle-L'ouverture Publishers, 1972.

Rushdie, Salman. "The Empire Writes Back with Vengeance." *London Times* July 1982: 334-45.

Said, Edward W. *Orientalism. New* York: Pantheon Books, 1978.

– – –.*The World, the Text and the Critic.* Cambridge: Harvard UP, 1983:31-53.

– – –. "Intellectuals in the Post-Colonial World." *Salmagundi.* 70. 71, 1986:44-66.

– – –."Representing the Colonized: Anthropology's Interlocuters." *Critical Inquiry*, 15.3 (1989):205-225.

– – –. *Culture and Imperialism.* London: Chatto and Windus, 1993.

Schipper, Minneke *Imagining Insiders: Africa and the Question of Belonging.* New York: Cassell, 1999.

Spivak, Gayatri Chakravorty. "Theory in the Margin: Coetzee's *Foe* Reading Defoe's *Crusoe/ Roxana.*"*English in Africa.* 17.2.1990: 1-23.

– – –."Can the Subaltern Speak?" *Colonial and Post-Colonial Theory.* Patrick Eds. Williams and Laura Chrisman. New York: Columbia UP, 1994. 66-111.

Tiffin, Helen. "Post-Colonial Literatures and Counter-Discourse." *KUNAPIPI,* 9. 3, 1987.17-34.

Valdiz, Moses M. "Caliban and his Precursors: The Politics of Literary History and the Third World." *Theoretical Issues in Literary History.* Ed. David Perkins. Cambridge: Harvard UP, 1991. 206-226.

Viola, André. "J.M Coetzee: Romancieur Sud Africaine." *Journal of Commonwealth Literature.* L' Harmattan. 6, 1999. 69-78.

Walder, Dennis. *Post-Colonial Literatures in English History, Language, Theory.* Oxford: Blackwell, 1998.

Zukogi, Maikudi Abubakar. "The Post-Colonial Text as Counter-Discourse: A Re-reading of Armah's *Two Thousand Seasons.*" A Paper Presented at the 15th International Conference of African Literature and the English Language (ICALEL), University of Calabar, Nigeria. May 7-11, 2002.

Chapter 3

FEMALE SILENCING: ANDREAS, HEAD, VERA

Works Cited

Andreas, Neshani. *The Purple Violet of Oshaantu*. Oxford: Heinemann, 2001.

Baumann, Hermann. *Schöpfung und Urzeit des Menschen im Mythus der Afrikanischen Völker*. Berlin: Dietrich Reimer, 1964.

Braidotti, Rosi. "Mothers, Monsters, and Machines." *Writing on the Body: Female Embodiment and Feminist Theory*. Ed. Katie Conboy et al., New York: Columbia UP, 1997.

Case, Dianne. *Toasted Penis and Cheese*. Wynberg: Kwagga, 1999.

Cixous, Hélène. "The Laugh of the Medusa." *Feminisms: An Anthology of Literary Theory and Criticism*. Ed. Robyn R. Warhol and Diane Price Herndl. New Brunswick: Rutgers UP, 1997.

Duras, Marguerite. *La pluie d'été*. Paris: POL, 1990.

Eppel, John. "Suffering and Speaking Out." *The Zimbabwean Review* 3.3 1997.

Gray, Stephen. "The Unsayable Word." *Mail & Guardian* Mar. 1997.

Head, Bessie. "Life." *The Collector of Treasures and other Botswana Village Tales*. Ed. Bessie Head. Oxford: Heinemann, 1992.

— — —. "The Collector of Treasures." *The Collector of Treasures and other Botswana Village Tales*. Ed. Bessie Head. Oxford: Heinemann, 1992.

— — — . *Maru*. Oxford: Heinemann, 2000.

Hoogestraat, Jane. "'Unnameable by Choice': Multivalent Silences in Adrienne Rich's Time's Power." *Violence, Silence, and Anger: Women's Writing as Transgression*. Ed. Deirdre Lashgari. London: UP of Virginia, 1995.

Leibowitz, Stacey, et al. "Child Rape: Extending the Therapeutic Intervention to Include the Mother-Child Dyad." *Southern African Journal of Psychology* 29.3 1999.

Mills, Alice, and Jeremy Smith. *Utter Silence: Voicing the Unspeakable*. New York: Peter Lang, 2001.

Phiri, Virginia. *Desperate*. Harare: Virginia Phiri, 2002.

Samuelson, Meg. "'Grandmother Says We Choose Words, Not Silence': Trauma, Memory and Voice in the Writings of Yvonne Vera." MA thesis. U of Leeds, 1999.

— — —. "Reclaiming the Body: A Memory for Healing in Yvonne Vera's Writing." A Symposium on Zimbabwean Literature: Scanning Our Future, Reading Our Past. U of Zimbabwe, Harare. 1-12 Jan. 2001.

— — — . "A River in My Mouth: Writing the Voice in Under the Tongue." *Sign and Taboo: Perspectives on the Poetic Fiction of Yvonne Vera*. Ed. Robert Muponde and Mandivavarira Maodzwa-Taruvinga. Harare: Weaver Press, 2002.

— — — . "Re-membering the Body: Rape and Recovery in Without a Name and Under the Tongue."*Sign and Taboo: Perspectives on the Poetic Fiction of Yvonne Vera*. Ed. Robert Muponde and Mandivavarira Maodzwa-Taruvinga. Harare: Weaver Press, 2002.

Shostak, Marjorie. Nisa: *The Life and Words of a !Kung Woman*. Cambridge, Massachusetts: Harvard UP, 2001.

Signori, Lisa F. *The Feminization of Surrealism: The Road to Surreal Silence in Selected Works of Marguerite Duras*. New York: Peter Lang, 2001.

Stone, Elena. *Rising from Deep Places: Women's Lives and the Ecology of Voice and Silence*. New York: Peter Lang, 2002.

Stories of Courage Told by Women. Women's Shelter Project 2000. Gaborone: Lightbooks, 2001.

Trinh, T. Minh-ha. "Not You/Like You: Postcolonial Women and the Interlocking Questions of Identity and Difference." *Dangerous Liaisons: Gender, Nation & Postcolonial Perspectives*. Ed. Anne McClintock, et al. London, Minneapolis: U of Minnesota P, 1997.

Veit-Wild, Flora. "Gebrochene Körper: Körperwahrnehmungen in der kolonialen und afrikanischen Literatur." *Fremde Körper: Zur Konstruktion des Anderen in europäischen Diskursen*. Kerstin Gernig. Ed. Berlin: dahlem UP, 2001. 337-355.

Vera, Yvonne. *Nehanda*. Harare: Baobab Books, 1993.

— — — . *Without a Name*. Harare: Baobab Books, 1994.

— — — . *Under the Tongue*. Harare: Baobab Books, 1997.

— — — . *The Stone Virgins*. Harare: Weaver Press, 2002.

Vigne, Randolph, (ed.) *A Gesture of Belonging: Letters from Bessie Head, 1965-1979*. London: SA Writers, 1991.

Watzlawick, Paul. *Wie wirklich ist die Wirklichkeit? Wahn, Täuschung, Verstehen*. München, Zürich: Piper, 1998.

Wicomb, Zoë. *David's Story*. Cape Town: Kwela Books, 2000.

Chapter 4

WRITING BACK: ACHEBE, DANGAREMBGA

Works Cited

Achebe, Chinua. "The African Writer and the English Language." *Chinua Achebe's Things Fall Apart: A Casebook*. Ed. Isidore Okpewho. Oxford: Oxford UP, 2003. 55-65.

– – – ."An Image of Africa." *The Massachusetts Review* 18.4 1977. 782-794.

– – – .*Things Fall Apart*. 1958. Oxford: New Windmills-Heinemann, 1971.

Adam, Ian and Helen Tiffin, eds. *Past the Last Post: Theorizing Post-Colonialism and Post-Modernism*. New York: Harvester Wheatsheaf, 1991.

Adams, David. *Colonial Odysseys: Empire and Epic in the Modernist Novel.* Ithaca: Cornell UP, 2003.

Aegerter, Lindsay Pentolfe. "A Dialectic of Autonomy and Community: Tsitsi Dangarembga's *Nervous Conditions.*" *Tulsa Studies in Women's Literature* 15.2 1996. 231-240.

Appiah, Kwame Anthony. *In My Father's House: Africa in the Philosophy of Culture.* New York: Oxford UP, 1992.

Ashcroft, Bill, Gareth Griffiths and Helen Tiffin. *The Empire Writes Back: Theory and Practice in Post-colonial Literatures.* London: Routledge, 2002.

Ashcroft, W.D. "Intersecting Marginalities: Post-colonialism and Feminism." *Kunapipi* 11.2 1989. 23-35.

Beckham, Jack M. "Achebe's Things Fall Apart." *The Explicator* 60.4 2002. 229-231.

Begum, Khani. "Construction of the Female Subject in Postcolonial Literature: Tsitsi Dangarembga's *Nervous Conditions.*" *Journal of Commonwealth and Postcolonial Studies* 1.1 1993. 21-27.

Boehmer, Elleke. *Colonial and Postcolonial Literature*: Migrant Metaphors. New York: Oxford UP, 1995.

Booker, Keith M. *The African Novel in English: An Introduction.* Portsmouth: Heinemann, 1998.

Briault-Manus, Vicki. "The Interaction of 'Race' and Gender as Cultural Constructs in Tsitsi Dangarembga's *Nervous Conditions.*" *Commonwealth Essays and Studies* 26.2 2003. 23-32.

Carroll, David. *Chinua Achebe: Novelist, Poet, Critic.* Basingstoke: Macmillan, 1990.

Cobham, Rhonda. "Problems of Gender and History in the Teaching of Things Fall Apart." *Chinua Achebe's Things Fall Apart: A Casebook.* Ed. Isidore Okpewho. Oxford, Oxford UP, 2003. 165-80.

Coroneos, Con. *Space, Conrad and Modernity.* Oxford, Oxford UP, 2002.

Dangarembga, Tsitsi. *Nervous Conditions.* New York: Seal, 1989.

Darby, Phillip. "Postcolonialism." *At the Edge of International Relations: Postcolonialism, Gender and Dependency.* London: Pinter, 1997. 12-32.

Davies, Carole Boyce. "Motherhood in the Works of Male and Female Igbo Writers: Achebe, Emecheta, Nwapa and Nzekwu." *Ngambika: Studies of Women in African Literature.* Ed. C. B. Davies and Anne Adam Graves. Trenton: Africa World, 1986. 241-56.

Dodgson, Pauline. "Coming in From the Margins: Gender in Contemporary Zimbabwean Writing." *Post-Colonial Literatures: Expanding the Canon.* Ed.

Deborah L. Madsen. London: Pluto, 1999. 88-103.

Eagleton, T. Criticism and Ideology: *A Study in Marxist Literary Theory.* London: Verso, 1976.

Gandhi, Leela. *Postcolonial Theory: A Critical Introduction.* Sydney: Allen & Unwin, 1998.

Gikandi, Simon. "Chinua Achebe and the Invention of African Culture." *Research in African Literatures* 32.3 2001. 3-8.

Goonetilleke, D.C.R.A. *Joseph Conrad: Beyond Culture and Background.* Basingstoke: Macmillan, 1990.

Harris, Michael. *Outsiders & Insiders: Perspectives of Third World Culture in British and Post-Colonial Fiction.* New York: Peter Lang, 1992.

Harrow, Kenneth W. *Thresholds of Change in African Literature: The Emergence of a Tradition.* Portsmouth: Heinemann, 1994.

Hawkins, Hunt. "Conrad and the Psychology of Colonialism." *Conrad Revisited: Essays for the Eighties.* Ed. Ross C. Murfin. Alabama: Alabama UP, 1985: 71-87.

Hogan, Patrick Colm. "Culture and Despair: Chinua Achebe's *Things Fall Apart.*" *Colonialism and Cultural Identity: Crises of Tradition in the Anglophone Literatures of India, Africa and the Carribean.* Albany: State U of New York P, 2000: 103-35.

Huggan, Graham. "African Literature and the Anthropological Exotic." *The Post-Colonial Exotic: Marketing the Margins.* London: Routledge, 2001. 34-57.

Innes, C.L. " A Less Superficial Picture: Things Fall Apart." *Chinua Achebe.* Cambridge: Cambridge UP, 1990. 21-41.

Jameson, Fredric. "Third-World Literature in the Era of Multinational Capitalism." *Social Text* 15, 1986. 65-88.

Jeyifo, Biodun. "Okonkwo and His Mother: *Things Fall Apart* and Issues of Gender in the Constitution of African Postcolonial Discourse." *Chinua Achebe's Things Fall Apart: A Casebook.* Ed. Isidore Okpewho. Oxford: Oxford UP, 2003. 181-99.

Kalu, Anthonia C. *Women, Literature and Development in Africa.* Trenton: Africa World, 2001.

Katrak, Ketu H. "Decolonizing Culture: Towards a Theory for Postcolonial Women's Texts." *Modern Fiction Studies,* 35.1 1989. 157-79.

King, Pamela. 'Like painting, Like music...': *Joseph Conrad and the Modernist Sensibility.* Brisbane: Pamela King, 1996.

Knowles, Owen and Moore, Gene M. *Oxford Reader's Companion to Conrad.* Oxford: Oxford UP, 2000.

Kortenaar, Neil Ten. "How the Centre is Made to Hold in *Things Fall Apart.*" *Postcolonial Literatures: Achebe, Ngugi, Desai, Walcott.* Ed. Michael Parker and Roger Starkey. Basingstoke: Macmillan, 1995. 31-51.

Linton, Patricia. "Ethical Reading and Resistant Texts." *Post-Colonial Literatures: Expanding the Canon.* Ed. Deborah L. Madsen, London: Pluto, 1999. 29-44.

McClintock, Anne. "The Angel of Progress: Pitfalls of the term 'Postcolonialism'." *Colonial Discourse/ Postcolonial Theory.* Ed. Francis Barker, Peter Hulme and Margaret Iversen. Manchester: Manchester UP, 1994. 253-66.

Miller, Christopher. *Blank Darkness: Africanist Discourse in French.* Chicago: U of Chicago P, 1985.

Nnoromele, Patrick C. "The Plight of a Hero in Achebe's *Things Fall Apart.*" *College Literature* 27.2, 2000. 146-56.

Nzenza, Sekai. "Women in Postcolonial Africa: between African men and Western Feminists." *At the Edge of International Relations: Postcolonialism, Gender and Dependency.* Ed. Phillip Darby. London: Pinter, 1997. 214-35.

Ogungbesan, Kolawole. "Politics and the African Writer." *Critical Perspectives on Chinua Achebe.* Ed. C.L. Innes and Bernth Lindfors, London: Heinemann, 1979. 37-46.

Okhamafe, Imafedia. "Genealogical Determinism in Things Fall Apart." *Genealogy & Literature.* Ed. Lee Quinby. Minneapolis: U of Minnesota P, 1995. 134-154.

Osei-Nyame, Kwadwo. "Chinua Achebe Writing Culture: Representations of Gender and Tradition in Things Fall Apart." *Research in African Literatures* 30.2 1999. 148-62.

Osei-Nyame, Jnr., Kwadwo. "The 'Nation' between the 'Genders': Tsitsi Dangarembga's *Nervous Conditions.*" *Current Writing: Text and Reception in Southern Africa* 11.1 1999. 55-66.

Pelikan Straus, Nina. "The Exclusion of the Intended from Secret Sharing in Conrad's *Heart of Darkness.*" *Novel* 20.2 1987. 123-37.

Povey, John. "The Novels of Chinua Achebe." *Introduction to Nigerian Literature.* Ed. Bruce King, New York: Africana Publishing Corporation, 1972. 97-112.

Quayson, Ato. "Feminism, Postcolonialism and the Contradictory Orders of Modernity." *Postcolonialism: Theory, Practice or Process?* Cambridge:

Polity, 2000. 103-131.

Rowell, Charles H. "An Interview with Chinua Achebe." *Chinua Achebe's Things Fall Apart: A Casebook.* Ed. Isidore Okpewho. Oxford, Oxford UP, 2003. 249-272.

Said, Edward. *Orientalism.* Harmondsworth: Penguin, 1985.

Schwartz, Nina. "The Ideologies of Romanticism in Heart of Darkness." *Dead Fathers: The Logic of Transference in Modern Narrative.* Ann Arbor: U of Michigan P, 1994. 31-54.

Skinner, John. *The Stepmother Tongue: An Introduction to New Anglophone Fiction.* New York: St. Martin's, 1998.

Spivak, Gayatri. "Can the subaltern speak?" *Marxist Interpretations of Culture.* Ed. Cary Nelson and Lawrence Grossberg, Basingstoke: Macmillan, 1988. 271-313.

Stratton, Florence. "How Could Things Fall Apart For Whom They Were Not Together?" *Contemporary African Literature and the Politics of Gender.* London: Routledge, 1994. 22-38.

Strobel, Susanne. "Floating into Heaven or Hell? The river journey in Mary Kingsley's Travels in West Africa and Joseph Conrad's *Heart of Darkness.*" *Being/s in Transit: Travelling, Migration, Dislocation.* Ed. Liselotte Glage. Amsterdam: Rodopi, 2000. 69-82.

Sugnet, Charles. "Nervous Conditions: Dangarembga's feminist reinvention of Fanon." *The Politics of (M)othering: Womanhood, Identity, and Resistance in African Literature.* Ed. Obioma Nnaemeka. London: Routledge, 1997. 33-49.

Suleri, Sara. "Woman Skin Deep: Feminism and the Postcolonial Condition." *Contemporary Postcolonial Theory: A Reader.* Ed. Padmini Mongia, London: Arnold, 1996. 335-46.

Tiffin, Helen. "Post-Colonial Literatures and Counter-Discourse." *Kunapipi* 9.3 1987. 17-34.

Traoré, Ousseynou B. "Why the Snake-Lizard killed his mother: inscribing and decentering "Nneka" in Things Fall Apart." *The Politics of (M)othering: Womanhood, Identity, and Resistance in African Literature.* Ed. Obioma Nnaemeka. London: Routledge, 1997. 50-68.

Uwakweh, Pauline Ada. "Debunking Patriarchy: The Liberational Quality of Voicing in Tsitsi Dangarembga's *Nervous Conditions.*" *Research in African Literatures* 26.1 1995. 75-84.

Veit-Wild, Flora. "'Women Write About the Things that Move Them.' A Conversation with Tsitsi Dangarembga." *Moving Beyond Boundaries,*

Volume 2: Black Women's Diasporas. Ed. Carole Boyce Davies, London: Pluto, 1995. 27-31.

Vizzard, Michelle. "Of Mimicry and Women: Hysteria and Anticolonial Feminism in Tsitsi Dangarembga's *Nervous Conditions.*" *SPAN.* October 1993. 202-10.

wa Thiong'o, Ngugi. *Decolonising the Mind: The Politics of Language in African Literature.* London: James Currey, 1986.

Watts, Cedric. "'A Bloody Racist': About Achebe's View of Conrad." *Yearbook of English Studies* 13 1983. 196-209.

Wren, Robert M. *Achebe's World: The Historical and Cultural Context of the Novels of Chinua Achebe.* Essex: Longman, 1981.

Wright, Derek, ed. "Introduction: Writers and Period." *Contemporary African Fiction.* Bayreuth: Bayreuth U, 1997. 5-15.

Yeats, W.B. "The Second Coming." *The Norton Anthology of Poetry. 4 ed.* Ed. Margaret Ferguson, Mary Jo Salter and Jon Stallworthy, New York: Norton, 1996. 1091.

Yegenoglu, Meyda. *Colonial fantasies: Towards a feminist reading of Orientalism.* Cambridge: Cambridge UP, 1998.

Chapter 5

CHILD HEROES: OYONO, WA THIONGÓ

Works Cited

Melone, Thomas, *Chinua Achebe et la Tragedie de I'Histoire,* Paris, Presence Africaine, 1973.12,77, 149.

Ngugi Wa Thiong'o, *Weep not, child,* Heinemann, 1962.

Ferdinand, Oyono *Houseboy,* London: Heinemann 1966,

Laye, Camara. *Une vie de boy. Paris:* Editions Julliard, 1956.

Robert, Marthe, *Roman des Origenes, Origenes du Roman.* Paris: Gallimard, 1972.

Chapter 6

FREE WOMEN: LOPES

Works Cited

Beyala, Calixthe. *C'est le soleil qui m'a brûlée.* Paris: Stock, 1987.

– – – . *Maman a un amant.* Paris: Editions, 1993.

Houque, Patrick. 'La femme, l'érotisme, le sacré.' *Eve, Eros, Elohin,* Paris: Denoel, 1982.

Evé, Mère. 'Chanson Savon Reward'. 25 Nov. 2005

<http://www.congopage.com>

Biaya, T. K. 'La culture urbaine dans les arts populaires d'Afrique: Analyse de l'ambiance zaïroise,' *Canadian Journal of African Studies* 30. 3, (1996): 345-370.

Dictionaire Suka Epoque. Lingala-Français. www.lingala utilisation dictionnaire.htm, 2007.

Gondala, Ch. Didier. 'Amours, passions et ruptures dans l'âge d'or de la chanson congolaise.' *Afrique cultures* 25 Nov. 2005 <http://www.africulture.com>

James, Jennifer. 'Prostitution.' Microsoft Student 2007 [DVD], Redmond, WA: Microsoft Corporation, 2006.

Lopes, Henri. *Dossier Classé*. Paris: Editions du Seuil, 2002.

– – –. *La Nouvelle Romance*. Yaoundé: Editions Clé, 1976.

– – –. *Le Chercheur d'Afriques*. Paris: Editions du Seuil, 1990.

– – –. *Le Lys et le Flamboyant*. Paris: Editions du Seuil, 1997.

– – –. *Le Pleurer-rire*. Paris: Présence africaine, 1982.

– – –. *Sans Tam-tam*. Yaoundé: Editions Clé, 1977.

– – –. *Sur l'autre rive*. Paris: Editions du seuil, 1992.

– – –. *Tribaliques*. Yaoundé: Editions Clé, 1971.

Obitaba, Erguonona. 'Prostitution in African Francophone Feminist Literature.' *Feminism in Francophone African Literature*. Ed. Sam Ade-Ojo Ibadan: Signal Educational, 2003. 208-235.

Ohlmann, Judith Sinanga. 'La Femme chez Calixthe Beyala et Henri Lopes: Objectivation et sublimation du corps.' Dans Nouvelles Études Francophones, 21.1. 2006.

Osazuwa, Simeon. *La dialectique du tragique et du comique dans Le Pleurer-rire d'Henri Lopes*. Thèse de maîtrise es Arts de l'université de Laval, Sainte-Foy, Québec, 1984.

Osazuwa, Simeon. 'Women Emancipation in the Work of Henri Lopes.' *Feminism in Francophone African Literature*. Ed. Sam Ade-Ojo, Ibadan: Signal Educational, 2003. 97-109.

Ridehalgh, Anna. *ASCALF Bulletin* 5. 1992. 19-20.

Robert, Paul. *Le Petit Robert*. Paris, Nouvelle Edition, 1978.

Sembene, Ousmane. *Les Bouts de bois de Dieu*. Paris: Présence Africaine, 1960.

Zanzi, Jean-Pierre Bwanga, Ndombezya, Olivier Nyembo et Mulunda, Nicodème Bondo. 'Des particularités lexicales et des emprunts dans l'œuvre romanesque de Zamenga Batukezanga' <http://www.unice.fr|ILF-

367

CNRS|ofcaf|21|Bwanga.pdf>

Chapter 7

TRADITION VS MODERNITY: CE, LAYE

Works Cited

Buckley, Hamilton Jerome. *Seasons of Youth. The Bildungsroman from Dickens to Golding.* Cambridge: Harvard University Press, 1974.

Ce, Chin. "Bards and Tyrants: Literature, Leadership and Citizenship Issues of Modern Nigeria." *African Literary Journal* B5 2005. 19 Dec. 2006.<http://www.africaresearch.org/Bards.htm>

– – –. *Children of Koloko* (PDF). Enugu: Handel Books Ltd., 2001.

Courlander, Harold. *A Treasury of African Folklore.* New York: Crown Publishers Inc., 1975.

Deleuze, Gilles, Felix Guattari. *Anti-Oedipus: Capitalism and Schizophrenia.* Trans. Robert Hurley, Mark Seem and Helene R. Lane, Athlone Press, 2000.

Emerson, Ralph Waldo. *Nature. American Literature* 1. Ed. William E. Cain. New York: Pearson Education Inc., 2004. 477-515.

Ewane, Kange F. *Semence et moisson coloniales: Un regard d'africain sur l'histoire de la colonisation.* Yaounde: Editions CLE, 1985.

Grants, Amanda. "Memory, Transition and Dialogue: The Cyclic Order of Chin Ce's Oeuvres." *Journal of African Literature and Culture.* IRCALC 2006. 11-29.

Jiménez, Deicy. Camara Laye's *"The Dark Child*: The undecided world of a mental mulatto." *LA CASA DE ASTERIÓN* 5.19 Barranquilla: Oct.-Nov.-Dec. 2004. 15 May 2006. <http://casadeasterion.*homestead.com /v5n19dark.html*>

Laye, Camara. *The Dark Child.* Trans. James Kirkup & Ernest Jones, New York: The Noonday Press, 1994.

Ngugi, wa Thiong'o. *Homecoming.* London. Heinemann, 1972.

Okolie, Maxwell. "Childhood in African Literature: A Literary Perspective." *Childhood in African Literature.* Eds. Eldred Durosimi Jones & Marjorie Jones. Oxford: James Currey Ltd., 1998. 29-35.

Plomer, William. "The Dark Child: The Autobiography of an African Boy by Camara Laye." *Current Concerns* 4 (2004). 25 Oct. 2005. http://www.currentconcerns.ch/archive/2004/04/20040414.php

Tala, Kashim Ibrahim. "The Critical Ideological Possibilities of African Orature." *Epasa Moto*. Vol. 1 No. 2. Eds. Etienne Ze Amvela & Charles Atangana Nama. Buéa: University of Buéa Press, Jan. 1995. 155-169.

Wood, Allen W. "Hegel on Education." *Philosophy as Education*. Ed. Amélie O. Rorty. London: Routledge, 1998. 1-28.

Chapter 8

CULTURAL TRANSLATION: AIDOO, ONWUEME

Works Cited

Aidoo, Ama Ata. *The Dilemma of a Ghost*. *Modern African Drama*. Ed. Biodun Jeyifo, New York: Norton, 2002. 242-275.

Azodo, Uzoamka Ada. "*The Dilemma of a Ghost*: Literature and Power of Myth." *Emerging Perspectives on Ama Ata Aidoo*. Ed. Ada Uzoamaka Azodo and Gay Wilentz. Trenton, NJ: Africa World Press, 1999. 213-240.

Bartlett, Juluette F. *Promoting Empowerment for Woman: Women between Modernity and Tradition in the Works of Tess Onwueme*. Diss. University of Houston, May 2002.

Bhabha, Homi K. "The Third Space: Interview with Homi K. Bhabha." *Identity: Community, Culture, Difference*. Ed. Jonathan Rutherford. London: Lawrence & Wishcart, 1990. 207-221.

Brown, Lloyd W. *Women Writers in Black Africa*. Westport, Connecticut: Greenwood Press, 1981.

Chamberlain, Lori. "Gender and the Metaphorics of Translation." *The Translation Studies Reader*. Ed. Lawrence Venuti. London: Routledge, 2000. 315-329.

Dunton, Chris. *Make Man Talk True: Nigerian Drama in English since 1970*. London: Hans Zell, 1992.

Elder, Arlene A. "Ama Ata Aidoo: The Development of a Woman's Voice." *Emerging Perspectives on Ama Ata Aidoo*. Ed. Ada Uzoamka Azodo and Gay Wilentz. Trenton: Africa World Press, 1999: 157-169.

Eveirthoms, Mabel I. E. *Female Empowerment and Dramatic Creativity in Nigeria*. Ibadan, Nigeria: Caltop Publications, 2002.

Gourdine, Angeletta KM. *The Difference Place Makes: Gender, Sexuality and Diaspora Identity*. Columbus: Ohio State University Press, 2002.

– – –. "Slavery in the Diaspora Consciousness: Ama Ata Aidoo's Conversations." *Emerging Perspectives on Ama Ata Aidoo*. Ed. Ada Uzoamka Azodo and Gay Wilentz. Trenton: Africa World Press, 1999: 27-

369

44.

Gyimah, Miriam C. "The Quest for Power and Manhood: Three (Neo) Colonial Male Characters of Ama Ata Aidoo." *Journal of African Literature and Culture*. 1.3 2006.

Lakoff, George and Mark Johnson. *Metaphors We Live By.* Chicago: UCP, 2003.

Odamtten, Vincent. *The Art of Ama Ata Aidoo: Polylectics and Readings Against Neocolonialism.* Gainesville, Florida: University Press of Florida, 1994.

Onwueme, Osonye Tess. *Legacies.* Ibadan: Heinemann Nigeria, 1989.

– – – . *The Missing Face.* San Francisco: African Heritage Press, 2002.

Rushdie, Salman. *Imaginary Homelands: Essays and Criticism 1981-1991.* London: Granta, 1991.

Trivedi, Harish. "Translating Culture vs. Cultural Translation." *www.91stmeridian.org.* May 2005 <http://www.uiowa.edu/~iwp/91st/may2005/index.html.>

Uko, Iniobong I. *Gender and Identity in the Works of Osonye Tess Onwueme.* Trenton, NJ: Africa World Press, 2004.

Chapter 9

REWORKING THE CANON: OSOFISAN

Works Cited

Adéyemi, Solá. "The Dictating Currents and the Questioning of Tyranny in Africa: an intertextual study of Fémi Osófisan's Yungba-Yungba and the dance contest." Mots Pluriels 13, 2000.11 Jan 2007 <http://www.arts.uwa.edu.au/MotsPluriels/MP1300sa.html>.

Amkpa, Awam. *Theatre and Postcolonial Desires.* London: Routledge, 2004.

Armstrong, Robert, Plant. "Tragedy –Greek and Yoruba: a Cross-Cultural Perspective." *Research in African Literatures* 7.1. 1976. 23-43.

Austen-Peters, Omale. "The Mytho-historical Base of Electre and Morountodun." *Humanities Review Journal* 3.1. 2003. 29-36.

Awodiya, Muyiwa P. "Form & Technique in Fémi Òsófisan's Plays" *African Literature Today 20*, 1996: 102-119.

Bal, Mieke. *Travelling Concepts in the Humanities: A Rough Guide.* Toronto, Buffalo, London: University of Toronto Press, 2002.

Boedeker, Deborah and Raaflaub, Kurt A. *Democracy, Empire and the Arts in Fifth-Century Athens.* Cambrdige, Mass.: Harvard University Press, 1999.

Brown, Wendy. *Politics out of History*. Princeton and Oxford: Princeton

University Press, 2001.

Chakrabarty, Dipesh. *Provincializing Europe*. Princeton and Oxford: Princeton University Press, 2000.

Crow, Brian. "African Metatheater: Criticizing Society, Celebrating the Stage." *Research in African Literatures* 33.1 2002. 133-143.

Crow, Brian and Banfield, Chris. *An Introduction to Post-Colonial Theatre*. Cambridge: Cambridge University Press, 1996.

Dunton, Chris. *Make Man Talk True, Nigerian Drama in English Since 1970*. New York: Hans Zell Publishers, 1992.

Frank, Haike. *Role-Play in South African Theatre*. Bayreuth African Studies 70. Bayreuth: Pia Thielman and Eckhard Breitinger, 2004.

Gibbs, James. "Antigone and After Antigone: Some Issues Raised by Femi Osofisan's Dramaturgy in Tegonni." *Portraits for an Eagle: Essays in Honour of Femi Osofisan*. Ed. Sola Adeyemi. Bayreuth African Studies 78. Bayreuth: Pia Thielman and Eckhard Breitinger, 2006.

Gilbert, Helen and Tompkins, Joanne. *Post-Colonial Drama: Theory, Practice, Politics*. London: Routledge, 1996.

Onwueme, Tess Akaeke. "Òsófisan's new Hero: Women as Agents of Social Reconstruction." SAGE V.1 (1988): 25-28.

Òsófisan, Fémi. "Ritual and the Revolutionary Ethos: The Humanist Dilemma in Contemporary Nigerian Theatre." *Okike 22* 1982. 72-82.

– – –. "Reflections on Theatre Practice in Contemporary Nigeria." *African Affairs* 97.386. 1998. 81-89.

– – –. "'The Revolution as Muse': Drama as Surreptitious Insurrection in a Post-Colonial, Military State." *Theatre Matters: Performance and Culture of the World Stage*. Eds. Richard Boon and Jane Plastow. Cambridge: University Press, 1998.

– – –. *Tègònni: an African Antigone*. Recent Outings: comprising Tègònni: an African Antigone *and* Many Colours Make the Thunder-King. Ibadan: Opon Ifa Readers, 1999.

– – –. "Theatre and the Rites of 'Post-Negritude' Remembering." *Research in African Literatures* 30, 1999. 1-11.

– – –. *The Nostalgic Drum: Essays on Literature, Drama and Culture*. Asmara (Eritrea) & Trenton (NJ): African World Press, Inc., 2001.

Raji, Wumi. "Africanizing Antigone: Postcolonial Discourse and Strategies of Indigenizing a Western Classic." *Research in African Literatures* 36.4 2005.135-154.

371

Richards, Sandra. L. *Ancient Songs Set Ablaze: The Theatre of Femi Òsófisan*. Washington DC: Howard University Press, 1996.

Sophocles. *Antigone*. Trans. Reginald Gibbons and Charles Segal. Oxford: Oxford Univeristy Press, 2003.

Spivak, G. Chakravorty. "More on Power/Knowledge." *Outside in the Teaching Machine*. London: Routledge, 1993.

Steiner, George. *Antigones: The Antigone Myth in Western Literature, Art and Thought*. Oxford: Oxford University Press, 1984.

Tiffin, Helen. "Post-colonial literatures and counter-discourse." *Kunapipi* 9.3 1987. 17-34.

Wetmore Jr., Kevin J. *The Athenian Sun in an African Sky: Modern African Adaptations of Classical Greek Tragedy*. Jefferson, North Carolina, London: McFarland & Company, 2002.

– – –. *Black Dionysus: Greek Tragedy and African American Theatre,* Jefferson, North Carolina, London: McFarland & Company, 2003.

Chapter 10

CONFLICT AND TURMOIL: UWAYS

Works Cited

al-Adīb al-Sūdānī: Ahmad al-Mubārak 'Isā (ed) A. M. Ahmad Khartūm: Dār Izza, 2007.

A. al-Jurjāni: *Dalāil al-'Ijāz* ed. R. Rashid 3rd ed. Cairo; 1946.

– – –. *Asrār al-Balāgāh* Ed. H. Ritter Istanbul, 1954.

al-Amīn: "Is-ām al-Mar'ah al-Sūdāniyah fī majālat al-Ilmī wal 'Amal" in *al-Mar'ah wa al-Ibdā' fī al-Sūdān* (Khatrum: Markaz al-Dirāsāt al-Sūdāniyah al-Dawliyah, 2001.

al-Hajj, T.U: *Tatawur al-Mar-ah al-* Sūdāniyah *wa Khusūsiyatiāh* Khartūm, 2007.

al-Azmeh. A: *Ibn Khaldun* American University Press, 1982.

al-Musawi. Muhsin: *The Postcolonial Arabic Novel: Debating Ambivalences* Leiden: E.J Brill, 2003.

al-Nahdah al-Sūdaniyyāh Khartoum 255, 1945.

Abu Deeb. Kamal: *al-Jurjāni's Theory of Poetic Imagery*. England: Aris and Phillips Ltd., 1979.

Abdul. M. K: "Mustafa's Migration from the Said: An Odyssey in Search of Identity." *Middle Eastern Literature* 10.1998.

Achebe, C: "The Novelist as Teacher" *African Literature: An Anthology of Criticism and Theory*. Ed. T. Olaniyan and A. Quayson, Oxford: Blackwell:

2007.

Adonis: *An Introduction to Arab Poetics.* Trans. C. Cobham. London: Saqi Books, 2003.

Ahmed. A. M: "Multiple Complexity and Prospects for Reconciliation and Unity: The Sudan Conundrum." *The Roots of African Conflicts: The Causes and Costs.* Ed. Alfred Nhema and Paul Tiyanbe Zeleza. Ohio: Ohio University Press, 2008.

'Ajūba. Mukhtar: *al-Qiah al-Qaīrah fī al-Sūdān* Khartūm: Dār al-Tālif wa Tarjamah, 1972.

Amyuni, M. T: "The Arab Artist's Role in the Soceity: The Three Case Studies: Naguib Mahfouz, Tayeb alih and Elias Khoury." *Arabic and Middle Eastern Studies* Vol. 2 No. 2 1999.

Antonius. G: *The Arab Awakening: The Story of the Arab National Movement* New York: Capricorn Books, 1946.

Bakhtin M: *The Dialogic Imagination: Four Essays* Ed. Michael Holquist trans Caryl Emerson and Michael Holquist Austin: U. of Texas Press, 1981.

Bhabha, H: *Nation and Narration* London: Routledge1990.

Bickford, S: "Beyond Friendship: Aristotle on Conflict, Deliberation and Attention." *Journal of Politics.* 28.2. 1996.

Birnbaum, L. C: *dark mother: African Origins and godmothers.* San Jose: Universe, 2002.

Deng, F. M: Scramble for Souls: Religious Intervention among the Dinka in Sudan." *Proselytization and Communal Self Determination in Africa.* Ed. A. Na'im, New York: MaryKnoll, 1999.

– – –. *Africans of Two Worlds: The Dinka in the Afro-Arab Sudan.* Yale: Yale University Press, 1978.

Effendi, Abdel Wahab: "Discovering the South:" Sudanese Dilemma for Islam in Africa." *African Affairs.* 89.1990.

Fanon, Frantz. *The Wretched of the Earth.* New York: Grove Press 2004.

– – – . *Black Skin White Mask.* New York: Grove Press, 1967.

Eibner, John: "My Career Redeeming Slaves." *Middle East Quarterly,* December 1999.

Foucault. A. M: *The Care of the Self: The History of Sexuality.* New York: Vintage Books, 1988.

Jacobson. R: *Language in Literature.* Ed. Krystyna Pomorska and Stephen Rudy, Cambridge: The Belknap Press, 1987.

Jameson, F: *The Political Unconscious: Narrative as a Socially Symbolic Act.* Ithaca: Cornell UP, 1981.

Hafez, Sabry: The Transformation of Reality and the Arabic Novel's Aesthetic Response." *Bulletin of the School of Oriental and African Studies, University of London* 57. 1. 1994.

Les Temps Modernes. 1.1 Oct., 1954.

Muhammad, A. *Nafathāt al-Yarā' fil Adab wa tārīkh wa' Ijtimā'* Khartūm; 1958.

Mazrui, Ali. "The Multiple Marginality of the Sudan." *Sudan in Africa*. Ed. Yusuf F. Hasan, Khartoum: Khartoum University Press 1971.

– – –. "Africa and Islamic Civilization: the East African Experience." *Islamic Civilization in Eastern Africa*. Ed. A.B Kasozi, Istanbul: IRCICA 2006.

– – –."Authority Versus Sexuality: Dialectics in Woman's Image in Modern Sudanese Narrative Discourse." *Hawwa* 2.1 2004.

– – –."*al-Sud*" "African Fiction: Rethinking Ayi Kwei Armah and Ihsan Abdul Quddus" *Journal of Oriental and African Studies*, Vol. 40, 2005.

– – –."Themes and Styles in Arabic Short Stories in Sudan 1930-2000." Ph. D thesis, University of Ibadan, 2001.

Prunier, A: *DarFur: The Ambiguous Genocide*. New York: Ithaca, 2005.

Nuseibah, Hakim Zaki: *The Idea of Arab Nationalism*. Ithaca: Cornell University Press, 1958.

Said, Edward: *Beginnings: Intention and Method*. New York: Columbia University Press, 1985.

– – –.*The World, the Text and the Critic*. Cambridge: University of Massachusetts, 1983.

– – –.*Culture and Imperialism*. London: Chattos and Windus, 1993.

Ṣālih al-Tayyib: *Mawsim al-Hijrah ilā Shimāl* Beirut: Dār al-'Awdah, 1969.

– – –."Nahw Ufuq Ba'īd" *al-Majallat*, No. 758. August, 1989.

Radhakrishnan, R: "Nationalism, Gender and Narrative of Identity." *Nationalities and Sexualities*. Eds. A. Parker, M. Rusco, D. Sommer and P. Yaiger, New York: Routledge, 1992.

Trinh. T, M: *Woman Other, Native Other: Writing Postcoloniality and Feminism* Bloomington; Indiana UP, 1989.

'Uways, Khalid I: *al-Ruqs taht al-Maar*. Khartūm: 2001.

Women and Law in Sudan: Women's seclusion in Private and Public life Sudan, Women and Law Project, 1999.

Chapter 11

SURREALISM IN DIASPORA: Bessora

Works Cited

Adamowicz, Elza. "Ethnology, Ethnographic Film and Surrealism."

Anthropology Today, Vol. 9, No. 1 (1993).

Adiaffi, Jean-Marie. *La carte d'identité*. Paris: Hatier, 1980.

Bessora, *53 cm*. Paris: Serpent à plumes, 1999.

– – –. "The Milka Cow." *From Africa: New Francophone Stories,* ed. Adele King. Lincoln: University of Nebraska Press, 2004.

Breton, André. *L'amour fou*. Paris: Gallimard, 1937.

– – –. *Manifestes du surréalisme*. Paris: Gallimard, 1962.

Célérier, Patricia-Pia. "Bessora: de la 'gautologie' contre l'impérité." *Présence Francophone*. 58.2002. 73-84.

Césaire, Aimé, Suzanne Césaire and René Ménil. *Tropiques 1941-1945*. Paris: Jean Michel Place, 1978.

Clifford, James. "On Ethnographic Surrealism." *Comparative Studies in Society and History*. 23. 4. 1981.539-564.

Dayal, Samir. "Diaspora and Double Consciousness." *The Journal of the Midwest Modern Language Association*.29.1.Spring 1996.

Foster, Hal. "Convulsive Identity." *October*.57.1991.18-54.

Foucault, Michel. *Surveiller et punir*. Paris: Gallimard, 1975.

Lionnet, Françoise. *Postcolonial Representations: Women, Literature, Identity*. Ithaca: Cornell University Press, 1995.

Richardson, Michael. "Surrealism Faced with Cultural Difference." *Cosmopolitan Modernisms*. Ed. Kobena Mercer. Boston: MIT Press, 2005.

Sembene, Ousmane. *Le Mandat*. Paris: Présence africaine, 1965.

Sharpley-Whiting, T. Denean. *Negritude Women*. Minneapolis: University of Minnesota Press, 2002.

Chapter 12

CHORIC/ANIMISTIC SELF: COUTO
Works Cited
Chamberlin, J. Edward. *Come Back to me My Language: Poetry and the West Indies*. Urbana: University of Illinois P, 1993.

– – –. *If This is Your Land, Where Are Your Stories?: Finding Common Ground*. Toronto: Alfred A. Knopf Canada, 2003.

Couto, Mia. *A varanda do frangipani: romance*. Lisboa: Editorial Caminho, 1996.

– – –. *Cada homen é uma raça: estórias*. Lisboa: Editorial Caminho, 1990.

– – –. *Estórias abensonhadas: contos*. Lisboa: Editorial Caminho, 1994.

– – –. *Contos do Nascer da Terra*. Lisboa: Editorial Caminho, 1997.

– – –. *Terra sonâmbula: romance*. Lisboa: Editorial Caminho, 1992.

Hyde, Lewis. *Trickster Makes This World: Mischief, Myth, And Art.* New York: Farrar, Straus and Giroux, 1998.

Iisuka, Takeshi. *The Quest for the Self: Zen in Business and Life.* New York and London: 1995.

Jeremias, Luísa. "O meu segredo é transportar a meninice." A Capital. Lisboa, 8 de Dezembro de 2000. 29 April 2002 <http://www.instituto-camoes.pt/arquivos/literatura/mcoutoentrv.htm>.

Ki-Zerbo, Joseph, ed. *General History of Africa. Vol. I: Methodology and African Prehistory.* London: Heinemann, 1989.

Kristeva, Julia. *Pouvoirs de l'horreur: essai sur l'abjection.* Paris: Éditions du Seuil, 1980.

– – –. *The Kristeva Reader.* Ed. Moi Toril. New York: Columbia UP, 1986.

Ngũgĩ, wa Thiong'o. *Decolonizing the Mind: The Politics of Language in African Literature.* London: Currey, 1986.

Plato. *Timaeus and Critias.* Trans. and Intro Desmond Lee. London: Penguin Books, 1977.

Pollard, Velma. *Dread Talk: The Language of Rastafari.* Kingston, Jamaica: Canoe P, 1994.

Rothwell, Phillip. *A Postmodern Nationalist: Truth, Orality, and Gender in the Work of Mia Couto.* Lewisburg: Bucknell University Press, 2004.

Suzuki, Daisetz Teitaro. *The Essentials of Zen Buddhism: Selected from the Writings of Daisetz T. Suzuki.* Ed. and Intro. Bernard Phillips, Westport, Conn.: Greenwood Press, 1973.

Walcott, Derek. *Collected Poems, 1948-1984.* New York: Farrar, Straus and Giroux, 1986.

Whorf, Benjamin. *Language, Thought, and Reality: Selected Writings.* Cambridge: M.I.T. P, 1964.

Chapter 13

COMPLEMENTARY REALISM: ACHEBE, CE

Works Cited

Achebe, Chinua. *Anthills of the Savannah.* London: Heinemann, 1987.

– – –. *Morning Yet on Creation Day.* Ibadan: Heinemann Educational Books, 1975.

Amadiume, Ifi. "Class and Gender in *Anthills of the Savannah.*" *PAL Platform,* 1989.

– – –. *Male Daughters, Female Husbands: Gender and Sex in African Society.*

London: Zed, 1987.

Asouzu, I. I. *The Method and Principles of Complementary Reflection in and Beyond African Philosophy.* Calabar: University of Calabar Press, 2004.

Berry, Wendell "Writer and Region." *What Are People For?* San Francisco: North Point Press, 1990.

Bostrom, Nick. "The Simulation Argument: Reply to Brian Weatherson." *Philosophical Quarterly* 2005. 55. 218. <http://www.simulation-argument.com/weathersonreply.pdf>

Ce, Chin. *The Visitor.* Enugu: Handel Books, 2004.

– – – . "A Griot of his Time: Chinweizu in Contemporary African Poetry." *Journal of African Poetry* 4. 2007. 13-21.

Davidson, Basil. *The Black Man's Burden.* Ibadan: Spectrum Books, 1993.

Ejizu, Christopher. "The Traditional Igbo Perception of Reality. Its Dialectics and Dilemma." *Bigard Theological Studies*, Vol 9. No1 Jan-Jun 1989.

Eke, Kola. "Full Moon: The Romanticism of Chin Ce's Poetry." *Journal of African Poetry* 4. 2007. 123-139.

Finnegan, Ruth. *Oral Poetry in Africa.* Cambridge: Cambridge University Press, 1977.

Gakwandi, Shatto Arthur. *The Novel and Contemporary Experience in Africa.* London: Heinemann Educational Books, 1977.

Grants, Amanda. "Background and Poetry of Chin Ce." *Africa Research International.* <http://www.africaresearch.org/Cepoetry.htm>

– – – . "Memory, Transition and Dialogue: The Cyclic Order of Chin Ce's Oeuvres." *Journal of African Literature and Culture* 3. 2006 11-21.

Nwala, T. Uzodinma. *Igbo Philosophy.* Lagos: Lantern Books, 1985.

Okuyade, Ogaga. "'Locating the Voice': The Modernist (Postcolonial) Narrative Maze of Chin Ce's *The Visitor.*" *The Works of Chin Ce: Critical Supplement (V)1.* Ed. Irene Marques. IRCALC, 2007. 135-157.

Said, Edward. "Collective Passion." *Al-Ahram Weekly Online* 20-26 Sept. 2001. 13 May 2007. <www.ahram.org.eg/weekly>

Sofola, Zulu. *The Artist and the Tragedy of a Nation.* Ibadan: Caltop Publications, 1994.

Stratton, Florence. *Contemporary African Literature and the Politics of Gender.* London: Routledge, 1994.

Section B1.

Chapter 14

GRIOT TRADITIONS: CHINWEIZU

Works Cited

Achebe, Chinua. *Morning Yet on Creation Day*. London: Heinemann, 1982.

Aiyejina, Funso. 'Recent Nigerian Poetry in English: An Alter-native Tradition.' *The Guardian*. Lagos, 1985.

Alternbernd, Lynn and Lewis, Leslie. *Culture and the Nigerian Novel*. Ed. Oladele Taiwo, London: Macmillan, 1982.

Amah, Stanley. 'Chinweizu: Proclivity to the Profane.' *Journal of the Association of Nigerian Authors*. 1986.

Awoonor, Kofi. *The Breast of the Earth*. Enugu: Nok Publishers, 1975.

Chinweizu. *Anatomy of Female Power.* Lagos: Pero Press, 1990.

– – –. *Energy Crisis and other Poems* Lagos: Nok Publishers, 1978.

– – –. *Invocation and Admonitions* Lagos: Pero Press, 1986.

– – –. *The West and the Rest of Us*. London: Random House, 1978.

Chinweizu, Jemie, Madubuike. *Toward the Decolonization of African Literature*. Enugu: Fourth Dimension, 1980.

Egudu, R. N. 'The Art of Igbo Written Poetry.' Seminar, Igbo Art and Music, University of Nigeria, Nsukka. 21-25 August, 1976.

Emezue, G. M. T. *Comparative Studies in African Dirge Poetry*. Enugu: Handel Books, 2001.

Finnegan, Ruth *Oral Poetry.* London: Cambridge University Press, 1979.

Irobi, Esiaba. "A glance at the observatory.' *The Guardian*. Lagos. April 2, 1986.

Obiechina, Emmanuel. *Journal of the Association of Nigerian Authors* 1986.

Ogunba, Oyin. 'Traditional African Poetry.' *Journal of the Nigeria English Studies Association*. Vol 8. No 2, December 1976.

Onwudinjo, Peter. 'Approaches to the teaching of Poetry.' *Critical Theory and African Literature*. Ed. Ernest Emenyonu, Ibadan: Heinemann, 1987.

Osofisan, Femi. 'The Assassin as a Critic.' *Journal of the Association of Nigerian Authors* 1986.

Oyortev, Zagbo. *Africa Events*. Vol. 3. No. 7. July 1987.

Soyinka, Wole. 'For Christopher.' *Don't Let Him Die: An Anthology of Memorial Poems for Christopher Okigbo 1932-67.* Eds C. Achebe and D. Okafor. Enugu: Fourth Dimension, 1978.

Ugonna, Nnabuenyi. 'The Growth of Igbo Poetry.' Seminar. Igbo Literature. University of Nigeria. August 12-15, 1981.

Chapter 15

POWER AND POLITICS: MAPANJE

Works Cited

Mapanje, Jack. *The Last Of The Sweet Bananas*: *New and Selected Poems,* Tarset: Bloodaxe and Wordsworth Trust, 2004.

Chapter 16

FOETAL SEARCHING: BRATHWAITE

Works Cited

Aiyejina, Funso. "Africa in West Indian Literature: From Claude McKay to Edward Kamau Brathwaite." Ph.D Thesis, University of West Indies, 1980.

Ajayi, Sesan. "The Theme of Exile in Caribbean Literature." *Undergraduate Text in English Language and Literature*. Ed. Lekan Oyegoke, Ibadan: Paperback Publishers, 1991. 18-29.

Asein, Samuel. "The Concept of Form: A Study of Some Ancestral Elements in Brathwaite's Trilogy." *African Association of the West Indies Bulletin* 4. 1971. 12-29.

Ashcroft, Bill, Griffiths, Gareth, & Tiffin, Helen. *The Empire Writes Back: Theory and Practice in Post-Colonial Literatures*. London: Routledge, 1989.

Brathwaite, Edward. "Imehri." *Savacou* 2. Sept. 1970.1-18.

Brathwaite, Edward. *The Arrivants*. Oxford: Oxford University Press, 1981.

Brown, Lloyd. "The African Heritage and the Harlem Renaissance: A Re-evaluation." *African Literature Today* 9. 1978. 21-35.

Brown, Stewart. "Writing in Light: Orality-thru-typography, Kamau Brathwaite's Sycorax Video Style."*The Pressures of the Text: Orality, Texts and Telling of Tales*. Ed. Stewart Brown, Britain: BPC Wheatons Ltd. 1995. 67-85.

Coulthard, G.R. *Race and Colour in Caribbean Literature*. London: Oxford University Press, 1962.

Dabydeen, David, et al. *A Reader's Guide to West Indian and Black British Literature*. Austria: Rutherford Press, 1988.

Dash, Michael, "Edward Brathwaite." *West Indian Literature*. Ed. Bruce King, London: Macmillan, 1970. 16-34.

Dathorne, O. R. "The Theme of Africa in West Indian Literature." *Phylon* xxvi. 3.1965.34-45.

Egudu, R.N. *Modern African Poetry and African Predicament*. London: Macmillan, 1978.

Gates, Henry Louis, Jr. *The Signifying Monkey - A Theory of African-American Literary Criticism*. New York: Oxford University Press, 1988.

Gikandi, Simeon. *Writing in Limbo: Modernism and Caribbean Literature*. London: Cornell University, 1992.

Gilroy, Paul. *The Black Atlantic: Modernity and Double Consciousness*. Cambridge: Harvard University Press, 1995.

Hulme, Peter. *Colonial Encounters: Europe and the Native Caribbean, 1492-1797*. London: Routledge, 1992.

Irele, Abiola. "The Poetry of Edward Brathwaite." Third Ife Festival of the Arts, 4th-18th Dec. 1970: 22.

Ismond, Patricia. "Walcott Versus Brathwaite." *Caribbean Quarterly*. 17. 2&4. Sept-Dec. 1974: 49-66.

King-Aribisala, Karen. "African Homogeneity: The Affirmation of a 'United' African and Afro-West Indian Identity." *African Literature and African Historical Experiences*. Ed. Ernest Emenyonu, Ibadan: Heinemann, 1991: 35-51.

King, Bruce. *The New English Literatures-Cultural Nationalism in a Changing World*. London: Macmillan, 1980.

Nketia, J. H. *Funeral Dirges of the Akan People*. New York: Negro Universities Press,1969.

Okigbo, Christopher. "Heavensgate." *Labyrinths*. London: Heinemann, 1971.

Oloruntoba-Oju, Omotayo. "Literature of the Black Diaspora." *New Introduction to Literature*. Olu Obafemi, ed. Ibadan; Y-Books, 1994. 131-145.

Raji-Oyelade, Aderemi. "The Troikan Consciousness in Edward Brathwaite's *The Arrivants*." *The Black Presence in Caribbean Literature. Ed.* Austine Akpuda. Enugu: Samdrew, 2005. 126-136.

Richards, David. "West Indian Literature." *Encyclopedia of Literature and Criticism*. Ed. Martin Coyle, Peter Garside, Malcolm Kelsall and John Peck, eds, London: Routledge, 1991. 1198-1208.

Steele, Shelby. *The Content of Our Character: A New Vision of Race in America*. St. Martin's Press: New York, 1990.

Chapter 17

NEO ROMANTICS: CE

Works Cited

Abrams, M.H. *A Glossary of Literary Terms*. Forth Worth: Holt, Rinehart and Winston, 1981.

Bowra, C.M. *The Romantic Imagination*. Oxford: Univ Press, 1973.

Byron, Glennis. *Dramatic Monologue*. London: Routledge, Taylor and Francis, 2003.

Ce, Chin. "Bards and Tyrants: Literature, Leadership and Citizenship Issues of Modern Nigeria." *Africa Literary Journal* B5. 2005. 3-24.

– – –. "Riddle and Bash: The Creative Wit of Alaa's Children." *Africa Literary Journal* B4. 2003. 99-125.

– – –. *Full Moon*. Enugu: Handel Books, 2001.

Langer, Susanne. K. "Poetic Creation." *The Critical Tradition: Class Texts and Contemporary Trends*. Ed. David H. Richter, Boston: Bedford Books, 1989. 534-542.

Leech, G.N. "Linguistics and Figures of Rhetoric." *Essays on Style and Language: Linguistics and Critical Approaches to Literary Style*. Ed. Roger Fowler, London: Routledge and Kegan Paul, 1966. 135-153.

Raghavacharyulu, D.V.K. *The Critical Response*. Madras: Macmillan, 1980.

Wordsworth, William. "Preface." *Wordsworth and Coleridge: Lyrical Ballads*. Eds. R.L. Brett and A.R. Jones, Cambridge: Univ Press, 1963. 241-272.

Wright, David. "Introduction." *The Penguin Book of English Romantic Verse*. Wright Harmondsworth: Penguin, 1968: XI-XXVII

Chapter 19

POETIC HUMANISM: ENEKWE

Works Cited

Achebe, C. *Things Fall Apart*. London: Heinemann, 1958.

Enekwe, O. O. *Broken Pots*. Enugu: Afa, 2004.

– – – ., ed. *Harvest Time* Enugu: Snaap, 2001.

Fanon, F. *The Wretched of the Earth*. Britain: MacGibbon, 1965.

Kermode, F., eds. *Oxford Anthology of English Literature*. New York: Oxford, 1973.

Landry, G. et al. *Materialist Feminisms*. Massachusetts: Blackwell, 1993.

Nwoga, D.I. (ed.) *West African Verse*. United Kingdom: Longman, 1967.

Ngugi, wa Thiongo *Petals of Blood*. London: Heinemann, 1977.

Olusunle, T. "Hew-man Rights." *Fingermarks* Ibadan: Kraft, 1996.

Sallah, T. *New Poets of West Africa*. Lagos: Malthouse, 1995.

Widdowson, H.G. *Stylistics and Teaching of Literature*. London: Longman 1975.

Yankson, K.E. *An Introduction to Literary Stylistics*. Nigeria: Pacific, 1987.

Chapter 20

GUINÉ-BISSAU / CARRIBEAN: CABRAL, TCHEKA, PROENCA, YTCHYANA, BORGES AND MILLER

Works Cited

"Amilcar Cabral." *Microsoft Encarta Research Library, MERL* (CD-ROM). Redmond: Microsoft Corporation, 2003.

Ana Raquel Lourenço Fernandes et al., trans and ed. *Para Vasco; Poemas da Guiné-Bissau (For Vasco: Poems of Guinea Bissau)*. Coventry: Heaventree Press, 2006.

Fanon, Frantz. *The Wretched of the Earth*. New York: Penguin Books, 1962.

Miller, Kei. *Kingdom of Empty Bellies*. Coventry: Heaventree Press, 2005.

Sartre, Jean Paul. "Preface." *The Wretched of the Earth*. Frantz Fanon, New York: Penguin Books, 1962.

INDEX

A

Achebe, Chinua
    Achebe's 21-27, 30, 36, 38,
40, 67, 68-69, 75, 80, 85-86,
127, 176, 239, 240, 243-
245, 247, 250-252, 255,
258-260, 278
African
    culture 139, 145
    Diaspora 303
    empires 293
    experience 71
    gods 293
    mythology 302
    narrative 331
    poetry 299
    story, The 40
    towns 293
    womanhood 103
    writer 120
    writers 91
    Lusophone 345
African-American 137
Africanism 77
Africanist vision 267
Afrocentric 264
    scheme 138
Aidoo, Ama Ata
Aidoo's 137, 140, 142, 143, 145,
146, 154-156
Algeria 20
al-Sudan 175, 178, 195,
Andreas, Neshani

Andreas' 51-52
anthropomorphic imagery 306,
309, 313,
Antigone
    choice of 159
Armah, Ayi Kwei 330
Asein, Samuel 299
Asouzu, I. I. 240
Attridge, Derek 42
Attwell, David 41
Ayinde, O. 175

B

Bakhtin 71
Bala, I. 279
Banda, Hastings 282
Bards 135
Bartlett, Juluette 151
Bessora,
Bessora's 199, 200-205, 207,
208, 210, 211-213
Beti, Mongo 89
Bhabha, Homi 30
Biafran struggle 338
"Bildung" 120, 122
bildungsromane 122, 123
Black
    Americans 130
    Consciousness 37
    Empowerment 322
    literature 303
    Rennaissance 37

tradition 123

Blake, William 330

Blyden, Edward Wilmot 129

Borges, Eunice 345, 350

Bostrom, Nick 239

Botswana 57

Brathwaite, Edward

Brathwaite's 289, 291-299, 300, 303

Browitt, Jeff 30

Buckley, Jerome 122

Buddhism 215

C

Cabral, Amilca 346

Cabral, Vasco

    Cabral's 345, 345

Cameroonian 85

Capitalism 128

Caribbean 220

    literature 293

    poetry 345

    society 354

    writers 303

    artist 290

cartes 199, 200, 208, 210, 211, 213

Case, Dianne 51

Ce, Chin

    Ce's 237, 240, 241, 243, 252, 253, 258, 260, 263, 305, 312, 315, 317, 318

Chamberlin, Edward J. 217, 220, 226,

Child education 128

    heroes 85

childhood 87

Chinweizu

    Chinweizu's 263, 264, 265, 267, 268, 271, 273, 275, 277, 278

chora 223, 227

choric self 231, 232

Coetzee, J.M.

    Coetzee's 35, 40, 41, 42, 43, 44-48

colonization 30, 31, 33, 36, 47

Complementary

    Realism, theory of 237, 240

    novel 102

Conakry 126

Conflict 175,

    of Gender 192

    of Nation 194

    Racial 189

Congoland 103

Congolese 103

Couto, Mia

    Couto's 215-221, 223, 227, 229, 230-232- 235

Crisis

    world of 264

Crusoe 31-35, 41-47

Cultural translation 138

culture

    postcolonial 39

D

Dangarembga, Tsitsi

    Dangarembga's 67, 68,

69, 76, 78, 80, 82, 83
Deleuze 131
diasporic authors 199
Differences 96
Diop, David 294
dramaturgy 161
dramaturgy
    context 168

E
Egyptian 190
Eke, K 305
Emenyonu, Ernest 38
Emezue, G.M.T. 237, 345
Enekwe, Osmond Ossie
    Enekwe's 327-329, 330-
    334, , 328, 340, 341,
    342
Eurocentric 68
European 36
exoticism 205, 206

F
Fanon, Frantz 19, 28, 20, 32, 333
Female Emancipation 114
Francophone 199, 201, 202
Free Women 104
French Cameroons 90
    colonialist 20
Fugard, Athol 158

G
Ghana 291
Gikuyu 20, 21, 24
Gondala, Didier 104, 105

Grants, Amanda 119, 252
Griot traditions 345
Guattari 131
Guinea Bissau 345
Gyimah, Miriam 144

H
Head, Bessie
Head's 51, 52, 53, 64,
Hobbes, Thomas 330
Humanism
    poetic 329
hybridity 211

I
ideological 153
Igbo, literary tradition 268
    rhetoric 268
    traditional 268
    poet-diviner 278
Ikiddeh, Ime 36
Iloh, N. 103
Imperial
    Crown 91
imperialism 32, 35-36, 42
Invocation, bards 271
IRCALC Editors 5, 303
Irele Abiola 302
issues
    postcolonial 41

J
Jameson, Fredric 38

K

Kahengua, Kavevangua
    Kahengua's 319, 320,
    321, 323, 325-327
Kehinde, A. 39, 289
Kenyan 16, 17, 18, 28
    people 16, 17
    politicians 17
Kenyatta, Jomo 18, 24,
King-Aribisala, Karen 290
Kumasi 294

L

Lesbitt, L. N. 15
Lewis, A. 67
Liberian war 333
Lopes, Henri
    Lopes'103, 107, 108,
    110, 112, 114-117

M

Malaba, M.Z 320
Malawian, culture
    history 281
Mamman Vatsa 340
Mandela, Nelson 323
Manichaean 69
'manichaeism delirium' 39
Manichean opposition 165
Mapanje, Jack
Mapanje's 279, 281-285, 287
Marate, G. N. 127
Marques, I. 215
Martriach 146

Mau-mau 92
Mazrui, Ali 255
Mbiti, John 125
Melone, Thomas 85
Miller, Kei
    Miller's 345, 351
Milner, Andrew 30
mise-en-abîme 219, 227,228
modernity 139, 150
Mozambique 218, 235

N

Namibia, in poetry 320
Ndoumba
    Characteristics 106
    Concept of 104
    life of 108
    women 107
Negritude 37
    movement 121
Neo Romantics 305
neo-colonialism 16, 18, 27
New Age thinker
    See Bostrom, Nick
Ngugi, wa Thiong'ó
    Ngugi's 20, 24, 26, 88-
89,   91, 98, 102
Niger
    lower 23
    river
Nigeria 22, 28
Nigerian audience 164
    predicament 161
    theatre 161

Nwokora, L. N. 85

O

Odamtten 144
Ogaga, Okuyade 252
Ohlmann, Judith Sinanga 117
Okigbo, Christopher
      Okigbo 263, 274, 277,
      299
Omotoso, Kole 289
Onwudinjo 266
Onwueme, Tess
      Onwueme's 137, 140,
      146-150, 152, 153, 154,
      156
Orabueze, F 329
Orientalism 77
Ósofisan, Femi
      Ósofisan's 157, 158,
      159, 160, 163, 168, 171-
      174
Other, the 143
Ousmane, Sembène 116
Oyono, Ferdinand
      Oyono's 85, 87-92, 95,
      102

P

Pan-African 138, 139, 140, 146, 154
Pan-Africanism 138
Pan-Africanist 138, 145
Paradigm
      complementarist 238
Penner, Dick 44
Phiri, Virginia 52

Poetic humanism
      See Humanism
postcolonial 15, 16, 20, 21, 28,
31, 67
postcolonial culture
      See culture
power and politics 279
Proenca, Helder
      Proenca's 345, 349
psychoanalysis 215
R
Rastafari 220
realism
      complementary 240,
423,   245
      spiritual 240
Resemblances 88
Resistance, South African 346
Romantics 306, 307
Rothwell, David 216
Rushdie, Salman 39
Rwanda genocide 333

S

Sharpley-Whiting, Denean 203
Said 39
Şālih, al-Tayyib 177
Satre 78
Schipper 37
Secovnie, K. 137
Senghor, Leopold 36, 294
Sofola, Zulu 237, 241, 247, 253
Sophocles, 158, 159, 162, 163-
167, 171
Soyinka, Wole 264

Spivak, Gayatri 39, 68
Sudanese
conflict 175, 176
Military College 180
Surrealism 199, 201, 202
surrealist
movements 202
techniques 201

T
Tcheka, Tony
Tcheka's 345, 349
Toko, D. M. 120
totem 125
traditional education 123
identity 150
traditions, griot 263
translation
See cultural translation
Trivedi, Harish 138

U
universality 86
"Ur-text" 70
Uways
Uways'175, 176,
180,181, 183, 184, 185,
187, 190,191, 193, 195,
196

V
Van Weyenberg, A. 157
Vassanji, M.V.
Vassanji's 16-17, 24
Velikovsky

Immanuel 238
Vera, Yvonne
Vera's 51, 52, 54, 59, 60,
62
Von Daniken Erich 238

W
Weiss, B. 51
West African 140, 148
West Indian 352
Western colonisation 120
colonizers 26
education 22, 24
god 23
identity 15, 16 25
literature 48
modernism 264
nation(s) 17, 18
religion 23
style 82
world 29
evolutionist 71
Westmoreland, J 199
Wetmore, Kevin 159
Widdowson, G 332
Widening
frontiers 138
woman-centered 80
Wordsworth, William 306
Wright, David 305
write back 52
writing back 67

Y

Yeats, W. B. 21, 22
        Yeatsian 72
Ytchyana
        Ytcyana's , 345, 347

Z

Zanzi et al 105
Zeitgeist 175

LaVergne, TN USA
19 October 2009
161313LV00001B/1/P